118

Cambridge studies in sociology 7
THE ARISTOCRACY OF LABOR

Cambridge studies in sociology

1 *The Affluent worker: industrial attitudes and behaviour* By John H. Goldthorpe, David Lockwood, Frank Bechhofer and Jennifer Platt
2 *The Affluent worker: political attitudes and behaviour* by John H. Goldthorpe, David Lockwood, Frank Bechhofer and Jennifer Platt
3 *The affluent worker in the class structure* by John H. Goldthorpe, David Lockwood, Frank Bechhofer and Jennifer Platt
4 *Men in mid-career: a study of British managers and technical specialists* by Cyril Sofer
5 *Family structure in nineteenth century Lancashire* by Michael Anderson
6 *Workers on the move: the sociology of relocation* by Michael Mann

Cambridge papers in sociology

1 *Size of industrial organisation and worker behaviour* by Geoffrey K. Ingham
2 *Workers' attitudes and technology* by D. Wedderburn and R. Crompton
3 *Perceptions of work: variations within a factory* by H. Beynon and R. M. Blackburn

THE "ARISTOCRACY OF LABOR"

The position of skilled craftsmen in the American class structure

GAVIN MACKENZIE

Fellow of Jesus College and Lecturer in Sociology
University of Cambridge

CAMBRIDGE UNIVERSITY PRESS

Published by the Syndics of the Cambridge University Press
Bentley House, 200 Euston Road, London NW1 2DB
American Branch: 32 East 57th Street, New York, N.Y.10022

© Cambridge University Press 1973

Library of Congress Catalogue Card Number: 73-80484

ISBNS:
0 521 20286 8   hard covers
0 521 09825 4   paperback

First published 1973

Photoset and printed in Malta by St Paul's Press Ltd

To the memory of
George Alfred Mackenzie and Leonard Alfred Marlow

Contents

Preface ix

1 Introduction *page* 1
The worker in American society 1
The community of Providence 7
Methodology 12

2 The job 19
Market situation: income 19
Other components of market situation 22
Promotion and mobility 27
A business of one's own 31
Job satisfaction 34
Conclusion 44

3 Family structure and patterns of socialisation 45
The family unit 46
Patterns of socialisation 51
Educational and occupational aspirations
and achievements 57
Conclusion 72

4 The organisation of life style 74
The home and the neighbourhood 74
Leisure time and leisure activities 81
Conclusion 94

5 Political behaviour and attitudes 95
Party identification and voting behaviour 96
Perceptions of party support 101
The bases of party support 106
Conclusion 114

6 Perceptions of class and class structure 116
Self-placement in class structure 117
Images of class structure 120
The bases of social class 125
The class situation of clerks and craftsmen 133
The class situation of skilled and
* non-skilled workers* 136
Class consciousness 138
Conclusion 147

7 The web of associations 149
Patterns of interaction 149
The content of interaction 152
Conclusion 160

8 Conclusions 162

Appendix: The interview schedule 176

Notes to the text 188

Bibliography 200

Index 206

Preface

This book is concerned with an analysis of change in the middle levels of the American class structure. In particular it attempts to determine whether the line separating the working class from the middle class is becoming increasingly blurred, leading to the *embourgeoisement* of large numbers of skilled blue collar workers. The emergence (or more accurately, re-emergence) of debate on this issue in recent years has in no sense been confined to the United States. Indeed discussion of the 'new' working class, or of the thesis that an identifiable and distinct working class is ceasing to be a feature of advanced capitalist society has become a major point at issue among Western sociologists generally. It is hoped that this book will contribute to that discussion.

Two preliminary caveats should be made. First, in what follows I shall often make reference to *trends*, to *processes* and to *changes* that are taking place within the American class structure. Such an approach is not without danger. Ideally, any study that tries to document a process of change should do so with reference to trend data. This I am unable to do. Instead, I have had to rely on the results of previous research carried out on certain aspects of the American class structure. To the extent that my findings differ from those of earlier studies I have felt justified in regarding this as indicative of change. In certain instances however, historical data have been less than complete, in which case I have been forced to fall back upon 'ideal type' characterisations of the traditional American working class. This is an inadequacy that is by no means limited to this particular piece of research, and one for which there is no really satisfactory remedy. Nevertheless, I have been able to document a situation as it exists in a single American community. Whether this situation is different from that existing previously, or only from that *perceived* to have existed earlier, I am not able to prove.

Secondly, while my ultimate concern is with changes in the *American* class structure, I am not unaware of the restrictions imposed by a single case study. The findings presented and discussed in this book were collected in one community at a single point in time. Thus, while I would argue that those findings add considerable fuel to the debate on changes in the American class structure, it would be naive to claim to have resolved that debate. For similar reasons I have resisted the temptation to compare in a systematic manner the findings of this research project with those of similar ones conducted in other societies. The few studies that do exist were carried out in differing communities, using differing research techniques and samples.[1] To compare the situation found in a single American city with the results of a small number of European studies, and then attempt to make statements relating to changes in the class structure of industrial society *per se* would, at this time, be both presumptuous and premature.

Chapters 1, 2, 5, 6 and 8 of this book were originally submitted in different form, in partial fulfilment of the requirements for the Ph.D. degree at Brown University. The major debt accummulated in the writing of that dissertation was to the Chairman of the thesis committee, Sidney Goldstein. His gentle and candid guidance at every stage of the project (and indeed throughout my career as a graduate student) is genuinely appreciated. The other two members of the thesis committee, Ely Chinoy and Dietrich Rueschemeyer both devoted many hours advising and encouraging me in the exercise. I am very grateful. I should also like to record my indebtedness to Kurt Mayer, who, before returning to his native Switzerland in 1966, did much to acquaint me with the uniqueness of the American class structure. Ed. Brown the Secretary-Treasurer of the Rhode Island A.F.L.–C.I.O. attempted to do the same thing with regard to the American labour movement. I hope he was successful.

The research was initially supported by an N.S.F. Doctoral Research Grant. Subsequently aid has been received from Smith College, the University of Leicester and the Nuffield Foundation. I wish to thank each of these institutions and foundations.

The study would not have been possible if nearly 300 Providence residents had not agreed to be interviewed, or if 15 interviewers had not been willing to spend their summer evenings administering the interview schedule. I should like to thank both these groups of people. In the preparation and processing of the data I benefited from the skills of Carol Spielman, Connie Noons and Peter Nokes, while Laurette Mackenzie provided invaluable encouragement and assistance.

Finally, I would like to express my indebtedness to the following persons, all of whom have commented, often at length, upon earlier versions of the manuscript: Frank Bechhofer, Anthony Giddens, John Goldthorpe, Geoffrey Ingham, and Sandy Stewart. In addition I am grateful to Mary Margaret McCabe and to Patricia Skinner, Editorial Director at Cambridge University Press. My greatest debts however are to Ilya Neustadt and Lesley Bower. The former made me realise how much the study of sociology 'is an endlessly exciting and rewarding task'. The reasons for my gratitude to the latter are more diffuse.

Gavin Mackenzie

1 Introduction

The Worker in American Society

The 1950s ushered in a period of rapid and extensive changes in the pattern of American life. Widespread affluence, and the breakdown of income differentials between occupational groups, appeared to be fast becoming a reality, while the emergence of the mass produced, middle income suburb brought together people from differing occupational, religious or ethnic backgrounds; people who traditionally had been segregated residentially. Change was also apparent in the workplace, most notably in the rationalisation and mechanisation of large numbers of white collar jobs. In the midst of all this, television became almost standard equipment: by 1955 seven out of every ten American homes had at least one set and television viewing took up more leisure time than any other activity.

Increasing recognition of the nature and extent of these and other developments gave rise to a good deal of conjecture as to their impact on the class structure of the United States. In particular social scientists and social commentators alike became concerned with the analysis of changes that might be occurring in the structure and composition of the working class. While there has been no shortage of speculations and hypotheses regarding the nature of such changes, discussion, for the most part, has focused on the blurring or disappearance of what was 'perhaps the most fundamental cleavage in American society',[1] and the consequent absorption into the middle class of large numbers of blue collar or manual workers.

The idea of the American worker becoming bourgeois, however, is not new. Indeed the last quarter of the nineteenth century was the scene of lively, and often bitter debate on the subject. Much of the discussion revolved around the issue of American 'exceptionalism'. Sheer size, an abundance of raw materials, an ethnically diversified population and the absence of a hereditary aristocracy meant that the United States had to be regarded as a society distinct from those of Western Europe. The question that arose was whether therefore, 'America stood *above* class antagonisms and struggles',[2] and whether therefore capitalism would ever be superseded in that society. While little agreement was reached on this latter question there was a good deal of unanimity regarding the existence of middle class or 'bourgeois' aspirations amongst a substantial segment of the working class. For example, the Central Committee of the Furniture Workers' Union of North America warned in 1879 that:

> The natural and justifiable longing of every person for well-being and independence has, among many working men, been developed in a wrong direction. They imitate the so-called higher classes in the maxim 'Everyone for himself and God for us all.' Yet they do not imitate them in combining for a common interest of their class...
>
> Through the unexampled prosperity of American industry and commerce after the Civil War, which lasted for half a decade, the working people learned to think and act in a capitalist way...There was no lack of farseeing leaders in these decades who admonished their fellows to stick to their organisations to which they owed so much. But the capitalist spirit of society had taken hold of the masses, and the voice of the leaders was disregarded.[3]

The 'unexampled prosperity' of the American worker was also seen by other writers, notably Marx and Engels, as being one of the bases of his identification with the bourgeois ethos. In a general exposition on the theory of 'Wages, Price and Profit' written in 1865, Marx explained the relatively high standard of wages in the United States by reference to the fact that in this society 'the law of supply and demand favours the working man'.[4] Similarly, writing some years later and discussing the particular features of the United States that presented 'very great and peculiar difficulties for a steady development of a workers' party', Engels commented '...through the protective tariff system and the steadily growing domestic market the workers must have been exposed to a prosperity no trace of which has been seen here in Europe for years now...'[5]

Engels also placed importance on the tendency for workers, newly arrived in the United States, to dissociate themselves from the societies that had been left behind, and consequently to over-identify with the American capitalistic ethos:

> It is remarkable, but quite natural, that in such a young country, which has never known feudalism and has grown up on a bourgeois basis from the first, bourgeois prejudices should also be so strongly rooted in the working class. Out of his very opposition to the mother country – which is still clothed in its feudal disguise – the American worker also imagines that the bourgeois regime as traditionally inherited is something progressive and superior by nature and for all time, a *non plus ultra*.[6]

Furthermore, he added, this process was reinforced by the opportunities that existed for upward mobility in nineteenth century America – opportunities which were seen as being greater than those available in Europe. Craftsmen were perhaps in the most favourable position, the move from employee to entrepreneur in the same skilled trade being both common and straightforward. 'For America after all was the ideal of all bourgeois...a country *rich, vast, expanding*... Here everyone could become, if not a capitalist, at all events an independent man, producing or trading, with his own means for his own account.'[7]

These then are some of the reasons advanced in explanation of the 'bourgeois tendencies' of large numbers of American workers in the last decades of the nineteenth century. It is, however, important to realise that most of those who participated in the discussion saw these as only short-run factors. America was undoubtedly an exceptional country: it was therefore not surprising that her working class should *temporarily* exhibit exceptional features. Nonetheless, the future pattern of economic growth meant that the role of the small entrepreneur in manufacturing would diminish considerably. Large corporations were already in evidence, requiring vast amounts of capital for plant and machinery. The opportunities for upward mobility could be expected to dwindle accordingly. Similarly the increasing mechanisation and improvement of production techniques was gradually reducing the bargaining power of manual workers: their 'unexampled prosperity' could not be expected to last forever. And finally, with the ending of large scale immigration from Europe, a 'native' American labour force would become established. Working class consciousness could then be expected to develop. Certainly Marx and Engels were under no illusions as to the ultimate fate of American capitalism:'...the American working class is moving, and no mistake. And after a few false starts they will get into the right track soon enough.'[8] Indeed, 'Once the Americans get started it will be with an energy and violence compared with which we in Europe shall be mere children.'[9]

Nonetheless, as I have already noted, in recent years discussion of the middle class worker has been reactivated. And while contemporary discourse is more varied than that of the previous period, and by no means limited to Marxists or writers from the left, there are important similarities between some of the claims of nineteenth century theorists and certain of the hypotheses advanced by present day scholars and commentators. In particular, current debate has been stimulated by the rapid post-war increase in the earnings of blue collar workers, an increase which has been relatively less pronounced for substantial numbers of clerical and other non-manual employees.

Awareness of this change in the economic fortunes of both skilled and non-skilled manual workers led a number of writers – particularly Kurt

B. Mayer – to suggest that 'the traditional dividing line between manual workers and white collar employees no longer holds, because large segments of the working class now share a "white collar" style of life and many also accept middle class values and beliefs'.[10] In terms of constant (1959) dollars, Mayer pointed out, median family incomes rose 50 per cent during the 1950s alone. This meant that the proportion of families receiving less than $5,000 per annum fell from 80 per cent in 1949 to 42 per cent in 1959. At the same time families earning between $5,000 and $10,000 rose from 17 to 43 per cent during the same period, while those numbers fortunate enough to receive in excess of $10,000 increased from 3 to 15 per cent of the total. To be sure, in 1959 around one fifth of families were earning less than $3,000 per annum – Michael Harrington's 'other America' – but this must not be allowed to detract from the fact that the vast majority of Americans, manual and non-manual workers alike, were now enjoying an income that previously had been the prerogative of the established middle class. This meant that in terms of the distribution of income 'American society has changed its shape from the traditional pyramid to a diamond bulging at the middle and somewhat flat at the bottom'.[11]

Following on from the assumption that changes in the distribution of income must have a 'fundamental impact' upon class structure, Mayer therefore felt able to claim that America was becoming a middle class or even 'classless' society. Increasing numbers of manual workers would now be able to adopt a middle class life style, purchase their own homes and furnish them with consumer durables that had previously been beyond their means. Furthermore, to the extent that home-ownership has often entailed a move to suburbia, then we have, so it has been suggested, a clear and unambiguous explanation for the blurring or disappearance of traditional class lines.

While the process of suburbanisation has been going on in the United States since the first half of the eighteenth century, the mass produced suburb, offering homes (and often mortgages) well within the reach of the manual worker, is very much part of the economic boom following the end of the Second World War. Indeed, the rise of such suburbs has been termed 'one of the major social changes of the twentieth century'.[12] The purchase of a house in such a tract has often meant, for a blue collar worker living in the East at any rate, a move away from a traditional working class area near the central city. In many instances, such areas were also ethnic enclaves, the Italian community described in Gans's study of South Boston being an extreme example.[13] Migration to suburbia from such a neighbourhood will, in most cases, bring about the disruption of old friendships and weaken extended family ties. And at the same time as the hold of family and friends is weakened, so the argument went, the new suburbanite is exposed to new pressures; pressures which are by their very nature middle class. For working class arrivals to suburbia will have as neighbours people from a variety of backgrounds and occupational situations, many of them white collar.[14] Affluent workers will therefore become increasingly exposed to a middle class ideology and style of life, both of which they will gradually come to adopt. The most fervent exponent of this view was undoubtedly William H. Whyte, who, in the mid 1950s, argued that newly emerged suburbs had become the 'second great melting pot'. Indeed the 'expansion of the lower limits of the middle class...is so pronounced in the new suburbs that it almost seems as if they were made for that function'.[15]

In this connection a good deal of importance has been attached to the impact of the mass media. Lenski, for example, has claimed that '...not only has the middle class been increasing in size relative to the working class, but its social standards are permeating the working class more and more with each passing year, thanks to the growing influence of the mass media. As a result, an ever increasing number of people who are objectively manual workers think and act like the middle class.'[16]

The conditions giving rise to renewed debate on the middle class worker were thus largely distinct from those associated with the debate in the latter part of the nineteenth century, and result in differing conclusions. For none of the social scientists or commentators addressing himself to the problem of the *embourgeoisement* of blue collar workers sees this process as transitory in character. Notions of 'false consciousness' or predictions concerning a reversal of the process are totally absent from the literature. Indeed, one scholar has recently argued that the reverse is the case: '...in the Unites States...class consciousness among manual workers is a transitional phenomenon – characterising workers not yet accustomed to the modern metropolis and the modern work place'.[17] But this does not mean that American social science has accepted without question the arguments put forward by writers such as Mayer, Bernard, Whyte, or Wilensky.

Criticism of the *embourgeoisement* thesis in America has taken two forms. First, a number of authors have suggested that the blurring of class lines is more apparent than real. While they have recognised that large numbers of manual workers are enjoying a new found affluence, often expressed in the purchase of homes, cars, or consumer goods, they point out that these material gains on the part of the working class can only be viewed as part of a general 'upgrading' of American life styles. In other words, as manual workers have, in the post-war years, come to adopt what was previously a middle class life style, members of this latter class have *also* altered behavioural and consumption patterns. Class differentials, and barriers, have therefore remained intact.[18] There has, in addition, been a small amount of research into particular aspects of the thesis that workers are becoming accepted into the middle class. Comparison of the life styles of manual and non-manual groups in that most notorious of new suburbs – Levittown, Long Island – showed, for example, 'no indication that the suburban situation in any way modifies class patterns'.[19] Indeed, one writer has gone further, suggesting not only that the manual/non-manual line of demarcation remains as the most significant cleavage within the American class structure, but also that skilled craftsmen form an 'autonomous status group' within the working class.[20]

A second group of writers have accepted the idea that significant changes are occurring in the middle ranges of the American class structure, but have gone on to argue that these do not involve an expansion of the lower limits of the middle class. In particular, it has been suggested that lower level clerical workers have become progressively detached from the established middle class and are in the process of becoming absorbed into the upper reaches of the traditional working class. The increased rationalisation and mechanisation of clerical tasks is thought to be obliterating many of the features that have, in the past, kept the work situation of the white collar worker quite distinct from that of the manual employee. At the same time it would appear that, with an increasing emphasis being placed upon technical and professional qualifications, opportunities for clerical workers to rise to managerial or executive positions are dwindling fast. Both these developments, it is argued, are making the class position of clerical workers more and more similar to that of wage-earners.[21] At the same time, as larger numbers of children from blue collar homes gain high school diplomas, recruitment from the working class ranks to fill positions in white collar occupations must increase accordingly. This may be leading, we are told, to the large scale 'importing' of traditional working class values into the lower levels of the established middle class. This means that 'contrary to the popular theorising about the "bourgeoisification of the workers", the actual process is one of "proletarianisation" (or more realistically for the United States, "liberalising") of the lower middle-class ranks'.[22]

These were the main arguments being advanced by the mid 1960s concerning the changing class position of the affluent worker, and, to a lesser extent, the clerk in American society. To the observer, however, the striking characteristic of this debate was the almost total absence of anything more than rudimentary empirical data. At best, points of view were bolstered with recourse to the secondary analysis of existing (and often aged) information, or to statistics (often taken from the U.S. Census) relating to only one aspect of class situation. At worst, the 'fact' that changes *had* taken place was accepted unquestioningly, and used to 'explain' other developments in the social structure.[23] Neither of these alternatives could be regarded as satisfactory. Accordingly, in 1967, the author initiated a study aimed at evaluating, on the basis of substantial evidence, some of the various claims and counterclaims that had been put forward in the preceding years. In the remainder of this chapter I say something about the city in which the investigation was carried out and the form which it took.

The Community of Providence

Providence is the capital of the smallest and most densely settled state in the Union, Rhode Island.[24] In 1965 the city's population numbered just over 187,000. In 1940 the figure was 253,504. This shrinking in size is not a phenomenon confined to Providence by any means, and is linked to the move to the suburbs that, as already pointed out, has become a feature of American society. In this particular case it is reinforced by a significant amount of migration away from the city and state altogether. This latter process is associated with the economic difficulties that have beset Rhode Island in recent years. In contrast to the rest of the country, in Providence the median age of the city's residents has steadily increased over time. During the past twenty or so years this has not been the national pattern. For the United States as a whole, the post-war 'baby boom' resulted in the median age of the total population being pulled down to 29.5 years in 1960. During the same period it rose from 31.7 to 31.9 in Rhode Island. Indeed in Providence in 1960 13 per cent of the population were over 65 years of age while only 25 per cent were below 15. The comparable proportions for the total society were 9 per cent and 31 per cent respectively.

The age structure of Providence can be explained with reference to two main features of the city. First, as already pointed out, the population is declining. Movement to suburbs within the state, and out of the state completely is specially selective of young single people and couples, often with children. Secondly, the high degree of urbanisation and manufacturing, both influencing the large percentage of married women in the labour force, has kept the birth rate of Providence below average. This is so despite the large numbers of Catholics in the city and state.

For the first hundred years or so of its existence, Providence was peopled almost completely with English colonists. This monopoly was slightly threatened towards the end of the eighteenth century with the arrival of small numbers of Huguenots, Portuguese Jews and Swedes. But it was not until around 1830 that significant numbers of foreign born began to arrive and settle in the area, and especially in Providence. By the middle of the nineteenth century 16 per cent of the people of Rhode Island had been born abroad. Of this 16 per cent almost three-quarters were Irish. However, in the period 1860–90, the Irish were replaced by French-Canadians as the major ethnic group settling in Rhode Island. Finally, after the wave of French-Canadian immigration had reached its peak around 1890, it was superseded by the arrival of large numbers of Italians in the state, nearly all of whom settled in the capital city.

These three main waves of immigration were such, that in the period between 1840 and 1910, Rhode Island and Providence moved from a situation where almost the entire population was of English Puritan stock to one where a third were foreign-born, and 70 per cent were of foreign origin. Not only did these waves of immigration make their presence felt in terms of nationality, but also with regard to religion, as all three of these recent groups of arrivals were Catholic. Thus the homogeneous Anglo Saxon Protestant population of 1840 found itself by 1910, as well as being only one of several national groupings in the city, practising a minority religion. The state census of 1905 showed the majority of the population to be Catholics. This situation remains at the present time.

With the coming of the First World War and the subsequent imposition of immigration quotas by the Federal Government, the days of rapid increase in numbers of foreign born settling in the state, and the days of rapid increase in the growth of Providence as a city were over. From around 1910, there has been a steady decline in the numbers of people born abroad. By 1960 only 12 per cent of the people of Providence were not Americans by birth. But the three great waves of immigration have still not become completely absorbed: 44 per cent of the city could still be classified as foreign born or of foreign stock, i.e. having a paternal grandfather born outside the United States. As would be expected, given their relatively late arrival, Italians comprise the largest single group amongst Providence's ethnic minorities. In 1960, 38 per cent of foreign stock in the city were of Italian descent. This number represented about 16 per cent of the city's total population. In contrast the Irish and French-Canadians only accounted for roughly 5 per cent each. The only other national groupings of measurable size in the Providence of the 1960s are British, Russians (predominantly Jews), Portuguese and Poles.

In contrast to this large ethnic population, the number of blacks in Providence is not large. In Rhode Island non-whites make up something over 2 per cent of the total population, while in Providence the figure is nearer 6 per cent. As in other major American cities, non-whites are concentrated in certain areas of the town. However, in contrast to many other cities, these areas are to nowhere near the same extent *exclusively* inhabited by black people. In 1960, the three census tracts with the heaviest concentrations of non-whites contained 56 per cent, 44 per cent and 22 per cent respectively. Taking into account the large segment of Providence's population that is of foreign stock, this relatively small percentage of non-whites is not difficult to explain. As Goldstein and Mayer have pointed out, 'Rhode Island has never been as attractive to Southern

Negro migrants as other industrial centres of the North because of the presence of a large working class immigrant population.'

Providence and Rhode Island were in the vanguard of the development of manufacturing in the United States, and the region continues to be one of the most highly industrialised in the country. Until the end of the nineteenth century, Rhode Island was one of the leading centres of textiles manufacture. A variety of cloths was produced, but primarily cottons, woollens and worsteds. However, since 1920, the cotton industry especially has been in a permanent state of decline, as firms have gradually moved out of the state and relocated in the South. This movement has not left the rest of the region's economy unaffected. The woollen and worsted industries were not influenced by this exodus in the 1920s, but since the end of the last war they too have been losing to competition from the South. The decline of the textile industry has therefore become a fact of life for both Rhode Island and Providence. In 1919 the textile industry employed 75,000 people, over half of the manufacturing labour force of the state. In 1965 the comparable figures were 21,000 and 18 per cent respectively.

The nineteenth century also saw the emergence of a number of metal working trades in Rhode Island, primarily engaged in the manufacture of specialised tools and machinery for the developing textile industry. However, diversification took place relatively early, and for the whole of this century a large variety of goods has been produced in the area. Nevertheless, decline in the textile industry brought about a severe contraction in the metal working trades, especially those that were most directly concerned with the building of textile producing machines. But this was not the only branch to suffer. The domination of the industrial scene by cloth manufacturing was such that its demise affected nearly all sectors of the state's economy. However, the economic boom brought along by the Second World War and lasting through until the 1950s was enjoyed almost entirely by the metal trades of Rhode Island. Between 1939 and 1947 the number of people engaged in the production of all kinds of machinery almost doubled: from 9,500 to 18,400. Today metal and machining production constitutes the single largest source of employment in Providence. Within the Providence–Pawtucket Standard Metropolitan Statistical Area (S.M.S.A.) in 1960, just over one quarter of the manufacturing labour force was employed in the metal trades. The comparable figure for the textile industries was just one fifth. In 1966 the metals and machining industries in Rhode Island employed over 37,000 people.

Towards the end of the eighteenth century a jeweller by the name of Nehemiah Dodge began making jewellery in Providence out of cheap alloy, rather than gold. Today the American low and medium price jewellery industry is centred in the Providence–Attelboro area. In 1967 there were 85 costume jewellery factories in Providence alone. Around

18,000 workers are engaged in the manufacture of various kinds of jewellery and silverware, constituting around 16 per cent of the manufacturing labour force. Finally, fourth in rank among Rhode Island's industries is the production of rubber and plastics. Again, the manufacture of rubber goods has long been associated with the state. And although initially the industry was virtually limited to the production of the Providence shoe – a type of footwear made of vulcanised rubber – it is, at present, fairly diverse, turning out a wide variety of products. Within the Providence–Pawtucket S.M.S.A. around 6 per cent of the labour force are concerned with the industry, comprising over 8,000 workers.

These four main industries form the industrial basis of Providence and Rhode Island, together with lesser manufactures such as food processing, optical goods and chemical products. Two features are striking: first, the very high degree of industrialisation in the state; secondly, the pronounced dependence on only a few industries, one of which has been in a state of decline for a long time. In 1950, 44 per cent of the labour force were engaged in manufacturing. By 1967 this figure had dropped to 38 per cent. Within this 38 per cent total textiles are coming to play a lesser role and, correspondingly, the metal industries a more important one, even though, in absolute terms, they have grown little during the 1960s. Nevertheless, there are signs that Providence is at last recovering from a period of economic insecurity and weakness, that has lasted – interrupted only by period of wartime artificial expansion – since the 1920s. In 1950, 7.5 per cent of the male labour force were unemployed. By 1966 the figure had dropped to 4.2 per cent.

The fact that the region has not enjoyed prosperity for the large part of this century is reflected in several demographic characteristics of its population. Rhode Island has proportionately fewer adults who have completed high school, or graduated from college, than the other New England states, or, for that matter, the country as a whole. Similarly, Rhode Island and Providence both have a significantly larger percentage of the labour force in manual or blue collar occupations than is the case for the rest of the country. Whereas for the United States, the segment of the workforce that is urban blue collar has fallen below 50 per cent, in Providence in 1970 56 per cent of the workforce were still in this category.

Table 1 shows the relative proportions of the labour forces of selected cities that are in white and blue collar occupations. In terms of total labour force, Providence has a smaller proportion of non-manual workers than any of the other cities shown with the exception of the automobile city, Flint, Michigan. As far as the female labour force is concerned Providence, of *all* metropolitan areas shown, has the smallest percentage engaged in white collar occupations. Indeed, there is a significantly higher proportion of females in the labour force in Providence than for the nation as a whole. These women are employed largely in non-skilled

Table 1. *Total labour force in white and blue collar occupations for selected cities, 1970*

	Male labour force		Female labour force		Total labour force	
	White collar	Blue collar	White collar	Blue collar	White collar	Blue collar
	Percentage					
San Jose, Cal.	49	50	68	32	56	44
Atlanta, Ga.	43	57	58	42	50	50
Boston, Mass.	43	57	70	30	55	45
Pittsburgh, Penn.	40	60	66	34	50	50
PROVIDENCE, R. I.	38	62	53	47	44	56
Savannah, Ga.	36	64	57	43	45	55
Hartford, Conn.	32	67	63	37	46	54
Flint, Mich.	27	73	56	44	38	62
Total U.S.A.	41	54	60	38	48	48

SOURCE: Computed from United States Census, 1970, series PC(1). In some cases percentages do not total 100 per cent because of exclusion of farm-workers and farm managers. Service workers have been classified as blue collar.

operative jobs in textile and jewellery firms. It is the existence of these two industries that largely explains the disproportionate numbers of female blue collar workers in Providence.

Despite the relatively small proportion of white collar people in Providence, the city does not contain an unusual number of really low-income families. In fact the state has comparatively fewer low-income families than the rest of the country, while Providence approximates to the norm, with just over one fifth of all families having a family income of less than $3,000 in 1960. With regard to income distribution for the rest of the city, the median income in 1960 was $5,069 and for the U.S.A. as a whole, $5,657. Over half of the residents earned a family income of between $3,000 and $7,000 per annum in 1960. This is lower clustering than one would expect to find elsewhere. At the same time a smaller segment of families earn incomes of above $10,000 than is the case in comparable cities in the United States. In 1960, 10 per cent of all family units earned such an income.

Finally, it is relevant that mention be made of the 'political atmosphere' of Providence and Rhode Island. The state is regarded by students of state politics as being a 'two-party competitive state'. While in general terms this is true (of the last thirteen presidential elections Rhode Island voted with the nation eleven times), as a statement it obscures several important dimensions of the situation. In fact, the Providence political scene of the mid 1960s had two striking features: the first was the tremendous hold the Democratic party had over the city; the second the tremendous hold the Irish had over the Democratic party. Of the 11 Senators Providence sends to the State Senate none were Republicans in 1967.

Of the 22 representatives it sends to the House of Representatives only two were Republicans in 1967. In the Presidential election of 1964 86 per cent of the Providence vote was for Johnson. Control of this Democratic strength is still very much in the hands of the first major wave of immigrants to Providence in the 1840s – the Irish. Of the 26 councillors in Providence in 1967 13 were Irish; this excludes the mayor, who is also Irish. There are in Providence 120 city committeemen: 71 of them are Irish; the party chairman is also Irish. Of the 13 ward chairmen 10 are Irish. This does not mean the political situation has always been like this, and nor is the picture as completely one-sided as these figures might suggest. Between 1963 and 1968 Rhode Island had a Republican Governor. Nevertheless, in the 1966 election – the last one where he was successful – his share of the vote in Providence was significantly lower than in the state as a whole (55 per cent as against 63 per cent).

Methodology

The Sample Frame and the Interview
The data for the study were obtained from a stratified random sample containing 333 cases. Of this number, interviews were successfully completed with 276 respondents. This represents a response rate of 83 per cent. The original sample was drawn from the 1966 edition of Polk's *Providence City Directory*, which lists all persons who live or work in the city of Providence. For the purpose of the research I required only male heads of households, married and presently living with their wives, and who were in one of the craft or white collar occupations listed below. This information was given by the Directory for each person listed, as well as their home address and the name of their employer. The actual sample is made up of:

> 35 Bricklayers and Masons
> 49 Cabinet makers and Masons
> 56 Electricians
> 54 Toolmakers
> 44 Clerks
> 38 Managers

The survey instrument was a structured interview schedule administered to the male head of household by a trained interviewer. That schedule in its final form contained 193 questions, many of them split into two parts. Both 'closed-ended' and 'open-ended' questions were included. The schedule itself is reproduced in the Appendix.

Before being approached by an interviewer, each potential respondent received a letter explaining that his name had been randomly selected for inclusion in a study being carried out by the Department of Sociology at Brown University. The letter was on University letterhead. The purpose of the study was described as being an investigation into the 'way of life' of the 'average American' in the mid 1960s. Within four days of receiving this letter, potential respondents were approached in person by an interviewer. If at all possible, the interview was obtained at that time. Otherwise, unless the person refused to take part in the survey, an appointment was made for a future date. Potential respondents who at the first meeting with an interviewer refused to co-operate, were sent a second letter. This attempted to show how important it was that *everybody* in the sample should take part. A second interviewer was then sent to the person's home to conduct the interview. Several of these second attempts were successful. Interviews lasted from one and a quarter to four hours. The average length was a little over two hours. Finally, blacks and people born abroad were excluded from the sample, as the nature of the study precluded any analysis of the interplay between racial and class situations, or between class structure and the process of early acculturation or assimilation. As the *City Directory* did not give this information, inter- viewers were instructed to follow a skip-pattern should a potential respondent fall into one of these groupings. In such cases, the schedule was then discarded.

The Occupational Categories

The four particular craft groups were chosen so as to yield some variation on factors such as type of work tasks, work situation (factory versus individual production) and age of the craft. While it was not feasible to control for these factors in any systematic way, the four groups chosen do, to an extent, provide that variation.

In these terms, toolmakers were selected as representing a craft calling for a very high level of skill (in general the apprenticeship lasts seven years), and where the worker has a high degree of autonomy in the work situation. Toolmaking is definitely a factory job, yet, as is shown below, the size of factory differed considerably within the sub-sample: while 29 per cent worked in factories employing less than 50 men, 28 per cent were in establishments with more than 500 employees. The majority of the toolmakers interviewed were engaged in making individual tools, working from blueprints. These tools were then used primarily in mass production industry, stamping out such things as buckles, watch parts and cases, and especially, jewellery.

Cabinet making and carpentering are much older trades than tool- making, yet neither appears to have resisted new techniques or methods to any extent. The variety of work tasks would seem to be greater within this woodworking group than among the toolmakers. Several of the cabinet makers worked in small shops making individual cabinets, or other furniture to order, while a good proportion of the carpenters worked mainly outside on heavy construction work. Similarly the degree of spec- ialisation differed considerably from one man to another: one cabinet maker worked only on the fine detail work (carving or inlay) on pieces of furniture, while several carpenters said they did everything concerned with the woodwork side of the construction industry generally. As would be expected, given the variety and nature of woodworking, few of the cabinet makers and carpenters in our sample worked in or for firms employing more than 250 people. This situation stands in contrast to that of the toolmakers.

The bricklayers and masons have much in common with the wood-workers, insofar as both groups are part of the construction industry and therefore not heavily involved in large scale organisations. An important difference however, is the degree of variety inherent in the two sets of occupations. From the responses of the bricklayers and masons we inter-viewed it would seem that their work offers less scope for variety or individuality. The vast majority of the people we talked to simply laid bricks, blocks or stone. To be sure, buildings differ one from another in form, but the actual tasks involved in bricklaying do not. The exception to this appears to be in the smaller jobs these men occasionally had to carry out, such as making patios, stone fireplaces or decorative tiling. But such tasks were the exception rather than the rule.

The electricians in the study represent the most recently developed set of skills of the four craft groups. In terms of variation in work tasks and the level of mastery, electrical work has more in common with tool-making than the building trades represented in the sample. A proportion of the electricians we interviewed were engaged primarily in wiring new homes and other buildings, but others were concerned with the repair and maintenance of V.H.F. equipment or airplane and submarine electrics. Linked with the variety of work carried out by these craftsmen, roughly equal proportions of the sub-sample worked in 'small', 'medium' and 'large' firms.

Virtually every lower level white collar worker was listed as a clerk, office worker or office clerk (in addition there were two bank tellers). Again the types of work tasks differ. As will be seen in chapter 2, there is considerable variation within the clerical group in terms of the extent to which the office is mechanised. While most clerks work with at least one machine, usually a desk calculator, several still carry out the majority of their duties without recourse to mechanical aids, while others, during their working day, use a whole variety of equipment. Similarly the content of work tasks varies considerably. Some of the lower level clerical workers we talked to performed only a few narrow and defined tasks. One man, for example, kept the records on the maintenance of the trucks owned by his firm; another accepted, and then forwarded com-plaints on inoperative street lights. Other clerks carried out even more delimited functions; one respondent simply processed in and outgoing mail; several members of this group were payroll clerks or expeditors. On the other hand a large proportion of the clerical sample were in jobs that did provide for a diversity of work experience. Several described their jobs as comprising 'varied office work', while a few were in positions that clearly afforded a good deal of autonomy. A clerk in the Licence Bureau, for example, spent his day researching around licence applications as well as the characters of people applying for particular licences. Other men had similar jobs working for agencies such as the Veteran's Administration and the Medicare programme.

The sub-sample of managers was obtained so as to provide a stable middle class control group, against which the situation of clerks and craftsmen could be compared. As might be expected, the term 'manager' covers a variety of titles and positions. In fact only individuals in middle or lower level managerial positions were included in the list from which the sample was drawn. Titles such as Administrative Assistant, Executive Assistant, Assistant Production Manager, Assistant General Manager, Assistant to the President therefore appear frequently. Similarly, the work tasks performed by members of this group were diverse, although all could be classed as being of an 'administrative' or 'executive' nature. Perhaps the most important difference within the category is the extent to which diffuse as opposed to specific and delimited functions are performed. Several men described their jobs as involving general administration, supervising so many people, or sharing in the overall running of an organisation. Others had posts which, while more specialised, still left scope for a degree of variability. One respondent, for example, did the accounting for plant machinery – the buying of new equipment, repairs and the disposal of used machinery. Two men were involved in production control, while another two were on the public relations side of industry. Finally, a few of the managerial respondents were in occupations that must be regarded as being highly specialised. One man we talked to was concerned only with the way in which space was used in his organisation. Another concentrated on the expansion of his company, with special reference to the possibilities of mergers or acquisitions of other firms.

Characteristics of the Sample

Several of the features peculiar to Providence, outlined earlier in this chapter, are manifested in this particular sample, some of the characteristics of which are presented in Table 2.

The fact that Providence contains an aging population is not specially evident from the age composition of the total sample. For the nation as a whole 29 per cent of the male labour force were over 50 years old in 1965, a figure almost identical to that found within the craft sub-sample. This is not the case however, for the two white collar occupational groups. Indeed nearly three fifths of the clerical workers were above this age. This gives credence to my earlier statement that the opportunities for clerical workers to rise to managerial or executive positions are diminishing. If the opposite

Table 2. *Selected sample characteristics*

	Brick-layers and Masons	Cabinet makers and Carpenters	Elec-tricians	Tool-makers	Total Craft	Clerks	Managers
	Percentage						
Age							
20–34	36	27	32	21	29	20	20
35–49	38	43	39	40	40	22	40
50 and above	26	30	29	39	31	58	40
Education							
Grammar or some high school	71	53	52	46	54	25	11
High school graduate	23	35	46	41	38	43	8
Some college or college graduate	6	12	2	13	8	32	81
Ethnicity, i.e. paternal grandfather's birthplace							
U.S.A.	12	6	21	19	16	21	24
Ireland	6	6	4	—	4	9	21
Canada	—	8	2	—	3	16	3
Italy	66	51	43	43	49	40	18
Other	16	29	30	38	28	14	34
Religion							
Protestant	6	18	13	26	16	16	29
Catholic	91	74	79	70	78	84	55
Other	3	8	8	4	6	—	16
Employment							
Employed	83	78	96	98	90	100	95
Self-employed	17	22	4	2	10	—	5
Size of firm							
Under 50	67	60	36	29	45	39	40
50–249	18	32	35	35	31	29	26
250 and above	15	8	29	36	24	32	34
Father's occupation							
Blue collar	80	82	78	73	78	83	44
White collar	9	4	6	14	8	12	35
Self-employed	11	14	16	13	14	5	21
Wife's current occupation							
Blue collar	20	24	14	18	19	11	5
White collar	6	24	23	18	19	32	16
Not employed	74	52	63	64	62	57	79
*Total per cent	100	100	100	100	100	100	100
Total number	35	49	56	54	194	44	38

* Totals for all characteristics equal 100 per cent.

were the case we should expect the age composition of this lower level white collar group to be balanced in favour of the younger age groups. There is, however, no reason to suppose that the age composition of the white collar sample represents a source of bias. While intuitively one might expect older people to be more conservative and set in their ways, and thus less likely to respond to change in market or work situation, sociological support of this position is scant.[25] Furthermore, as will become apparent, on none of the objective or subjective components of social class analysed in subsequent chapters does the variable of age exert any significant effect.

While the general level of education throughout the sample is relatively high, there is a significant gap in the standards reached by clerks and craftsmen. However, it must be realised that within the craft sub-sample the proportion of young workers who have graduated from high school is much higher than the proportion of older men who have done so. This is also the case for the nation as a whole. In the present study 66 per cent of the craft sample under the age of 35 had graduated from high school, as against only 31 per cent of those aged over 50. Therefore, if education should prove to be an important factor making for the breakdown of class differentials it must be borne in mind that the educational standards of skilled workers are rising swiftly.

The ethnic and religious composition of the sample is what one would expect given the history of immigration to Providence and Rhode Island. By far the largest ethnic group represented is the Italian, with the managerial category containing disproportionately fewer of this group and more 'native' Americans than the other two occupational groups, especially the skilled craftsmen. Given the fact that individuals of foreign stock are represented heavily in all of the occupational sub-samples, I would not expect this to provide a major source of bias *within* this particular study. Indeed, in this connection Providence is not dissimilar from other large New England towns. It does however provide cause for concern in any attempt to generalise from the situation in Providence to the American class structure *in toto*.

Table 2 also shows that 10 per cent of the craft sample are self-employed. This may appear surprising. Nonetheless my decision to include these people in the study was a conscious one, and stems from a careful consideration of their characteristics, as compared with those of the large majority who are employees. The nature of the work tasks carried out by the self-employed was identical to those performed by those who did not work for themselves. Virtually every one of this former group either worked by himself or employed no more than one other person. If anything, these people worked longer days than those working for an employer. Furthermore, in the analysis of each of the components of social class examined in this monograph, self-employed craftsmen were initially separated from the rest of the skilled craft group in order to ascertain whether or not any difference existed between the two sub-groups. In not one case did such a difference appear. Accordingly I have included in the total craft category those few skilled men who do work for themselves.

Earlier in this chapter, in the discussion of the ways in which it had been suggested the affluent worker might be exposed to middle class values and behavioural patterns, attention was directed towards the family. It is evident, however, that for the craft sample as a whole, exposure to the middle class via the working wife is not going to assume significant proportions. Only around one fifth of the craftsmen in the study currently have wives in white collar jobs. To be sure, over half of these skilled men are married to women who *at some time* have been employed in offices but, as we shall see, little significance can be attributed to this. In addition emphasis was placed upon the potential importance of the class *background* of routine non-manual and manual workers. Intergenerational mobility was regarded as being relevant insofar as it may lead to the *importation* of middle class values into the working class by downwardly mobile manual workers, or, and more likely, the carrying of working class values into the middle class by upwardly mobile white collar employees. In fact, as can be seen in Table 2, very few of the manual workers in the sample were brought up in homes headed by a white collar worker. However over 80 per cent of the clerks we interviewed had themselves been upwardly mobile from a blue collar household. If the subsequent analysis suggests that changes are occurring in the middle ranges of the American class structure, the class backgrounds of the clerical sample may well assume a degree of importance.

We have seen that the choice of locale for this study is in the centre of a highly urbanised and industrialised area. As a community it contains disproportionate numbers of both foreign stock and manual employees, while in political terms the region is strongly Democratic, and the Democratic party is run largely by people of Irish descent. The population is aging, and there is a good deal of out-migration. In economic terms there has been, and to a lesser extent continues to be, an over-dependence on only a few industries. As a result Providence cannot be regarded as being a wealthy or affluent city. The sample drawn reflects these various characteristics. Finally, in *any* piece of sociological investigation conducted in a single community, distinctive features of that community present difficulties to the researcher, especially insofar as he may be inhibited from generalising from that particular locale to the society as a whole.* The analysis that follows take explicit account of this fact.

---

* I am therefore, rejecting the notion that one can find the 'ideal' community in which to conduct a piece of research – a community that can be regarded as a microcosm of the total society. The avoidance of certain unusual characters will almost certainly be associated with exposure to others. In this regard I cannot agree with Warner and his associates who feel able to claim that 'To study Jonesville is to study America.' For 'Jonesville is in all Americans and all Americans are in Jonesville, for he that dwelleth in America dwelleth in Jonesville, and Jonesville in him.' Such assertions do little to foster our understanding of social class in the United States. See W. Lloyd Warner *et al.*, *Democracy in Jonesville* (New York, 1949), p. ix.

2   The Job

'After building a home I feel an accomplishment, something to last 100 years or so. I feel I've done something for society.'

'I like creating and building things, I like to use my hands and brains, it's constructive work; very satisfying when you see the metal tool that I've built myself as per blueprint instructions.

Market Situation: Income

I have already noted that discussion of changes taking place in the middle ranges of the American class structure was stimulated by the increasing evidence that the income differential between the upper levels of blue collar workers and lower grade clerical workers was fast disappearing. This evidence, crude as it was, began to appear in the 1950s. Given the interrelationship between the economic system and class structure, several sociologists, most notably Mayer, were led to suggest that this crucial shift in the distribution of income represented a first step in the acceptance of large numbers of blue collar workers into the existing middle class.

Traditionally, as has already been pointed out, a fundamental line of demarcation in the American class structure has been that separating manual from non-manual workers. This line of demarcation was noticeably evident in the income differential that separated the two groups. The extent of this differential, and its gradual disappearance, has been clearly documented by Burns who has brought together data bearing on the comparative economic position of skilled manual and white collar employees between 1890 and 1952.[1] The data presented by Burns are important for two reasons. First, they show clearly the extent of the difference in income between clerks and craftsmen and the way in which this gap has gradually closed. Secondly, they indicate that changes in the volume of economic activity appear to affect the manual worker's wage packet more drastically than the non-manual worker's. During the boom years of the First World War the pay of manual workers rose at a faster rate than that of white collar workers. Similarly in the deflation period of

1920-2, whilst both groups' income dropped, it was that of the blue collar group which dropped the more sharply.

More generally, Burns shows that between 1890 and 1915 clerical workers earned more than twice as much as manual workers. Gradually during the first half of the twentieth century, allowing for fluctuations brought about by the trade cycle, the earnings of blue collar workers closed with those of lower level white collar employees. In 1949 there was virtually no difference between the average weekly earnings of the two groups, while in 1952 manual workers had an average weekly wage of $69.24 cents as against $66.63 cents for clerical workers.

These same trends observed by Burns were also detected and documented in rather more detail by Mayer.[2] In 1956 for example, the latter was able to reveal the rather surprising fact that amongst families earning more than $7,500 per annum, over one third were headed by individuals in manual occupations. Mayer also stressed the importance of the working wife in 'lifting' large numbers of blue collar families into higher income brackets.[3]

In the present study respondents were asked for details of their income before taxes for the year 1966, both for themselves and for their wives in those cases where she was working. Mean annual incomes for husbands only are shown in Table 3.

These average income figures show that the trend documented by Burns and Mayer has continued, so that the earnings for the craft group as a whole are considerably higher than for the clerical group. In addition it is clear that there is considerable variation *within* the craft group from one skill to another. For example, toolmakers and electricians earn considerably higher incomes than the crafts associated more closely with the building trades. This difference is in some cases well over $2,000. An interesting comparison is between the average income of those husbands whose wives

Table 3. *Mean annual income for male head of household*

	Brick-layers and Masons	Cabinet makers and Carpenters	Elec-tricians	Tool-makers	Total Craft	Clerks	Managers
Husband's income (non-working wife)	$7640	$6670	$8750	$9000	$8110	$6390	$12170
Husband's income (working wife)	6230	6230	6950	7590	6800	6000	9750
Total husband's income	7110	6470	8110	8400	7590	6180	11650
Total number	35	49	56	52	192	39	37

do not work and whose income is therefore total family income, and those who do have working wives and who, consequently, have a total income which is considerably higher than that they themselves earn. In all cases the average income of those men who do have working wives is substantially lower than that of those who do not. In the case of electricians the gap approaches $2,000. These differences give important clues as to the factors underlying wives remaining in or returning to the labour force after marriage. These points will be taken up in the following chapter.

In an increasing number of families, husband's income will not be the sole source of support but will be supplemented by the earnings of a working wife. Indeed, as I have already pointed out, Mayer saw the working wife as being a crucial factor in explaining why such a large proportion of manual families was now able to attain middle or even upper middle level incomes. It is important, therefore, that we make some comparison of the relative extent to which wives do augment their husband's total income.

My findings do indeed bear out Mayer's assertion that the working wife does make an important contribution toward the family income of skilled workers. However, this phenomenon is by no means limited to the wives of craftsmen. Indeed the clerical group has a much higher proportion of families where the wife works than do any of the manual categories. Two fifths of the craft group as a whole have working wives (amongst the electricians the figure is 35 per cent whilst for the cabinet makers and carpenters it is 45 per cent). In the case of the clerks 54 per cent of the families have a wife in the labour force. As might be expected in the managerial group, less than one quarter have wives who work.

In Table 4 are presented the family incomes both of those families where the wife does work, and those where she does not, as well as the total family incomes of the sample. (The total family incomes where the wife does not work is, of course, the same as husband's income alone – see Table 2 above.) It is evident that the wives of electricians and clerks make the

Table 4. *Mean annual income for total family*

	Brick-layers and Masons	Cabinet makers and Carpenters	Electricians	Tool-makers	Total Craft	Clerks	Managers
Family income (non-working wife)	$7640	$6670	$8750	$9000	$8110	$6390	$12170
Family income (working wife)	8230	8770	10260	10090	9430	9050	13000
Total family income	7860	7610	9300	9460	8650	7820	12350
Total number	35	49	56	54	192	39	37

largest average contribution, amounting, in both cases, to over $3,000. However, because the average income of husbands who do have working wives is less than those who do not, the additional income gained by the wife does not raise the total family income as much as might be expected in all cases. For example, the total family income of the electricians who do not have working wives is only $1,500 less than those who do, although wives contribute an average of $3,300 within this particular group. On the other hand, the wives of clerical workers earn sufficiently more than the wives of skilled building workers, so that the total family income of these white collar families is appreciably higher than for two of the four craft groups.

It is evident that if there does exist an income differential between clerks and craftsmen, it is a differential in favour of the latter. This is the situation whether we compare husband's wage or salary alone, or total family income, although the superior earning powers of clerical wives do reduce the size of blue collar advantage in those families where both husband and wife are in the labour force.[4]

Other Components of Market Situation

Annual income cannot be regarded as the sole determinant of life chances or market situation. Other dimensions of occupational role can also be important, primarily because of their ability to influence income, especially in the long run. It has often been in terms of these other factors that clerks have shared a far more advantageous position than blue collar workers.

Traditionally white collar workers have enjoyed a much greater degree of job security, and earnings which fluctuate far less from one week to the next than have manual workers. Whilst white collar workers have usually been considered as part of overhead costs, blue collar workers have been seen as variable costs, closely tied to a firm's production schedule or general level of economic activity. This means that the demand for blue collar workers' services has expanded and contracted, and this has been reflected in level of earnings and unemployment. American unions have been striving towards the goal of a guaranteed annual wage for manual workers for a very long time. Foote noted as long ago as 1953 the increasing demands of labour unions for a continuous income, and saw this as the most convincing evidence to date of what he regarded as a move towards 'the professionalisation of labour'.[5] And stability of income has not been the only benefit of white collar employment. Manual workers have always been paid by the hour rather than the week and have had to punch a time clock and work longer or more inconvenient hours – the shift system being the epitome of this. In the mid 1960s for example, General Motors was still paying its blue collar employees on the basis of every tenth of an hour

Table 5. *Length of notice employer must give to terminate employment*

	Brick-layers and Masons	Cabinet makers and Car-penters	Elec-tricians	Tool-makers	Total Craft	Clerks	Managers
	Percentage						
One day or less	87	73	61	36	61	31	30
One week	—	16	13	30	16	7	—
2 weeks	3	5	14	30	15	18	33
4 weeks or more	10	6	12	4	8	44	37
Total per cent	100	100	100	100	100	100	100
Total number	30	38	56	54	178	44	35

worked. Several of these differences have also, of course, been important in status as well as economic terms: clerks arriving at work an hour later than manual workers being seen both as an economic and as a prestige advantage.

My findings indicate that there still exists a substantial difference between white and blue collar workers with regard to these secondary aspects of market positions. Skilled craftsmen remain in occupational situations less secure, less privileged and with fewer safeguards than those experienced by lower level clerical employees.

In Table 5 data are presented regarding the length of notice, or amount of pay in lieu of notice, that respondents' employers would *have* to give if they wanted to dispense with their services. It is evident that, with the possible exception of the toolmakers, few of the craftsmen we interviewed enjoy anything approaching a level of formal job security, being liable to virtually instant dismissal. In contrast, it comes as little surprise that the majority of individuals in both clerical and managerial groups cannot be dismissed without at least a full week's notice. This sets both white collar categories off sharply against all four craft groups. However, this security is to a degree affected by the fact that almost one third of both the white collar groups are liable to dismissal upon notice of a day or less.

As an additional measure of job security respondents were also asked to say how safe, in their own estimation, were their present jobs. While in theory it may be possible to dismiss a man at a day's notice, in reality the situation may never come about because of a scarcity of skill, informal agreements, and so forth. Not only does this provide an additional source of information on job security, it is also relevant in that it provides clues as to respondents' *perception* of the situation. This is important insofar as it may affect attitudes towards, or degree of satisfaction with, the job. The pattern of responses to this question is shown in Table 6. In fact it indicates that the perceived *de facto* situation is somewhat less drastic or insecure than the *de jure* situation. Indeed, with the possible exception of the

Table 6. *Perceived level of security of present job*

	Brick-layers and Masons	Cabinet makers and Car-penters	Elec-tricians	Tool-makers	Total Craft	Clerks	Managers
	Percentage						
Completely secure	29	21	47	31	33	55	39
Quite secure	35	58	46	63	52	34	52
Not very secure	15	2	5	2	5	7	3
Not at all secure	6	7	2	—	3	4	3
D.K.	15	12	—	4	7	—	3
Total per cent	100	100	100	100	100	100	100
Total number	35	49	56	54	194	44	38

bricklayers and masons, the proportion of each occupational group in the sample considering its present job to be 'not very secure' is minimal. Despite the fact that so many could, in theory, be dismissed with an hour's notice, few appear concerned that this is a possibility. Clerks nonetheless appear to remain in a preferential position to craftsmen, although this must not be allowed to minimise the fact that 85 per cent of the sample of blue collar workers regard their present job as being at least 'quite secure'.

From other evidence available it would seem that these optimistic evaluations are not without foundation. Of the 194 craftsmen in the sample only 34 had been put out of work through no fault of their own at any time in the five years previous to 1967. Of these 34 craftsmen 26 were either woodworkers or bricklayers and masons. Only two toolmakers and six electricians (and one clerk) have been 'laid off' during the period 1962 to 1967. The single most important reason for this redundancy was the weather or seasonal factors. Thirteen of the 16 bricklayers and masons concerned said they had been made unemployed because of winter conditions, which made work impossible. This is clearly a factor peculiar to the building trade and one that is going to continue to place building workers in a disadvantageous position in the foreseeable future. Nonetheless 82 per cent of the craft group as a whole and 96 per cent of toolmakers and 89 per cent of the electricians have not been put out of work in the last five years. The confidence expressed by the craftsmen in general, and these two groups in particular, cannot therefore be regarded as being overly unrealistic.

An integral aspect of stability of incomes is the presence and size of sickness benefits attached to a particular occupation. Again this is an area where in the past white collar workers have held the advantage. This advantage has yet to disappear. Eighty-six per cent of the clerical sample and all but one of the managers were in jobs that continued to pay them if they were unable to work because of illness. Amongst the total craft group, however, only 32 per cent were in this enviable position. Again it is the woodworkers and stoneworkers who are the least privileged while the toolmakers and electricians are in a position closer to that enjoyed by the clerks. Forty-six per cent of electricians and 37 per cent of toolmakers received sick pay from their employer in the event of illness. In addition, those firms that do provide sickness benefit for skilled blue collar workers appear to have adopted reasonably generous programmes. Of the 26 electricians who receive sickness payment, 18 (69 per cent) go on receiving if for more than three months in the event of illness. The comparative figures for clerks and managers are 61 per cent and 59 per cent respectively. For the craft group as a whole 42 per cent of those who are paid in the event of illness can go on receiving that pay for a period of over three months.

While the blue collar respondents are still in a considerably disadvantageous position in terms of the provision of sick pay, this is not the case with regard to firms providing and contributing to health schemes for their employees. Virtually all the white collar workers in the sample worked for firms that contribute to one of the major health insurance schemes (usually Blue Cross), while one third of the clerical group and about half of the managerial group work for employers who, in addition, contribute to Major Medical insurance. However, four fifths of the total craft group are also enrolled in a health insurance scheme by their employer or to a lesser extent by their union. Indeed 65 per cent of electricians and 96 per cent of toolmakers have employers who contribute to health insurance schemes for them. Again the situation of the woodworkers and bricklaying groups is less fortunate. Approximately one third of these groups are not involved in schemes provided by either management or union.

The situation that has existed in the past, with white collar workers receiving a guaranteed income after retirement in the form of a pension, and manual workers having to exist on Government programmes only, would appear to be changing rapidly. Only 18 per cent of the clerks and 11 per cent of the managers do not receive a pension upon retirement. For the craft group, while the comparable proportion is certainly larger, it is not inordinately so. Thirty-five per cent of the total craft group do not receive a pension. In the case of the electricians the figure is only 16 per cent. The majority of skilled blue collar workers are therefore in a position long considered to be the prerogative of white collar personnel. The nature of the pension, however, does differ both between the white and blue collar groups and within the four craft groups. Both clerks and managers receive their pensions from their employer, as does virtually every one of the pension-receiving toolmakers and almost half of the pension-receiving electricians. On the other hand, amongst bricklayers and masons, and cabinet makers and carpenters, employers do not pay pensions after retirement. This is linked to the casual nature of the building industry. Those bricklayers and woodworkers who do receive pensions collect them from their unions, who have, in this case, developed their own schemes in response to the mobility from one job to another characteristic of these trades.

However, job security and sickness and retirement benefits are not the only rewards that have in the past been associated with non-manual, as opposed to manual work. Features such as the length of working week, the method of payment, and the presence or absence of shift-working, must be included in any discussion of comparative market situation. Such aspects of a particular job may be less tangible than, for example, size of income or pension, but they are rewards nevertheless. And in terms of such rewards there is again a clear line of demarcation separating the blue from the white collar members of the sample.

Over three quarters of the clerks work a five day week, a situation enjoyed by only 44 per cent of the toolmakers. For the craft group as a whole, about three fifths do not work on either Saturday or Sunday. Virtually the entire sample works a normal day. This is even the case amongst toolmakers working in a factory. Only one out of the 54 toolmakers was involved in any kind of shift work. All the wood and stone workers worked regular hours and only four out of 56 electricians were employed on a shift basis. These men, however, were working on submarines at nearby Greenwich, Connecticut, which made their work situation somewhat different. One would not find such a widespread working of 'office hours' amongst a sample of non-skilled assembly line workers. Not surprisingly, none of the clerks or managers worked other than a normal daily routine.

There is considerable variation within the craft group and between this group and the clerical workers with regard to the working of overtime. Only one third of the clerks ever work overtime as against 78 per cent of the toolmakers. For the total craft sample 57 per cent usually work overtime. Amongst bricklayers and masons only one quarter do so. As would be expected the great majority of craftsmen receive extra payment for working overtime. But surprisingly, 61 per cent of the clerical group said they received overtime pay if they stayed at work longer than usual. This is certainly suggestive of a change in the employment situation of clerks. In the past as salaried workers they have been expected to work, like management generally, extra hours whenever necessary without remuneration.

As would be expected, given differences in the working of overtime and a five day week between clerks and craftsmen, there is still a significant disparity between blue and white collar respondents in terms of the number of hours worked a week, although again this difference is not as great as it has been in the past. The clerks worked an average of $40\frac{1}{2}$ hours per week (including overtime). Although bricklayers and masons worked an average of only 40 hours per week, for the craft group as a whole this figure was 44, and for toolmakers it was $47\frac{1}{2}$. For different reasons, management worked longer hours than clerks, and indeed had an average identical to that of the total craft group.

Similarly there is a considerable difference between the manual and non-manual groups in terms of method of payment. But this difference is not as marked as we might expect, or as it has been in the past. Over four fifths of the total craft sample are paid by the hour. Within this group there is not a great deal of variation. However, 39 per cent of the clerks are also paid at an hourly rate. This is somewhat surprising, and would seem to be another example of a trend towards the lessening of the clerical workers' privileged position. This would also seem to be the case as far as a formal method of checking arrival and departure from work is concerned, i.e., by punching a time clock. 93 per cent of toolmakers – the factory workers – have to punch a time clock, but also half of the other three skilled manual groups have to do likewise. As compared to this proportion, 36 per cent – over one third – of the clerical workers have to clock on and off work.

If these secondary dimensions of market situation are taken as a whole, the toolmakers emerge as the craft group most clearly divorced from the position occupied by the clerical group: they work longer hours, a $5\frac{1}{2}$ day week, and more overtime than any of the other occupational categories. Conversely, bricklayers and masons seem to be in a very similar situation to clerks on all of these aspects. With only one quarter of them doing overtime, this is the only occupational group to achieve an average working week of 40 hours. However, there is a price to be paid for this luxury. It will be remembered that toolmakers earn the highest average income of any of the craft groups (at the same time as they enjoy a greater amount of job security), while bricklayers and masons, along with the woodworkers, were lagging behind considerably on both counts.

Promotion and Mobility

One of the most important differences in the situation of white and blue collar workers has always been the differential opportunities for upward mobility inherent in the two types of job. Manual occupations have been characterised as possessing virtually no mobility opportunities, the exception being the possibilities of promotion to the position of foreman. But even these have been few and far between. Chinoy found, for example, that in a factory of 6,000 workers only 10 or 12 vacancies for foreman occurred per year.[6] In addition, advancement across the blue collar/white collar line from the factory floor to the office appeared non-existent. Conversely there has been in the past a high degree of upward mobility from clerical to managerial positions. Indeed, a substantial proportion of managers have been recruited from the ranks of lower level white collar employees. Such differential mobility opportunities have had a crucial significance for the class situation of blue and white collar workers. First, the possibilities of becoming a part of management via promotion has acted as an important source of middle class identification and therefore behaviour, on the the part of lower level clerical workers. (This will be taken up in Chapter 6.) Secondly, such potential differences in career patterns have meant that the market situations of manual and non-manual workers may increasingly diverge: the skilled worker, for example, will not expect his income to change very drastically once he has completed his apprenticeship, while the clerk may reasonably expect his own salary to increase each time he is promoted. Indeed, the notion of the 'income career' is often held up as one of the identifying features of white collar employment.

In this study I unfortunately had to rely on the respondents' assessment of the promotion possibilities in their particular occupations. There is however, no reason why we should expect this to introduce a bias in a particular direction. The pattern of these estimations is shown in Table 7.

It is readily apparent that amongst the craft groups the perceived opportunities for advancement are considerably greater than previous research would lead us to expect, and certainly more impressive than those existing in the factory studied by Chinoy. Exactly one half of the skilled craft respondents considered the chances of promotion in their present job to be 'fair' or 'good', with slightly more opting for the latter than the former choice. This is to an extent offset by the fact that one quarter of the total craft group – and over a third in the case of woodworkers – say that they have no chance at all of being promoted. It is also relevant that the group of factory workers, i.e. the toolmakers, have the lowest proportion with a 'fair' or 'good' chance of promotion whilst the electricians have the highest proportion of optimists and the lowest proportion of pessimists—only 13 per cent of them saying they have no chance of promotion.

Equally important are the responses of the clerical group to this ques-

Table 7. *Estimated chances of promotion in present job*

	Brick-layers and Masons	Cabinet makers and Car-penters	Elec-tricians	Tool-makers	Total Craft	Clerks	Managers
	Percentage						
Good	35	21	44	27	33	27	30
Fair	17	29	15	15	18	23	14
Poor	17	8	22	29	20	23	28
None	31	37	13	25	25	18	28
D.K.	—	5	6	4	4	9	—
Total per cent	100	100	100	100	100	100	100
Total number	29	38	54	52	173	44	36

tion. For despite the existing stereotype, only half of the clerks interviewed (exactly the same proportion as for craftsmen), condidered the opportunities for advancement in their present job to be 'fair' or 'good'. This is by no means as high a figure as I would have expected. Indeed, in terms of general perceived chances for advancement there is little difference between any of the occupational groups in the sample (i.e. comparing the proportions of each group's considering its chances to be 'good' or 'fair' against the proportion considering the possibility of advancement to be 'poor' or 'none').

Those respondents who did regard their chances of promotion as being 'fair' or 'good' were then asked what was the top position they could expect to reach. Here differences did emerge between the white and blue collar samples. While in roughly equal proportions clerks said they could expect to be either chief clerks, assistant managers or managers, very few craftsmen gave positions on the other side of the white collar/blue collar line from their own. Of the 87 craftsmen who thought they had at least 'fair' promotion prospects, only six were thinking in terms of promotion to a white collar position. Rather, the great majority (85 per cent) regarded the job of foreman as being the top position they could expect to reach.

As far as individual aspirations are concerned, 66 per cent of the clerks and 56 per cent of the craft group say they would like to be promoted. For managers the figure is 75 per cent. Of those toolmakers who would like promotion, 39 per cent think their chances are slim as compared to 32 per cent of clerks. The difference between the two groups is that while 86 per cent of the clerks who think they have a 'fair' or 'good' chance of promotion would like that promotion, only 66 per cent of the craftsmen in a similar position wish to move upwards. Furthermore, amongst those who do want promotion, the evidence is that the clerks have done far more to attain that promotion than craftsmen. Over half of the craftsmen who wanted promotion admitted they had done nothing that would help them achieve that goal. Only 31 per cent of the clerks had been similarly inactive, while two thirds of them had had talks with the management or taken evening courses. For the craftsmen the corresponding figure is only one third.

Turning now to an examination of those respondents who did *not* consider their chances of promotion to be at least 'fair', it is surprising that not one of the 78 craftsmen in this situation cited the barrier of the blue collar/white collar line as being the underlying reason. It would seem that this is something that is so natural and permanent that it is neither questioned nor discussed. Instead the major reason given by the craftsmen for their lack of promotion possibilities was the fact that very few positions ever fell vacant. In the great majority of cases they were talking about the position of foreman. The only other reason mentioned to any extent was given only by the bricklayers and masons and cabinet makers and carpenters. Forty four per cent of the former and 36 per cent of the latter groups said they had little chance of promotion because there was 'nothing higher' to which they could be promoted. This explanation, hardly mentioned at all by the electricians and toolmakers, is clearly related to the casual work situation of the building trades. It is also further evidence regarding my interpretation of the perception of the blue collar/white collar line by craftsmen generally. Clearly there *are* higher jobs where bricklayers and carpenters work. What these respondents mean then is that there is nothing open to *them*, i.e., they are recognising the fundamental importance of the blue collar/white collar line, but only in a particular and implicit way.

The only major reason given by the clerks and managers in explanation of their poor promotion possibilities was that there were few positions ever vacant. This is understandable in the case of managers and somewhat surprising in the case of clerks, insofar as it would appear to signal a move away from the situation that has traditionally existed. And yet there are sound sociological reasons why we may expect this move to gain in momentum. Increasingly, as managerial positions become more specialised and technical, then they will be filled by people with particular qualifications, qualifications other than simple a general clerical experience. For example, more and more banks are recruiting college graduates as trainee managers and specialists, and high school graduates as tellers. It seems plausible to assume that the chances of a teller being promoted to a managerial position are correspondingly decreasing. Indeed, as long ago as 1951 Mills argued that the 'individual ascent chances' of the American clerical worker had declined considerably during the twentieth century and predicted that they would continue to do so. This decline was a direct result, Mills suggested, of two more general processes at work in American society: an increasing emphasis on technical expertise and formal qualifications, and the concentration of white collar jobs into larger and larger units. Emphasis on qualifications must be linked with a growing tendency to recruit people for higher positions from *outside* the hierarchy. Administrative rationalisation, made possible by economies of scale, will be associated with a reduction in the ratio of managerial to clerical functions. Opportunities for promotion would thereby decline accordingly.[7]

I am suggesting therefore, that in terms of the level of promotion possibilities inherent in occupational role, lower level clerical workers are fast approaching the level of *stasis* that has, in the past, been the lot of the blue collar labour force. But this is *not* to say that the structural positions of the two groups are becoming merged. Very few craftsmen even considered the possibility that they might be promoted over the blue collar/white collar line, a line that in terms of promotion is not relevant to the aspiring clerk, 'To be sure, the white collar employee is at the bottom of the ladder, but at least he is already on the ladder.'[8] As such, the dwindling of class differences must not be confused with the dwindling of class barriers.

A Business of One's Own

For the American working man, the alternative avenue of upward mobility to promotion within his own factory or firm has traditionally been going into business for himself. While opportunities for advancement to the post of foreman have been few and far between, and movement into white collar jobs virtually non-existent, there has always been the compensatory opportunity of starting a small business of one's own. As such, this has been the goal of the majority of aspiring workers, especially those working in factories. To these men, a business of one's own has been regarded as offering prestige, independence, and perhaps above all, freedom from the constraints of a particular work situation. Unfortunately, however, the number of ex-blue collar workers failing in small business ventures has for a long time been equally large. Lack of the necessary capital, knowledge, skills or business acumen have, in the majority of cases, driven small businessmen back to the status of employees within a fairly short period of time.[9] And a number of the craftsmen in my sample are no exception.

No less than one quarter of the total number of craftsmen we interviewed have at some time in the past owned their own business and now no longer do so. Seventeen of the electricians presently working for somebody else have previously worked for themselves. For the other three craft groups between six and 11 men have formerly been in a like situation. Surprisingly, perhaps, so also have five clerks and seven managers. At the time of the interview, one tenth of the craft group were practising their trade independently. None of the clerks were doing so. This reflects an important difference between skilled workers and other blue collar and clerical employees. In nearly all cases the craftsmen will be able to set up business doing what he did when he worked for somebody else. The non-skilled or clerical employee, however, cannot simply utilise his talents as a business enterprise but will in most cases have to go into something completely different, a small store or gas station being the traditional goal. The majority of craftsmen working for themselves at the time of the research were cabinet makers and carpenters, and to a lesser extent bricklayers or masons. Only one toolmaker and two electricians were self-employed. This is not difficult to explain. In the case of the building trades, the cost of setting up a business for oneself is fairly low as compared to the cost of equipping a small machine shop to set up a small toolmaking concern.

Of the 174 craftsmen (90 per cent of the total) who were not working for themselves at the time of the interview, just over one fifth said they hoped to go into business for themselves in the future. This is not a very high proportion. In addition, the numbers of craftsmen wishing to tread this traditional path of opportunity were not evenly distributed among the four craft groups. The majority were bricklayers and masons or cabinet makers and carpenters – over a third of whom said they hoped to be able to set up their own business. Five of the toolmakers and nine of the electricians also hoped to follow suit, as did two of the clerks and three of the managers.

The motive for wanting to own their own business given most frequently by blue and white collar workers alike was the ambition to be one's own boss. But the reasons underlying this desire are not the same as those usually proffered by non-skilled factory workers. Chinoy, for example, found that so many of the automobile workers he studied wanted to go into business for themselves because '"being one's own boss" strikes a resonant chord among workers subject to the authority of the organisation and the mechanical domination of the machine'.[10] 'The alienation of this work does much to explain their widespread interest in a small business.'[11] As we shall see later in this chapter, the concept of alienation would seem to have little relevance in describing the orientation to work of the skilled craftsmen who are the subject of this study. To be sure, these men seek independence so as to gain more control over their work, but it is control over one limited dimension of the total work situation. And it is viewed in a positive light, rather than simply as the only alternative to an intolerable present work situation. Hardly anybody wanted to be his own boss in order to escape harsh or unfair supervision. (Not one of the craftsmen who wanted independence mentioned supervision as being one of the things he liked least about his job.) Rather, several craftsmen sought a business of their own because they saw this as the way to improve their standards of workmanship and thus the intrinsic benefits from the quality of the work they produced. For example, a cabinet maker who said his chance of being promoted to foreman was 'good', nevertheless wanted to be his own boss so that he could 'turn out a product the way it should be turned out'. Another cabinet maker who earlier complained that 'you have sometimes to do things not the way you would like to to meet competition and make money', wanted to work for himself so as to avoid having to do this unsatisfying and unsatisfactory work. Alternatively, an electrician employed by the state of Rhode Island said: 'I would like to get the credit for myself for what I do. In my job the boss is apt to get the credit for my work especially if I do a good job or something.'

The second most important reason given for the interest in small business was in order to increase income. A young toolmaker in his twenties, complaining about his present salary of between $6,000 and $7,000 per year, explained: 'I don't have to answer to anybody, you work twice as hard but the profits are yours.' A cabinet maker earning $2,000 a year more than this man explained: 'I'd enjoy working more, there is more profit when you own your own business so you don't mind working harder or putting in more hours.' In all, 16 of the 37 craftsmen who were planning to go into business for themselves said it was because of the financial advantages of independence. This, or the desire to be one's own boss, were the only two reasons given by those few electricians and toolmakers wanting to strike out on their own. These were also, by far, the most important reasons given by the bricklayers and masons and the cabinet makers and carpenters. In addition, one carpenter said he wanted to have something to pass on to his sons. Surprisingly, only two men, both cabinet makers, explained their desire to own their own business in purely 'achievement' terms. One, in his early thirties, and in a fairly small firm where he was 'under the owner', explained: 'I am aggressive and I want to get ahead – can't go any further in present job.' The other was the same age and earning the same income, but reckoned his chances of promotion to be 'fair' at his current job. This clearly wasn't good enough. This man wanted his own business so that he could 'advance more and not have to wait for promotions'.

Inasmuch as we are interested in a small business as an alternative to promotion within a firm, or mobility from one occupation to another, it is important that we go beyond mere verbalising on the part of respondents as to why they hope to become entrepreneurs. An attempt must be made to assess how serious are these hopes, and what the chances are of their being realised. This I did by asking all respondents who expressed the desire to go into business for themselves what steps they had taken to achieve this goal. Their replies lead me to suspect that for the great majority this aspiration is little more than a daydream. Of the 38 craftsmen who said they hoped to go into business for themselves in the future, 24 had done nothing at all in the way of planning or preparation. Of the remainder, six said they had been saving in order to get the necessary capital. Nonetheless, the amounts saved were not overwhelming: three had put by less than $5,000; a toolmaker had amassed between $5,000 and $7,500; while two cabinet makers had between $7,500 and $10,000. (One was at that time looking for an 'established business in the woodworking line' while the other had savings in the form of stocks which he intended to sell when he felt he had enough to go into business.)

The only other thing that had been done by any number of the craftsmen in the way of planning for their independence was the buying of equipment: tools, a truck, a lock-up garage. Indeed two men (a cabinet maker and a toolmaker) said they were already setting up small shops (one with a partner) and were in the process of equipping those shops, while another two were working toward that stage. A carpenter in his early twenties for example, had been taking extension courses, had bought 'very expensive' tools, and had 'just started to put money aside'; he had already saved between $2,000 and $2,500.

The other four craftsmen and the two clerks who claimed to be in the throes of preparation for entrepreneurship were either unrealistic or unconvincing. A bricklayer who said he intended to set up his own business 'in a few months' had less than $500 saved, while a carpenter in his sixties was taking a course on radio and television repair so that he could open a shop in that line. And despite protestations to the contrary, neither of the two white collar workers concerned had made serious plans. One was merely 'tempted to buy and run a cafe.' He had saved less than $2,500. The other clerk had no real intention at all. When asked if he had made any plans he said: 'too much of a gamble to invest money today.' This explanation may be at least partially explained by the fact that the respondent didn't have any money to invest anyway. But, of course, we cannot be sure.

In all then, out of the 38 craftsmen who said they were planning to go into business for themselves in the future, only 10 could really be taken seriously. For the majority of the craft sample this traditional avenue of mobility is not the attraction one might have expected, despite the limited opportunities for promotion within most firms. The reasons underlying this lack of interest in the 'American Dream' will become apparent in the following section of this chapter.

Job Satisfaction

The methodological and conceptual problems facing the sociologist attempting to analyse work experience in general, and job satisfaction in particular, are too well known to require documentation.[12] Nevertheless the measurement of job satisfaction provides, at present, the optimum way of *comparing* the manner in which individuals in differing occupations experience and relate to their jobs. And such a comparison must play a crucial role in any analysis of the class situation of blue and white collar workers. As Crozier has expressed it:

> Questions relating to satisfaction have...continued to be
> universally used, for they provide a measuring instrument,
> limited to be sure, but irreplaceable... But the spirit in which
> such questions are used is altogether different. [From the 'some-
> what naive positivism of the first researchers'.] It is no longer
> a question of getting measurements that are valid in and of
> themselves or through purely statistical exploration, but of
> gathering comparative elements susceptible to diverse inter-
> pretations.[13]

One of the more obvious sociological truths (produced as the result of not a few empirical studies) is the proposition that level of work satisfaction varies considerably from one occupation to another.[14] In general, the amount of intrinsic satisfaction endemic in a particular job increases as one ascends the occupational hierarchy. It is another example of the 'end in itself'–'means to an end' dichotomy. At one end of the scale is the professional – the academic or physician – who involves himself in his work because he is commited to the goals of that profession and hence derives intense satisfaction in striving to achieve those goals. At the other end is the assembly worker performing a repetitive, boring, and to him, meaningless task solely because the extrinsic rewards attached to that task are sufficiently attractive. The two occupational groups with which I am most concerned – clerks and craftsmen – fall somewhat in the middle of this continuum, but the line separating one from another has, in the past, been significant. 'The white collar employee is expected to be "company" oriented and like his work: but the loyalty of the manual worker is never taken for granted . . . In fact it has been asserted that "the natural state of the worker . . . is one of discontent".[15] The amount of satisfaction to be gained from any one occupation depends on a constellation of factors, many of them attributes of work situation. Following Blauner, we may distinguish several aspects of work situation which research has shown to be important in influencing degree of job satisfaction: control over the use of one's time and physical movement; control over the pace of the work process; control of the technical and social environment; freedom from hierarchical authority; membership of an integrated work group. Clearly, these components of work situation are closely interrelated. Other factors external to the workplace, but also important in influencing the degree of job satisfaction are membership in an occupational community, degree of job security, income, level of skill, and finally occupational prestige. This last factor is obviously a kind of composite index of several of the variables already mentioned.

Given this list of features important in determining the level of intrinsic satisfaction inherent in a particular work role, the enviable position enjoyed by non-manual employees is not difficult to explain. The office worker for example, has always had a far greater degree of freedom and autonomy in his work than his blue collar counterpart. The relations of each to authority have been qualitatively very different, as has the relative amount of income, prestige and job security. However, as I have already begun to show, on several of these dimensions there is no longer the difference between the lower level white collar and skilled blue collar jobs that used to exist, even in the recent past. It remains to determine whether or not these changes have led to significant shifts in the relative degrees of satisfaction clerks and craftsmen gain from their work. In attempting to do this respondents were asked five separate questions on job satisfaction, each aimed at tapping different dimensions of the general concept.

First, respondents were asked how *interesting* they found their job.

Table 8. *Amount of interest found in present job*

	Brick-layers and Masons	Cabinet makers and Car-penters	Elec-tricians	Tool-makers	Total Craft	Clerks	Managers
	Percentage						
Very interesting	66	69	82	61	70	61	79
Quite interesting	23	24	16	35	25	25	18
Not very interesting	6	6	2	4	4	11	3
Not at all interesting	6	—	—	—	1	2	—
Total per cent	100	100	100	100	100	100	100
Total number	35	49	56	54	194	44	38

The pattern of responses to this question is shown in Table 8. It is evident that the great majority of the total sample find their job 'very interesting'. Indeed, with the exception of the bricklayers and masons, and the clerks, over 90 per cent of each occupational group say they find their job at least 'quite interesting'. Only three respondents out of the entire sample - two bricklayers and masons, and one clerk – described their present job as being 'not at all interesting'.

The toolmakers do not express as great a degree of interest as one would have expected. Similarly one would not have predicted the fact that three of the four craft groups expressed a greater degree of interest in their work than did the clerks. Although previous research has shown clearly that within manual categories job satisfaction is highest amongst skilled workers, it has not been found to be higher than that within the clerical group.

Secondly, members of the sample were asked simply what they liked *best* and *least* about their jobs. Both these questions were open-ended. There were three main categories of response to the first of these questions: extrinsic factors such as pay, or job security; intrinsic factors such as the challenge offered by the work, the feeling of pride and accomplishment in doing a good job; and, finally, the opportunities the job provided to meet and come into contact with other people, primarily workmates, but also clients or customers. The percentage of each group giving each of these types of answers is presented in Table 9. The totals add up to more than 100 per cent because respondents often gave answers which fell into more than one category. One factor stands out clearly in this Table. The majority of all six occupational groups discussed the things they liked best about their jobs wholly or partially in intrinsic terms. There is clearly a close relationship between the frequency with which people describe the satisfaction of their job in intrinsic terms and the fact that the majority of respondents described their jobs as being 'very interesting'.

In reading the responses people gave to the question of what they liked

Table 9. *Aspects of present job which are best liked*

	Brick-layers and Masons	Cabinet makers and Carpenters	Elec-tricians	Tool-makers	Total Craft	Clerks	Managers
	Percentage						
Extrinsic benefits	37	18	17	23	23	30	19
People come into contact with	6	10	14	10	12	50	26
Intrinsic benefits	74	81	82	89	83	59	87
Other/Nothing	6	10	5	4	6	7	3
Total per cent	123	119	118	126	124	146	135
Total number	35	49	56	54	194	44	38

best about their job, the words 'challenge', 'stimulating', 'satisfaction', and 'variety' came up with a monotonous regularity. But the detail which the craftsmen especially go into, in explaining *why* the job is challenging or stimulating, gives the clear impression that these are not stock clichés reiterated unthinkingly. Compared, for instance, to the attitudes assembly line workers usually hold regarding their jobs, these men really give the impression of identifying with, and getting a lot of meaning out of, their occupations. Consider these responses:

A mason:
'Satisfaction – seeing a building go up from floor to roof. I've been part of it all.'

A cabinet maker:
'I like the feeling of creating something - can see something I have done – that is everything. It lasts for many years when you have made something good.'

An electrician:
'Challenging to see a forest, then houses, it's fabulous. Storeys, buildings, grow and you know you've been a small part in it.'

A toolmaker:
'You make different kinds of tools. It isn't monotonous – everything's different. Sometimes you have to plan out your own work – its a challenge. Its doing something different always.'

The bricklayers and masons group is clearly the 'odd man out' in the general craft category, having at the same time the lowest number of responses that can be classified as representing intrinsic, and the highest number indicating extrinsic satisfactions. More surprising is the fact that it is the clerical group which has the lowest proportion of intrinsic responses, and the second highest proportion of extrinsic answers. Nevertheless, while both the bricklayers and masons, and the clerks have relatively lower proportions of intrinsic responses, the absolute size of these proportions is still very high – 59 per cent in the case of the clerks and 74 per cent in the case of the bricklayers and masons.

In general terms the numbers of craftsmen describing the things they liked best about their jobs in extrinsic terms are not large. As would be expected, in the case of the skilled craftsmen those factors mentioned most often were the high pay and, to a much lesser extent, the hours. The two are not unrelated. With the very high rates of hourly pay which these men earn, large amounts of overtime are not essential to acquire a substantial wage. Amongst the clerical group pay is not mentioned to any extent. Rather, clerks talk about the traditional advantages of white collar employment – the hours, the benefits and the vacations that have long been associated with non-manual occupations.

The advantages of having good workmates and dealing with pleasant clients or customers are mentioned to a surprisingly small extent by the blue collar sample. Out of the total craft category only 19 men mentioned workmates or customers as being one of the two or three things they liked best about their jobs, while only one man, an electrician, saw the opportunities in his job to work with or meet people, as being *the* best thing about the job. Given the stress in the literature about the importance of being a member of a work group its lack of importance to our manual respondents is surprising. This can probably be explained in one of two ways; either because these men derive such satisfaction from the creativeness of their work as to make workmates less important; or because, in contrast to the assembly line worker, being part of a group is regarded as normal and therefore not particularly worthy of special comment. It is quite possible that the importance of working with people is only apparent in situations where for one reason or another the individual feels isolated.

For the clerk, however, and to a much lesser extent the manager, the people one either works with or comes into contact with at work clearly provide one of the most important sources of satisfaction in the job. Exactly half of the clerical group and one quarter of the managers mention the opportunities their work provided to associate in some way or other with people as being one of the things they liked best about the job. To some extent this must be seen as an alternative to some of the intrinsic benefits the craft groups described. In a clerical occupation there is certainly the opportunity to gain satisfaction from doing a good job, but the opportunities for creating, for 'overcoming a challenge', are present less in the semi-routinised work day of the clerk than of the craftsman. In these terms there is more likelihood that the clerk will turn to personal relationships as providing his main source of job satisfaction. A bank clerk liked best the hours, the benefits and 'meeting important people'. A clerk in the Veterans Administration commented: 'it gives you a certain satisfaction because you know most people come in because they have problems, and we feel pretty good if we can help to solve them'.

Equally important in building up a picture of the meaning people get out of their work, and what they look for in their occupational roles, is to find out what they like *least* about their present jobs. In contrast to the descriptions of what respondents liked best about their jobs, comments relating to the negative aspect of work situation tended to be somewhat more idiosyncratic and therefore more difficult to categorise.

Roughly one quarter of the three main groups could think of nothing at all they disliked about their work. This is probably a very high proportion. Yet for the bricklayers and masons it was only 14 per cent, while 60 per cent complained of specific extrinsic aspects of their job, a proportion that was not approximated by any other of the groups studied. This lends further weight to the picture that is emerging of this particular craft group having, relatively, the least agreeable work situation. Several men complained simply of the physically hard or dirty labour their job entailed. Lack of work in cold or bad weather is another hazard faced by tradesmen in the building industry. One man said that it was quite possible to go for two or three months without work, although this would appear to be unlikely for the majority of the bricklayers and masons in the sample. While the average income of this craft group was on the low side, it was certainly not low enough, as compared to the other craft groups, to indicate long periods of unemployment each year.

As already pointed out, extrinsic factors were not mentioned nearly so many times by other craftsmen as by bricklayers and masons. Nonetheless for the manual group as a whole complaints of an extrinsic nature were reported by just under one third of the respondents. For the two white collar groups this was not the case. Only nine per cent of clerks mentioned extrinsic factors as being things they did not like about their jobs, while for managers the figure was 16 per cent. A few of the woodworkers in the sample also mentioned the effect of rain or bad weather, but for the group as a whole however this was clearly not a major cause for complaint. Several of the toolmakers as well as members of other craft groups said that theirs was a dirty job, but one does not get the impression that this is as serious a grievance as is the weather to bricklayers. A carpenter remarked: 'I come home with sawdust – dirty hands but a clean cheque!' The physical exertion some of the craft jobs require is seen as a source of dissatisfaction by several craftsmen, especially the older ones.

Finally, the type of supervision was not often mentioned in responses to this question. Given the nature of skilled manual work, craftsmen are given a good deal of freedom from continuous supervision in comparison with individuals performing less skilled manual tasks. Nonetheless, eight craftsmen, five of whom were toolmakers, did complain about supervision. Again the self-awareness of their own skill, and their pride in that skill, are evident. A toolmaker said that he disliked 'being talked down to by bosses who really sometimes know less than me. I like to get credit for knowing what I'm doing. I like them to have faith and trust in my ability. When they don't, I'm displeased.'

Following on from this discussion of those aspects of their jobs they liked most and least, respondents were asked how *satisfied* they were with their present job. This question was seen as being one which would enable respondents to weigh up intrinsic interest and other sources of satisfaction to be found in the job against possible sources of dissatisfaction.

As can be seen from the pattern of responses to this question, presented in Table 10, the vast majority of the sample were at least 'quite satisfied' with their present job. Indeed, for two of the craft groups and the managerial group, over half of the people interviewed were 'very satisfied'. Again electricians present a picture, as a group, of getting the most out of their jobs, while clerks and two of the craft categories appear the least satisfied. But these are relative statements: the significant feature of Table 10 is the generally high levels of job satisfaction expressed by the total sample.

In general terms, then, any interpretation of the relationships between my respondents and their jobs, and hence the meaning or satisfaction they gain from these jobs, suggests that it is impossible to draw a line between the blue and white collar workers in the sample or that, if one is drawn, it has to be in the favour of the skilled craft category. All four craft groups had larger proportions describing their job as interesting than the number of clerical workers who did likewise. Two of the craft groups expressed a greater degree of satisfaction with their present job than clerical workers, while the other two exhibited an almost identical set of

Table 10. *Level of satisfaction with present job*

	Brick-layers and Masons	Cabinet makers and Carpenters	Elec-tricians	Tool-makers	Total Craft	Clerks	Managers
	Percentage						
Very satisfied	54	47	71	48	56	48	58
Quite satisfied	34	37	23	37	32	36	39
Somewhat dissatisfied	6	16	5	15	11	11	—
Very dissatisfied	6	—	—	—	1	5	3
Total per cent	100	100	100	100	100	100	100
Total number	35	49	56	54	194	44	38

responses. In discussing what they liked best about their jobs a greater proportion of clerks mentioned extrinsic rewards than three of the four craft groups, while significantly fewer of the clerks mentioned intrinsic satisfaction of one sort or another.[16] This was at least partially compensated for by the larger number of clerks valuing the opportunities their jobs provided for them to interact with people. But in many cases this was coupled with another extrinsic reward. Fewer clerks than any craft group (except bricklayers and masons) described the thing they liked best about the jobs *solely* in intrinsic or social terms.

In an attempt to explain this rather surprising pattern of findings, the data were reanalysed, this time controlling for several of the variables usually associated with degree of job satisfaction. However, in no single case did one variable have a clear influence on *general* degree of job satisfaction. Income, education, chances of promotion and job security all seem to have a positive effect on job satisfaction on *certain* of the four questions. But such effect was in most instances limited only to the white collar employees and even then was by no means substantial.

It would seem therefore that we must focus on the *nature of the job itself* in explaining both the relatively high level of satisfaction found amongst the craft workers and the relatively low level expressed by the clerks. This means that the intrinsic satisfactions inherent in craft jobs, rooted in the amount of freedom and control the craftsman has over his work situation, as well as in the nature of the tasks he is asked to perform, provide virtually *the* explanation of the degree of job satisfaction found amongst these blue collar workers.* In contrast, there is mounting evidence to suggest that the types of task that make up the duties of a

* I am still, of course, faced with the task of explaining differences in level of job satisfaction *within* the craft category. The electricians as a group clearly get more out of their jobs than the other members of the sample, no matter what dimension of work satisfaction is measured. Yet while 89 per cent of toolmakers described what they liked best about their jobs in intrinsic terms, less than half described themselves as being 'very satisfied' with their present job, and only one fifth did not have any complaints at all about their jobs. It would seem profitable here to distinguish between the satisfactions inherent in a particular occupation and the extent to which these potentialities are inhibited or realised in particular jobs. In these terms the electricians' work situation would appear to offer, intrinsically, a high degree of satisfaction, which in most cases electricians are able to realise. Toolmakers, on the other hand, perhaps because of authoritarian supervision, out of date machinery, or occasional routine or boring jobs, are not deriving as high a level of satisfaction as the nature of the work could provide. The concept of relative perceived deprivation is obviously relevant. Ninety per cent of the electricians who thought their jobs were 'very interesting' were also 'very satisfied' with them. For the toolmakers (and clerks) the comparable figure was only 67 per cent. Alternatively, bricklayers, who have a large number of complaints about their working conditions, are nonetheless relatively satisfied with their jobs, partly because of extrinsic compensating factors such as pay, but also, perhaps, because relative to other people with whom they work, they do very well.

lower level clerical worker are in and of themselves becoming less and less rewarding. And this reduction in the inherent interest attached to white collar duties can be seen as a direct result of the trend toward office mechanisation.[17]

Office machines became important in the United States during the First World War. Until that time the amount of machinery to be found in the office was negligible. The work of clerks and bookkeepers was barely rationalised, and, as in the larger offices different clerks usually had different tasks, there was little opportunity for comparison or uniformity. However, a little more than thirty years after the end of the Great War, Mills felt able to proclaim that 'the industrial revolution now comes to the office'[18] and indeed saw it as coming far faster than it had in the factories. The tremendous expansion of United States industry during this century, plus the increasing demands of the Government in its own right, heralded an enormous expansion in the amount of paper work. This vastly increased volume, plus the standardised nature of much of this new paper work created the necessity for machinery to be introduced into the office as rapidly as possible.

This swift and drastic change has clearly, at least for clerical workers in large offices, brought about a crucial change in certain aspects of work situation. The introduction of machinery has often brought with it change in the layout and shape of offices. The days of individual clerks working in their own offices on complete sets of tasks would appear to be diminishing. A glance at any Government agency, for example a tax office, with rows upon rows of men and women sitting at desks operating two or three machines leaves little room for doubt that this is happening.

> Machines and centralisation...also open the way to a full
> range of factory organisation and techniques; work can be
> simplified and specialised work standards for each operation
> can be set up and applied to individual workers...the number
> of routine jobs is increased and consequently the proportion
> of 'positions requiring initiative' is decreased. 'Mechanisation
> is resulting in a much clearer distinction between the managing
> staff and operating staff,' observed the War Manpower Com-
> mission. Finger dexterity is often more important than creative
> thinking, promotions consequently become relatively rare.[19]

For the large part of my clerical sample this process has not progressed as fast as Mills predicted, but there are clear indications that for a propor-tion of the clerical respondents at least, his forecast has become a reality. Bank tellers perform highly standardised routine and specific tasks with, as we have already seen, reduced opportunities for promotion. A clerk described his work situation as being 'all on a floor – different departments broken down by partitions – I am alone in my compartment'. The machinery this clerk (earning between $5,000 and $6,000 a year) operated included a multilith, a mimeograph, an addressograph, and an adding machine. A police clerk was in charge of the marking and keeping of records for the police training school as well as marking the multiple choice exams sat by the police recruits. A clerk in a large shipping firm described how 'all deposit slips are turned over to us, we have to check them out, run an adding machine all day'.

To repeat, this is not to say that all the clerks in the sample were in similar work situations. Clearly, many were in jobs that provided variety and satisfaction, with more 'creative thinking' than 'finger dexterity'. But for a number of these routine white collar workers this was not the case, and their situation was a far cry from that of the working clerk fifty years ago. Mills may have been premature in claiming that this stratum of old bookkeepers was 'being demoted to the level of the clerical mass',[20] but for a segment of the clerks in our study this has happened and there is no evidence to suggest that the trend will not continue.

Given these changes in the nature of clerical work, the lack of differentiation in terms of job satisfaction between clerks and craftsmen is not difficult to explain. Indeed it might well be asked why the clerks as a group appear as contented as they are. There are two reasons for this. First, the process of mechanisation is by no means complete. Secondly, on features such as promotion possibilities, security, and financial benefits, clerks remain in a superior position, albeit a declining superiority. And as we have already seen there is a positive relationship between these variables and level of job satisfaction within the two white collar groupings. However, should the situation of clerks continue to deteriorate on any of these aspects of employment, for example promotion prospects, and should such a deterioration go alongside increasing mechanisation, then we might expect the level of job satisfaction inherent in clerical work to decrease substantially in the years ahead.*

* An alternative viewpoint is held by Mumford and Banks. On the basis of an investigation into the effect of the introduction of a computer into a manufacturing company and a bank, already referred to, these researchers provide evidence that both work satisfaction and promotion possibilities declined with the advent of office mechanisation. However they feel able to predict as a consequence of this, that 'clerical work at a routine level will fall almost exclusively into the hands of girls and women' and further, that 'the few men remaining in clerical jobs will be "juniors" working their way up and the routine male clerk, as a career grade, will become extinct'. See Enid Mumford and Olive Banks, *The Computer and the Clerk* (London. 1967), espec. chap. 2. In the Unites States, at least, there is little evidence to support this assertion. To be sure, a larger and larger proportion of white collar workers are female. But the percentage of the male labour force engaged in clerical work is *also* rising, albeit slowly. In 1949 6.6 per cent of the male labour force were clerical and kindred workers. By 1968 this proportion had risen to 7.25 per cent.

Conclusion

It is evident that statements relating to the disappearance of economic differentials separating blue and white collar workers are as unrealistic as they are insufficiently precise. As always, reality is more complicated. The evidence that I have brought forward does show that on certain aspects of both market and work situations the positions of clerical workers and skilled craftsmen have been undergoing a process of convergence. This is evident not only in terms of the superior incomes enjoyed by craftsmen, but also with regard to other components of market situation, such as job security and, more important, the declining levels of intrinsic satisfaction inherent within the work of the contemporary clerk. At the same time, it would appear that lower level clerical workers are becoming increasingly isolated occupationally and materially from the established middle class, as represented by the role of the manager or executive. This is perhaps most evident in the declining opportunities for promotion from clerical to managerial positions within the enterprise. But such changes, important as they are, do not indicate that skilled craftsmen and routine clerical workers are approaching a state in which their economic positions will be indistinguishable. Indeed, as long as blue and white collar workers remain physically and socially separated from another in the division of labour, i.e. the work situation, then they will remain separate one from another along certain crucial aspects of economic and therefore class position. Nonetheless, the situation existing earlier in the century when all economic and occupational differentials fell neatly away from the watershed of the blue collar/white collar line is no longer a reality. In the chapters that follow my concern is with the ways in which these changes in the work and market situations of skilled craftsmen and clerks have affected their relative positions in the American class structure.

3   Family Structure and Patterns of Socialisation

'My sister, my father, my in laws all live in the area. I see them almost every day. We talk–discussions–argue like hell–their homes and mine. We enjoy it!'

'You are what you make of yourself. Now my son who is going to be a doctor will be able to make something real good for himself and his family. It will be worth all the hard work for me to see that happen.'

'Women should be educated–you bring up your children differently. You raise your children properly and with all these social functions that go on, like the P.T.A., I think a woman should be educated to get in with that stuff.'

'The man brings home the bread and butter. Women should be home washing rugs.'

There are at least two reasons why any analysis of changes in class structure should focus on the family unit. First, the dissimilar market and work situations enjoyed by manual and non-manual workers have, at least until recently, been reflected in clear and distinct differences in the structure and functioning of working and middle class families. Secondly, these differences have been especially marked with regard to patterns of socialisation, which, in turn, have been directly linked with the *perpetuation* of class distinctions from one generation to another. Insofar as blue and white collar parents, by virtue of their differing positions in the division of labour, bring up their children in differing ways, possessing differing skills, attributes and values, then the family must be seen as contributing toward the maintenance of inequality.* In order to reach a conclusion however tentative, regarding the blurring or

---

* This is not to put forward a naive functionalist perspective: to state that family structure is linked with the perpetuation of class differences is not to say that the nuclear family is a functional requisite of industrial societies, or that 'the socialising influence of the nuclear family (is) necessary for the flourishing of industrial society'. See David Lane, *The End of Inequality* (Harmondsworth, England), p. 137. I am merely arguing that in Western society at the present time one of the *consequences* of differential socialisation is the passing on of class differences from one generation to another.

breakdown of class lines, it is therefore important that we determine whether or not these dissimilarities in family structure remain.

The Family Unit

In common with other Western nations the United States witnessed a spectacular and general fall in birth-rate during the latter half of the nineteenth century. Insofar as this decline can be seen as being led by families in the upper echelons of the class structure, it enhanced the already considerable fertility differentials between classes that already existed. Indeed, at least one writer has suggested that in the period up to the First World War the inverse correlation between social class and fertility was more marked than has been the case before or since.[1] However in the years between the two wars this inverse correlation was reduced considerably in strength, and while the general drop in fertility continued, not all occupational groups declined at the same rate. The most notable exceptions were clerical and sales workers who, in the United States, had the lowest fertility of any occupational category. Finally the baby-boom immediately following the Second World War further contributed to a narrowing of class differences in family size, as, in general, the middle classes increased their fertility to a greater extent than did blue collar wage earners.

This pervasive breakdown of fertility differentials, in periods of falling and climbing birth-rates, has been interpreted by more than one demographer as merely another example of the *general* disappearance of class differences in American society: as the middle class way of life has diffused through the class structure, then so has the notion that fertility is something that can be controlled and therefore planned.[2] One advocate of this view has gone as far as to suggest that 'class fertility-differences are destined to disappear as a feature of the demographic structure of Western nations'.[3]

The reproductive behaviour of my own respondents suggests, as always, that such predictions should be treated with caution. While there are clear indications that the model family is one of moderate size for all six of the occupational groups, fertility differentials remain. And the pattern of these differentials is not dissimilar from that which has existed in the United States since the turn of the century. Of the three major groupings clerical workers exhibit the lowest level of fertility while managers appear to have families on average slightly larger than those of skilled craftsmen: this superiority is most marked in the proportion of managers having families of three or more children. Not only do members of the clerical sample have fewer children than members of either of the other two major occupational groupings, it is also probable that they are appreciably slower in starting their families. A comparison of those

Table 11. *Family size by duration of marriage*

	Brick layers and Masons	Cabinet makers and Carpenters	Electricians	Toolmakers	Total Craft	Clerks	Managers
Percentage							
Married less than ten years							
No children	—	7	11	15	9	18	29
One child	42	29	28	15	28	36	—
Two children	33	36	44	46	40	36	29
Three or more children	25	29	17	23	23	9	43
Total per cent	100	100	100	100	100	100	100
Average per family	1.83	1.86	1.72	1.85	1.81	1.45	1.86
Total number	12	14	18	13	57	11	7
Married more than ten years							
No children	4	6	18	10	10	15	16
One child	9	20	10	24	17	18	13
Two children	39	43	32	46	40	36	29
Three or more children	47	31	40	17	33	30	41
Total per cent	100	100	100	100	100	100	100
Average per family	2.56	2.20	2.45	1.98	2.26	2.00	2.32
Total number	23	35	38	41	137	33	31
Total							
No children	3	6	16	11	10	16	18
One child	20	22	16	22	20	23	11
Two children	37	41	36	46	40	36	29
Three or more children	40	30	32	19	30	25	42
Total per cent	100	100	100	100	100	100	100
Average per family	2.31	2.10	2.21	1.94	2.13	1.86	2.24
Total number	35	49	56	54	194	44	38

couples married less than ten years with those married for a longer period (based only on small numbers) – see Table 11 – shows that the difference between clerks and craftsmen is most marked in the earlier stages of marriage. It is realised that such a statement should properly be supported by trend data, rather than a comparison of different couples within the same occupational grouping. But the fact remains that the majority of the clerks in the sample who had been married for less than ten years had fewer than two children, while over three fifths of the craftsmen in a like situation had families of at least this size.[4]

The family policy exhibited by the clerical workers can be linked with at least two other features of their situation. First, as we shall see later in this chapter, these men cherish appreciably higher hopes for the educational and occupational success of their offspring than do the skilled craftsmen. It is at least plausible to suggest that such aspirations are not unrelated to this comparatively low level of fertility: the fewer the number of children the better the opportunities that can be provided by the parent. Indeed Arsene Dumont recognised this relationship over eighty years ago in his celebrated theory of capillarity: 'just as a column of liquid has to be thin in order to rise under the force of capillarity, so a family must be small in order to rise in the social scale'.[5] Secondly, despite these differences in the timing of births and in overall numbers of children, it should be emphasised that the fertility differentials existing between clerks and craftsmen and managers are not overwhelming. Over half of each group have either two or three children while only 13 per cent of the managers and craftsmen and 7 per cent of the clerks have four or more children. This is especially noteworthy given the religious and ethnic composition of the sample. It will be remembered that around half of both the clerical and craft groupings are from Italian or Irish backgrounds, and 84 per cent of the clerks and 78 per cent of the craftsmen are Catholic. In American society generally the continuing high levels of fertility among Catholics, including those of high status and education, have been referred to by one demographer as 'one of the striking findings of the postwar American studies'.[6] Yet despite the existence of a distinctive Catholic pattern of high fertility at the national level the average number of children per family for this group of predominantly Catholic clerical workers is only 1.84. In fact my findings are directly in accord with the situation found in Rhode Island generally which, despite a preponderance of Catholics, has lower than national fertility rates. This has been explained by reference to the high degree of urbanisation in the state and the disproportionaly large number of women in the labour force, conditions which offset the national Catholic fertility pattern to a considerable extent.[7]

It is evident that the majority of respondents are the heads of conjugal families of moderate size.[8] Large units, containing more than three children, were the exception. Furthermore, only 12 craftsmen, two clerks and two managers had relatives, other than their wives and children, living with them. In nearly every case, such relatives were elderly parents. This, however, must not be taken to mean that these people have become isolated from relatives outside of their immediate nuclear families, or that extended family ties are in the process of disappearing. Indeed, the opposite is the case. For, as Table 12 makes clear, the majority of craftsmen and clerks alike see relatives at least once a week, while 13 per cent of the blue collar group and 9 per cent of the clerks spend some time with relatives at least three times a week. Managers visit their kin to a lesser extent than either of these other two groups, although they too are clearly in a position far removed from that of the isolated nuclear family.

Over 90 per cent of the relatives reported as being seen most often were the respondent's or his spouse's parents, siblings or children.

Table 12.   *Frequency of seeing relatives*

	Brick-layers and Masons	Cabinet makers and Carpenters	Elec-tricians	Tool-makers	Total Craft	Clerks	Managers
	Cumulative percentage						
At least twice a week	42	38	31	43	37	32	8
At least once a week	60	56	55	63	59	62	45
At least once a fortnight	74	60	66	72	68	73	61
At least once a month	83	81	79	81	81	82	74
A few times a year	100	98	98	96	98	100	95
Never	—	2	2	4	2	—	5
Total per cent	100	100	100	100	100	100	100
Total number	35	49	56	54	194	44	38

Relatives further removed, such as uncles or cousins, were hardly ever mentioned. In addition, the proportions of blue and white collar employees seeing the husband's and wife's parents were almost identical: I was unable to find any signs of matriarchal structure. This was the case within Catholic and non-Catholic households. Perhaps the most formalised meetings with relatives take place on public holidays, such as Christmas and Thanksgiving. And here again managers appear to have as much and as narrow a contact with relatives from outside of their immediate family as do craft and clerical workers. Less than one fifth of either of these latter groupings do not spend such festivals with kin. In the case of the managers, the comparable figure is 21 per cent. Instead between 60 per cent and 70 per cent of each of the occupational categories get together with their parents or their children that have left home. Again, signs pointing to the existence of 'traditional' matriarchal family structure are little in evidence: only 12 per cent of the craftsmen stated that they were more likely to see the wife's rather than the husband's parents on such an occasion. Non-related friends are conspicuous by their absence: only two managers said they spend public holidays with friends as opposed to relatives; 4 per cent of craftsmen and 7 per cent of clerks gave similar responses.

Despite the extent of interaction with kin, the range of activities enjoyed at such times is limited. Less than 10 per cent of any occupational grouping mentioned doing things with relatives that took place outside the home. Well over two thirds of the respondents simply reported chatting or arguing when they saw relatives – discussing the rest of the family, children and grandchildren and their homes. A very few went to the beach or had picnics in the summer. Indeed, as we shall see in chapters 5 and 7, to the extent that other forms of leisure time activity take place, the likelihood is that they will be enjoyed in the company of non-related friends. To be sure, these manual and non-manual workers alike are involved in patterns of continuing and frequent (if somewhat restricted) interaction with kin. But this finding cannot be separated from the fact that they *also* spend the large part of their leisure time with non-related friends.

It would seem that the type of family structure found amongst skilled craftsmen (and to a lesser extent within the clerical grouping) is different both from the traditional extended familialism characteristic of American working class enclaves earlier in the century, as much as it is distinct from the isolated nuclear family units that have, for long, been associated with the established middle class. This situation is not difficult to explain. One would not expect, for example, Italian extended familialism to withstand completely the pressures to which it has been subjected in twentieth century America, especially those resulting from the process of social mobility. As Table 13 indicates, the majority of respondents do not share the same market and work situations as their fathers. Similarly, if one assumes that the wife's class situation is largely determined by that of her husband, we have reason to suppose that the majority of respondents' wives have also experienced a degree of social mobility.[9] Such movement must be associated with discrepancies in style of life and in value and consumption patterns between our respondents and their kin. It should not therefore be regarded as surprising that family ties have lost their

Table 13. *Parental occupations*

	Brick-layers and Masons	Cabinet makers and Car-penters	Elec-tricians	Tool-makers	Total Craft	Clerks	Managers
	Percentage						
Respondent's father							
White collar	9	4	6	14	8	12	36
Skilled blue collar	57	44	40	36	44	42	24
Non-skilled blue collar	23	38	38	37	34	41	19
Self-employed	11	14	16	13	14	5	21
Total per cent	100	100	100	100	100	100	100
Respondent's father-in-law							
White collar	12	16	8	8	11	18	37
Skilled blue collar	37	29	23	20	26	32	18
Non-skilled blue collar	45	39	44	51	45	34	24
Self-employed	—	12	18	19	13	5	21
D.K.	6	4	7	2	5	11	—
Total per cent	100	100	100	100	100	100	100
Total number	35	49	56	54	194	44	38

all-encompassing role. On the other hand, given the industrial structure of Rhode Island, the occupational mobility experienced by the majority of these people has not entailed a move away from the city such as might be necessitated by achievement in some professional field. In any event, the son of an unskilled manual worker who becomes a toolmaker, an electrician, or a clerk can pursue that vocation in Providence as well as in Hartford, Connecticut, or Des Moines, Iowa. For these people in the middle ranges of the American class structure the relationship between occupational and geographical mobility is therefore weak. And this is borne out by the data. 77 per cent of the total craft sample and 74 per cent of their wives were born in Rhode Island. Exactly four fifths of the clerks and their wives were in a like situation, while over 70 per cent of the managers and their marriage partners were also living in the state of their birth. One would therefore expect relationships to be retained with families of origin, albeit the fact that the quality of those relationships might be more circumscribed and less intimate than might have been the case in the early part of the century.

Patterns of Socialisation

As pointed out at the beginning of this chapter, it is in its role as the primary agent of socialisation that the family has often been viewed as exercising a conservative influence within class structure. In bringing up their children parents are concerned with fitting them with a set of skills, values and qualities that will enable them to assume adult roles in later life. And yet parents' conceptions of *which* skills values or qualities it is important to instil in their offspring will be crucially influenced by *their own* experiences and situation in the adult world. Insofar as middle and working class parents have occupied significantly different positions in social structure, they have practised distinct modes of child rearing, which have, in turn, contributed to the maintenance of class differences and boundaries within complex society. In the present section I am therefore concerned with determining whether or not some of the changes in the situation of clerks and craftsmen, discussed in the previous chapter, have been reflected in the convergence of socialisation patterns practised within the two groups. Such a question must be an integral part of any discussion of the collapse of class boundaries.

In an attempt to ascertain the way in which respondents viewed their parental roles they were asked what they thought were the two or three most important 'qualities of character' a parent should teach a child. The pattern of responses to this question is given in Table 14. It is evident that there is little difference between the proportions of managers, clerks and craftsmen who would like to see particular values embodied in their children's behaviour. Honesty, for example, would appear to be an

Table 14. *Desired qualities in a child*

	Brick-layers and Masons	Cabinet makers and Car-penters	Elec-tricians	Tool-makers	Total Craft	Clerks	Managers
	Percentage						
Honesty	56	65	57	75	64	54	77
Obedience	26	20	28	17	22	22	26
Good behaviour /manners	38	22	13	17	21	14	6
Respect for others	71	52	62	65	62	49	36
Morality	12	11	19	12	14	27	13
Religiosity	9	20	17	19	17	19	16
Self-confidence /discipline, aggression, perseverance	9	23	12	22	17	35	64
Ability to socialise	3	4	11	8	7	34	10
Total number	34	46	47	48	175	37	31

attribute recognised as being important by blue and white collar parents alike. Nevertheless, the craft sample especially lays stress on certain values that are not as highly regarded by the managers, and vice versa. And while these differences between blue and white collar respondents on individual items are not substantial, together they go to make up *orientations* towards child rearing that can be seen as being qualitatively different one from another. In particular, upper middle class managers appear more concerned with raising their children as *individuals* – with internalised values and standards of behaviour, which make them self-confident and give them independence and integrity. Craftsmen, on the other hand, are more concerned that their offspring should learn to conform to externally imposed rules or standards, that they should be respectable whilst showing respect for others.

This difference in the values managers and craftsmen wish to see incorporated in their children's behaviour is nowhere more evident than in the proportions of parents in the two groups assigning priority to character traits that, in the future, may be linked with occupational success. Over three fifths of the managerial parents regarded such a 'quality of character' as important, while only 17 per cent of the craftsmen did likewise. On the other hand, 62 per cent of this latter grouping considered it desirable that children should learn respect for others, especially those in authority such as one's parents, while only one third of the managers considered this necessary. Contrast, for example, the manager hoping that his children would possess 'honesty to himself and others, determination to do his best, self-reliance' with the toolmaker who expected 'respect, religion and obedience' or the bricklayer who wanted 'obedience, discipline and respect'.

It is more difficult to ascertain the existence of a theme or pattern underlying the values the clerical sample stated they wished to see incorporated into the behaviour of their children. In general these lower level white collar workers occupy a position midway between craftsmen and managers. However in certain respects this group was unique: for example, it is only amongst clerical parents that we find an appreciable number considering it important that their children learn to get along with other people. And while often expressing an adherence to goals similar to those of managers, these people often couched their replies in a language almost stereotypically lower middle class: 'to be polite, courtesy, keep out of trouble'; 'religion, respect for elders, dedication to the country'; 'obedience, dependability, being neat-appearing'; and 'respect for other people's property' are not atypical responses.

Given these differences between craftsmen and managers, it is perhaps surprising that the techniques of child rearing used by the two groups should have a good deal in common. Parents were asked firstly what was their response if one of their children did something he or she had been asked not to do, and secondly what happened if the child persisted in disobedience. These questions were open-ended and worded in general terms, in the expectation that respondents would themselves distinguish between differing kinds of crimes and punishments. This did not turn out to be the case: only two managers and virtually no clerks or craftsmen specified particular reactions to particular wrongdoings on the part of their children. Rather, responses to these two questions indicate that the majority of subjects have only a limited repertoire of disciplinary techniques which, depending upon the situation, they apply with varying degrees of severity. Serious misbehaviour will result in a child being scolded more loudly, confined to the back yard for a longer period of time, or spanked harder than he might be in the case of only a minor misdemeanour. Indeed, the simplicity and uniformity of disciplinary techniques, especially among the craft sample, is startling. An electrician who thought it most important that his offspring 'learn honesty, respect and obedience' used only two means to achieve these ends: putting soap in his children's mouths and, in extreme cases, sending them to bed. Similarly a carpenter always 'sat them (his children) in a chair and said "sit there until you realise you have disobeyed me"'. In fact around half of both the clerical and craft groups had only one form of response to disobedience. Less than one third of the managers exhibited such a limited approach to the use of punishment.

Information regarding parental reactions to children's misbehaviour is

Table 15. *Parental responses to child disobedience*

	Brick-layers and Masons	Cabinet Makers and Car-penters	Elec-tricians	Tool-makers	Total Craft	Clerks	Managers
	Percentage						
Physical punishment	47	48	32	44	42	35	42
Privileges withdrawn	32	50	47	48	45	57	58
Remove from situation	21	6	21	21	17	11	10
Scold, threaten	15	9	15	21	15	14	6
Reasoning and discussion	12	17	13	14	14	14	42
Total number	34	40	47	48	175	37	31

presented in Table 15*. It is evident that the disciplinary techniques used most often by these parents involve relieving a wayward child of something that is valued. This may involve, for example, confinement to the house or the taking away of toys or books. But the major weapon available to these parents was clearly the 'off' button on the television set, for depriving a disobedient child of a particular programme he enjoyed watching would seem to be the most common threat and punishment used by blue and white collar workers alike. Indeed one carpenter, when asked what he did when his children did something he had told them not to do, replied simply 'Turn off the T.V.'

It is significant that craftsmen, clerks *and* managers employ physical punishment as a disciplinary practice. This form of coercion has, in the past, been associated far more with working class than middle class parents.[10] However, my findings are in accord with those of the detailed study of child rearing techniques conducted by Kohn in Washington D.C. in 1957. This researcher found middle class mothers resorting to physical punishment as often as working class mothers, but in response to differing types of misbehaviour.[11] While, regrettably, my own data are not as detailed as those of Kohn, there are indications that this particular form of constraint is viewed differently by the blue and white collar workers in the Providence sample. Of the thirteen managers who reported ever using

* These data relate only to the first question on disciplinary techniques. This asked: 'What do (or did) you usually do if one of your children disobey(ed) you and does (did) something you have (had) clearly told him or her not to do?' The columns total more than 100 per cent because a proportion of respondents in each category used two forms of punishment at the same time, i.e. they might scold a child and remove him from a situation by sending him to his room. It is not considered necessary to present in tabular form the pattern of responses to the second question: 'And what happens(ed) if he/she does (did) it again?' For, as I have already pointed out, the large majority of respondents simply repeated the same form of punishment, often with greater severity.

physical punishment ten mentioned it as one aspect of their reaction to disobedience on a single occasion: 'I spank them and deprive them of privileges'; 'I punished him by taking away privileges and occasionally back of the hand.' Furthermore, for several managers physical punishment is by no means always regarded as the final deterrent: one man for example spanked his children and deprived them of a privilege if he was disobeyed. If that disobedience persisted the child was made to stand in the corner. In contrast, exactly one half of the craftsmen using physical punishment reported that this was their *only* reaction to disobedience. Only three clerks relied solely upon this form of disciplinary practice.

While there exists, at least superficially, a good deal of similarity in the use of punishment by the members of the sample, the managers do stand out as being the only group where a significant proportion of parents attempt also to reason with their children when they behave in an undesirable manner.[12] This is, of course, the technique that one would expect to find among a group of educated upper middle class parents and it is indeed surprising that the proportion of parents so doing is not larger. Nevertheless it was only among this group that I found any number of respondents who reported talking rather than reacting to their children, and indeed the majority of these people said that this was the *only* disciplinary technique they used. Thus an office manager always 'tried to point out to her that her actions were not proper – just re-emphasise again that it was not proper – just reason with her and try to make her understand. We never resorted to any physical punishment or taking away privileges.' Similarly, an upper level civil servant explained: 'I talk to them – explain what it is they are doing wrong – why it is wrong to do it,' and when asked what happened if the child persisted in misbehaviour commented: 'I can't recall that it did – I would again explain to them.'

It would, therefore, be difficult to argue that either our blue collar or lower level white collar parents view the rearing of children in a light, using the managers' responses as a yardstick, which could be described as 'middle class'. Indeed, the pattern of values given priority by large numbers of the skilled craftsmen and the techniques they employ to inculcate those values in the behaviour of their children, are not dissimilar from those emphasised by working class parents in *Middletown* over forty years ago.[13] While this could not be said of clerical parents, their orientation toward the rearing of children is clearly distinct from that of the managers. In explaining these differences, attention must be focused upon the relative positions of craftsmen clerks and managers in the division of labour, insofar as these may be linked with differing work situations and levels of education. Indeed, a number of earlier writers have been concerned with demonstrating the relationship between occupational role and the socialisation of children, and my own findings would appear to lend added weight to their arguments.[14]

In these terms, given the value structure of managerial and executive occupations, it is not surprising that parents in such positions should be the ones more likely to want to inculcate values such as self-confidence, perseverance and determination into their children's behaviour. For these are the very values that are associated with achievement in the occupational world of the upper middle class male. Little wonder that an Assistant Executive Director, having 'overall responsibility for my share of the organisation' should want his three children to learn 'self-discipline, common-sense and the will to succeed'. Similarly, it is in keeping that managers should use reasoning and discussion as a technique of socialis- ation to a greater extent than either clerks or craftsmen. Insofar as the occupational circumstances of upper level occupations are more likely to focus upon the *internalised* qualities of self-direction and initiative, it is more likely that such parents will train their children to understand *why* they should or should not think or behave in a certain way, rather than simply aim at securing conformity to externally imposed values or stand- ards. In contrast, while the skilled craftsman may be exercising a high level of skill (and as we have seen, gaining a good deal of satisfaction from the experience) he is required to make fewer decisions or independent judgements. In the majority of cases these will be made for him by fore- man, supervisor or manager. As such the relative emphasis placed upon conforming, upon good behaviour and respect for others as desirable qualities of character can be viewed as being linked with the values operant in the work situation of the skilled craftsman. This interpretation is lent added weight by the fact that the bricklayers and masons, the group in a work situation where initiative and independence in decision making are least pertinent, are the parents who most value the qualities of respect and good behaviour and pay least regard to those of independence or self- confidence.

The demonstration of congruence between the occupational situation of clerical workers with their patterns of child rearing is not as straight- forward as in the cases of craft and managerial parents. Nonetheless, given the kinds of work situation enjoyed by not a few of these lower level white collar respondents, and the routinised nature of many of their work tasks (discussed in the previous chapter), it is not surprising that only one third of them gave priority to qualities of character having to do with internalised self-direction, confidence or control. Neither is it difficult to suggest why the large majority of clerks resorted to coercion rather than discussion in securing their children's conformity to their wishes. But as I have stressed in the previous chapter, the work situation of clerical workers is changing, and these changes may well be reflected in orient- ations which are in part distinct from those of both craft and managerial parents, while sharing certain features in common with both.

The only other feature of parent's position in the social structure found to be related to child rearing techniques was level of education.[15] Of the twenty managers citing qualities of character having to do with internalised discipline, ambition or confidence eighteen were college graduates. Similarly, of the thirteen managers using reasoning and discussion as a means of socialisation, ten were college graduates while two of the remaining three had some college experience. The large majority of clerical and craft parents using such techniques are among the more highly educated within their respective groupings. For example, all of the craftsmen using reasoning and discussion in response to misbehaviour were high school graduates, while thirty of the thirty-nine stressing the need for obedience on the part of their children had not reached this standard. Again, these findings are in accord with those of earlier research. Kohn found a clear and positive correlation between parents' educational level and a desire on the part of those parents to teach their children *internalised* standards of behaviour, rather than conformity to externally imposed rules: 'Education is important because (teaching a child) self-direction requires more intellectual flexibility and breadth of perspective than does conformity; tolerance of non-conformity, in particular, requires a degree of analytic ability that is difficult to achieve without formal education.'[16]

Educational and Occupational Aspirations and Achievements

The goal of occupational or economic success and the value placed upon a college education as the principle avenue to such advancement are often held up as central tenets of the American value system. Yet social scientists have for long pointed out that both the motivation to advance occupationally, and to obtain the necessary formal education, is found to a much greater extent in middle class households than in those headed by a blue collar worker.[17] Again one can regard the traditionally working class family as operating in a conservative manner. Insofar as blue collar parents have placed little emphasis on the desirability of higher education or occupational achievements, they have set up almost self-imposed barriers to upward mobility for their offspring at the same time as they have reinforced the stability of the manual/non-manual line of demarcation.

However, my own data enable me to suggest that differential orientations towards education are no longer found (at least on the surface) among blue and white collar workers. This is the case both generally and, more specifically, with regard to their own children. Respondents were first asked what they thought was 'the minimum amount of education a young man must have to get on in the world these days'. The pattern of responses to this question is produced in Table 16. Perhaps the most striking feature of these data is the fact that for almost the entire sample, education *is* regarded as being necessary. Equally striking is the similarity

Table 16. Attitude towards education

	Bricklayers and Masons	Cabinet makers and Carpenters	Electricians	Toolmakers	Total Craft	Clerks	Managers
Desirable education for a 'young man'	Percentage						
High school graduate	49	47	52	56	51	48	53
Some college	9	14	18	19	15	16	16
College graduate	34	33	27	20	28	36	32
Doesn't matter/Other	9	6	8	5	6	—	—
Total per cent	100	100	100	100	100	100	100
Total number	35	49	56	54	194	44	38

Desired education for own sons and daughters

	Bricklayers and Masons		Cabinet makers and Carpenters		Electricians		Toolmakers		Total Craft		Clerks		Managers	
	Son	Daughter	Son	Daughter	Son	Daughter	Son	Daughter	Son	Daughter	Son	Daughter	Son	Daughter
High school graduate	—	23	10	25	—	20	4	33	4	25	—	—	5	—
Some college	10	23	3	21	4	28	8	14	6	22	—	13	—	5
College graduate	57	45	69	42	81	48	73	43	71	45	50	67	35	45
Graduate school	19	5	10	4	15	—	15	—	15	2	45	20	55	36
Other/Up to him or her	10	5	7	8	—	4	—	10	4	6	5	—	10	14
Total per cent	100	100	100	100	100	100	100	100	100	100	100	100	100	100
Total number	21	22	29	24	26	25	26	21	102	92	20	15	21	22

of viewpoints held by members of the various occupational categories. To be sure, slightly larger numbers of managers and clerks than craftsmen regard a college degree as essential, but the differences are not great. Within the four craft groupings the numbers regarding at least some college training as essential are not substantially outnumbered by people viewing a high school diploma as sufficient.

Those respondents having children in school or still too young for school were also asked to discuss their educational aspirations for their own children. And if one is impressed with the fairly high standards underlying their viewpoints on education in general, then one is doubly so by the heights of achievement these people hope will be scaled by their own children. Information regarding their aspirations is also presented in Table 16. Again, the similarity in the hopes of people from all six occupational groups is apparent: we have a situation where at least four fifths of every skilled or white collar category do not wish to see their sons finish their education without gaining at least a college degree. In the case of the electricians and the managers, the proportions are well over 90 per cent. Furthermore, it would appear that these aspirations are strongly felt. When questioned further, over 80 per cent of those individuals within each occupational group wanting either a son or a daughter to gain a college degree said that they held this desire 'very strongly'.

Nevertheless, these uniformly high levels of educational aspiration must not be allowed to obscure the fact that there exist two fundamental differences between the blue and white collar members of the sample. First, the numbers of craftsmen hoping that their children will pursue studies beyond the level of the batchelor's degree are small. Indeed only two skilled workers out of the 92 who had daughters still at school expressed the desire for those daughters to enter a Graduate School. In contrast around one half of both the white collar groups explicitly stated that they wanted a post-graduate education at least for male children, while around one third of the managers also hoped that their daughters would reap the benefits of such a training. This last point highlights the second major point of difference between the non-manual and the manual categories: the emphasis placed by this latter group on the desirability of a college education for daughters as well as for sons. For while over four fifths of both the clerical and the managerial parents desired a full-term college education for their daughters, less than half of the craftsmen had similar aspirations. Within all four craft groups, the viewing of a college education as less than essential for daughters is as stable as it is distinctive.[18]

Furthermore, these varying patterns of educational aspirations would appear to be associated with differing conceptions of the benefits to be reaped from formal education. Quite simply, blue collar parents are inclined to view education as vocational training, while for the clerks, and to a much greater extent, the managers, learning is more broadly conceived. We have two sources of information on this point: first, people were asked to explain their views on the education of women; secondly I asked a more general question on perceptions of the *value* of education.[19]

Discussions by blue and lower level white collar respondents of the value of learning generally produced a picture which highlights the enormous stress placed upon education as job training by these people. Over 70 per cent of both occupational groupings, when asked, 'what does the person who *is* educated have over the person who isn't?', couched their answers at least partially in terms of the greater job opportunities open to the educated person. And several of these answers are indicative not only of attitudes towards education but also of imagery of the occupational structure 'beyond' the level of the skilled craftsman. Thus a toolmaker explained: 'Educated people can get a better type of job – make more money, live in better homes, eat better; their standard of living would be higher', while another replied: 'More chance of better jobs – higher pay – *unless he knows a trade.*' Similarly, a clerk demanded: 'Can you become a lawyer or doctor without it?', while a carpenter commented: 'They turn out to be foreman or president in my book. He'll make more money – is more in the limelight.'

However, the importance placed upon education as vocational training by clerks and craftsmen alike must not be allowed to mask significant differences that exist between the two groups. While, as we have seen, the occupational benefits to be reaped from the high school or college diploma are by no means slighted by the clerks, only 25 per cent of them discussed the process of education *solely* in these terms. In contrast, 48 per cent of the skilled craftsmen took this restricted view. On the other hand, 37 per cent of these blue collar workers, but 58 per cent of the clerks, also referred to what they saw as some of the non-vocational benefits accruing from formal education. Indeed, several members of this latter group viewed learning only in such terms: 'education gives the ability to appreciate the beauties in life – and that has nothing to do with making money'; and 'It gives a broader perspective on life – he knows what's going on, how to apply himself, how to enjoy life a little more and get more things out of life.' This is not to suggest that such responses were totally absent within the four craft categories. A toolmaker, for example, said that education enabled one 'to appreciate the finer things in life', while another commented: 'knowledge, knowledge is power, knowledge is pleasure – he has less fear of life'. But, in contrast to the clerical workers, craftsmen voicing such sentiments were very much in the minority.[20]

Similar views of the educational process underlie the positions taken by these blue and white collar workers regarding the schooling of women. Indeed, in many cases almost identical ideas as to the functions of education are associated with radically differing opinions on the necessity for scholastic parity between the sexes. Turning first to those clerks and craftsmen who did subscribe to the notion of equality in educational opportunity, over 60 per cent of both groups considered education necessary for women so as to enable them to get decent jobs or earn high incomes. Moreover, 45 per cent of both groups gave this as the *only* reason for their viewpoint. In the words of a bricklayer: 'They should get at least a high school education – got to have at least that for a job.' Many responses were couched in terms of an awareness of the increasing demands and development of the technological society: 'today a woman has to be self-sufficient'; 'the way the world is nowadays they need as much education as they can get'; 'because they are more and more going into the business world and the businesses require it'; and 'even store clerks have to be high school graduates'. Whether it is welcomed or not, these people feel they cannot turn a blind eye to what is going on around them: 'Women are coming out of their kitchens...the more education, the better the job she gets.'

The only other reason given by a significant proportion of clerical and craft workers in justification of their desire for educational parity was again pragmatic. Around two fifths of both occupational groups justified their point of view on the grounds that the modern marriage demands an educated wife and mother. This is seen as making for both a better 'marriage dialogue' and a higher standard of child rearing. In the words of a bricklayer 'The children are with their mothers – they need an educated person to guide them.' Similarly, a clerk commented: 'Today's children require a mother who understands and who can explain more to them than in my day.' Not a few respondents evidenced awareness of the problem of communication between husband and wife should their levels of education differ considerably. A bricklayer explained: 'education for a woman gives her more understanding of her husband's way of life', while a carpenter demanded: 'How can she keep up with her husband if she's not as educated?' Finally, only 24 per cent of the craft group and 38 per cent of the clerks justified education for women in terms of its desirability as an end in itself – simply as producing a more cultivated individual. As we have already seen, the clerks especially are not unaware of some of the non-vocational benefits that may be gained from education. And yet these benefits were not mentioned to any extent when discussing the education of women. It would seem fair to surmise that not only do clerks and craftsmen view education as being less necessary for women than for men, they also see only certain aspects of education as being relevant in the case of women. And as has been already stated, those aspects are those which we can regard as being pragmatic: education as vocational training and education as making for a better marriage partner and mother.[21]

Despite these divergent views of clerks and craftsmen, it is evident that neither group approximate to what have in the past been seen as the traditional working or middle class attitudes towards education. The blue collar sample are far more aware of the desirability of educational achievement than has traditionally been the case within the working class; the clerks exhibit a higher degree of pragmatism in their view of education than that previously found within the middle class, and indeed than that expressed by the managers in my own sample.

We have seen that in terms of educational aspirations for sons and daughters this upper level white collar group strive toward higher levels of achievement than do their clerical counterparts. But it is their justification of these aspirations in particular, and their ideas concerning the purpose of education in general, that separate the two white collar groupings most markedly. For example, only one fifth of the managers subscribing to the notion of educational parity between the sexes mentioned vocationally linked reasons as a basis for this view.[22] Indeed, in more than one case the economic advantages of education were explicitly discounted: 'They (women) are human beings. An educated society requires women to be educated regardless of earning capacity or ability or need. It's just as important for women to be educated because they influence children – they determine attitudes in life for children.' This non-fatalistic view of marriage, as something that can be controlled, and the greater ease with which this can be accomplished by the educated women, stands out clearly in several of these responses on the education of women. A manager, himself a college graduate and with a wife of equal education, explained: 'Mothers are with their children more, and the wife can be of great value to her husband in handling numerous situations that might come up in married life.'

A similar picture emerges when one looks at the views expressed by managers with regard to the purpose or value of education in general. Indeed, in this instance, the isolation of this upper level white collar grouping is even more distinct. Only 8 per cent of the managers I interviewed discussed the value of education solely in vocational terms, while only around one third mentioned this at any point in their answer. Instead 84 per cent discussed the purpose of education in terms of the intrinsic benefits to be gained – the chance of getting more out of life, of being able to understand and enjoy music, the arts, or simply of being trained to think. And coming into a large number of the answers was a theme discussed a little earlier: that life could be manipulated or controlled to a degree and that education provided a formidable weapon for such action. The following responses are indicative:

> 'It broadens his outlook in life. It gives him a knowledge to rationalise his thinking; and this is so true – I found out for myself.'

'Ability to take decisions through training of the mind.
Better use of leisure – through books, art, music – which
exposed to in college.'

'An educated person gets much more out of life, enjoys the
finer things of life and is able to pass it on to their children.
I would say they have many more interesting friends because
they are better versed than an uneducated person.'

Such comments stand in stark contrast to some of the views of education
held by a large number of the clerks and craftsmen. Both these groups
have high educational aspirations for their children, but they are high
for predominantly one reason: that of occupational success. For despite
affluence and a high degree of satisfaction with their own jobs, these
skilled blue collar workers want their children to do better than they did.
And by 'better' they mean a non-manual occupation.

All respondents were asked to assume that a son of theirs was choosing
a job at the time of the interview, and required to say whether, in such
circumstances, they would prefer him to opt for a manual or non-manual
occupation. The pattern of responses is shown in Table 17. It is apparent
that despite the fact that 70 per cent of the total craft group claimed to
find their job 'very interesting', and despite 50 per cent of this same group
declaring themselves 'very satisfied' with those same jobs, only one quarter

Table 17. *Occupational preference for a son*

	Brick layers and Masons	Cabinet makers and Carpenters	Elec- tricians	Tool- makers	Total Craft	Clerks	Managers
	Percentage						
Preferred occupation							
Non-manual	60	60	54	57	57	68	66
Manual	20	20	37	22	26	7	11
Don't mind, don't know	20	20	9	21	17	25	23
Total per cent	100	100	100	100	100	100	100
Total number	35	49	44	54	194	44	38
Reasons for white collar preference							
Prestige	5	7	10	13	9	13	12
Extrinsic benefits	62	48	37	52	49	27	8
Intrinsic benefits	—	3	7	—	3	7	24
Income	19	21	23	13	19	27	8
Advancement potential	5	14	20	26	17	43	28
Other	29	28	20	23	24	17	40
Total number	21	29	30	31	111	30	25

would want a son of theirs to remain in manual work. This average figure would be lower if it were not for the electricians who, it will be recalled, exhibited the highest degree of job satisfaction of the four craft groupings.

Perhaps more surprising is the fact that those craftsmen who would want a son of theirs to remain in a blue collar occupation gave little indication that by this they meant a skilled trade, let alone their own particular craft. Out of the 50 craftsmen who reported a preference for a blue collar job for a son, only four explained this in terms of a clearly held, and positive, view of skilled manual work. A carpenter explained: 'I don't believe in a job that won't encompass the whole body – physically and mentally. This is carpentry – I would want him using both mind and body. Also a healthful occupation.' But such aspirations were rare: responses that could be categorised with reference to concepts such as craft pride or an occupational community were also totally absent. Instead the most frequent single explanation offered was economic: 18 craftsmen regarded manual work either as more remunerative or as more stable than white collar employment. In the words of a cabinet maker: 'Anything happens, you can always get a job if you do something with your hands. In time of depression a white collar worker can't get a job.' In addition eight craftsmen explained their preference for manual work in terms of relative levels of job satisfaction: 'There's more satisfaction – to be able to do something – make something with your hands.' But in general, as I have said, one cannot detect in the answers of those craftsmen wanting blue collar careers for their sons any reasoned or clear-cut set of arguments in justification of their standpoint. Not a few of the responses evidenced a lack of knowledge of possible alternatives to blue collar employment as much as anything else.

This is not, however, the case amongst the larger part of the sample – those preferring that any son of theirs follow a white rather than a blue collar vocation. Information regarding the reasons given for this preference is also shown in Table 17. It is apparent that few craftsmen would seem to be engaging in vicarious status striving: the prestige attached to the white collar and business suit appears to be irrelevant to around 90 per cent of those blue collar workers preferring a non-manual job for any son entering the labour market. Furthermore, it is also evident that for the large number of these people it is not so much the attractions of white collar employment that lie beyond their parental ambitions so much as some of the negative aspects of their own occupational experiences. Fully half of the craft sample in this case explained their preference for white collar employment for their sons in terms of one or more extrinsic aspects of white collar employment, which stood, in their eyes, in sharp contrast to the situation existing on the other side of the manual/non-manual line. Indeed, the very large majority of this group explained their preference *solely* in these terms. This was especially so in the case of the bricklayers and masons, who it will be recalled, were themselves in relatively the least enviable of work situations. And those features of white collar employment standing in the highest regard were almost without exception cleanliness, lack of danger, absence of fatigue or of exposure to the elements. The paucity of 'middle class' conceptions of the advantages of non-manual work – career prospects, prestige, autonomy – is startling. Consider the following responses:

A carpenter:
'I've seen myself the way I work manual, and I wouldn't want him to work the way I do. I'd rather he'd use his head than his back. Just wouldn't want him to work as I do.'

A cabinet maker:
'Everyone wants an easy job – to sit down all day is easier.'

A bricklayer:
'I do manual work and it's hard work. Non-manual is easier on your health–no hazards sitting in the office where it's warm.'

An electrician:
'I think the body can take so much, and in a period of years it won't be able to stand up if you do manual work.'

A toolmaker:
'Having done manual work all my life, I'd rather not have done it. It's harder work. So I'd rather see him in non-manual.'

In contrast, the impression is strong that many of the physical conditions of white collar employment, viewed covetously by manual employees, are taken for granted by the people enjoying those conditions. Only four clerks for example, discussed the advantages of white collar employment *solely* in terms of extrinsic features of the work situation. Instead 70 per cent of those clerks wishing a son of theirs to enter white collar occupation justified their choice by reference to the higher incomes or the opportunities for advancement inherent in such a career. The word 'opportunity' emerges repeatedly in an examination of this group's perceptions: 'Opportunities for greater salary, benefits'; 'More opportunities because of gaining more knowledge'; 'More room to move up' are typical of some of the responses.

Perhaps the striking feature of the managers' explanations of their preferences for white collar employment is the number of unclassifiable answers. To be sure, the intrinsic satisfactions and challenges inherent in non-manual work, coupled with the greater potential for advancement were mentioned by around one half of this group. Nonetheless, many of the responses suggest that a sizeable proportion simply were not able to justify what to them was something not open to debate: as such discussion of the relative merits of manual versus non-manual work has as much meaning as a debate on the advantages and disadvantages of insanity.

This preference for white collar employment remained even when respondents were asked to choose between a skilled craft occupation (a plumber earning $150 per week) and a modest clerical job (that of bookkeeper receiving $120 per week), although a proportion of those people initially exhibiting a desire that any son of theirs enter a white collar occupation nevertheless decided upon plumbing rather than bookkeeping. See Table 18. In general, those doing so chose this occupation because it is seen as providing a higher pay packet, with all the attendant advantages this brings. An electrician commented: 'It's interesting work and you can always go out and hustle a buck on the side if you have to. You can increase that from $150 to $250 – $100 tax-free.' In addition a number of respondents pointed to the superior intrinsic satisfactions to be gained from plumbing as an occupation ('a lot of merit in a day's work') as well as to the possibilities that exist for setting up one's own firm or small business. Thus a bricklayer who had earlier made it clear that he would want a son of his to get a college education and then embark upon a white collar career was not enthusiastic about the possibilities of bookkeeping, 'because a plumber's job is more rewarding than a bookkeeper's job, and not only money-wise. Myself, I would hate to be chained to a desk with a bookkeeper's job.' Similarly, a tool-

Table 18. *Specific occupational preference for a son*

	Brick-layers and Masons	Cabinet makers and Carpenters	Electricians	Tool makers	Total Craft	Clerks	Managers
	Percentage						
Preferred occupation							
Bookkeeper	54	53	41	43	47	50	53
Plumber	17	33	46	43	37	25	21
Don't mind; don't know	29	14	12	15	17	25	26
Total per cent	100	100	100	100	100	100	100
Total number	35	49	56	54	194	44	28
Reasons for bookkeeper preference							
Prestige	—	8	9	9	7	4	5
Extrinsic features	58	54	65	52	57	41	10
Advancement potential	79	58	61	70	66	68	70
Other	—	8	—	9	4	9	15
Total number	19	26	23	23	91	22	20

maker who earlier expressed the desire that his son would become a dentist – 'but generally non-manual because you live longer – better living' – when faced with the choice of plumbing or bookkeeping, chose the former on the ground that 'the possibilities of going into your own business or branching out more are better – a bookkeeper will be that all his life'. It is clear, in other words (and this is also evident in the responses of those who 'remain' with the bookkeeping job), that the large number of individuals stating a preference for non-manual over manual work were *not* thinking in terms of lower level bookkeeping tasks. A toolmaker who gave as examples of a desired non-manual job a doctor or a lawyer, went on to reply: 'Rather be a plumber – more money – than just running round an office,' while an electrician who had explicitly stated that he would want his son to become 'a professional' opted for a career in plumbing on the grounds that 'the bookkeeper has less chance of advancement'.

Turning to those respondents preferring a bookkeeping career for a son despite its modest salary, again the numbers choosing the white collar job for prestige or status reasons are minimal. Rather, the large majority of people would prefer their son to become a bookkeeper rather than a plumber not because of the advantages of bookkeeping *per se*, but because bookkeeping may lead to better things. It will be recalled that when discussing the advantages of non-manual occupations in general, only 17 per cent of the total craft group mentioned superior possibilities for advancement. At this point the extrinsic advantages to be gained from such a career were paramount. Such aspects remain important, but in these shallow waters of bookkeeping they take second place to the possibility of upward movement in the direction of managerial or professional status. The following comments are illustrative:

A mason:
'Better possibilities (as a bookkeeper). There's more future in office-type work – as an accountant or C.P.A. later.'

An electrician:
'Being a bookkeeper, he's learning as he goes, where as a plumber – he's down in the cesspool handling other people's crap. And as a bookkeeper he has a chance for advancement – might end up as head bookkeeper, making $175.'

A cabinet maker:
'Not a labouring job. It's white collar. You can better yourself by staying away from labour – eventually he would progress more. In the long run it would pay off.'

A clerk:
'Steady – he wouldn't have to work as hard. He could go on further – a plumber's always a plumber.'

A manager:
'The low salary hopefully is temporary, with room for advancement. No maximum to earnings – growth possible, while the plumber is limited. You've got to look at the future – what will he earn in ten years? A plumber will still be a plumber.'

It is evident therefore that despite high levels of affluence, pride in the possession of craft skills and the gaining of intrinsic rewards in the performance of those skills, the majority of the blue collar sample do not want their children to follow in their occupational footsteps. But it is also evident that the reasons underlying these parental aspirations are not connected with vicarious status striving: rather these people are keen that their sons should work in jobs where they will not experience the sorts of physical deprivations to which they themselves are being exposed in the work situation. To a mason, in his early sixties, and who earlier in the interview had complained about the strain of lifting bricks and stones all day as well as the rigours of winter storms, bad weather and slack periods, the advantages of bookkeeping over plumbing were very real: 'He'd be cleaner – he wouldn't be cold. He wouldn't be hot – or sweat. Better surroundings – the chance for advancement.' Everything, it would seem, is relative: an electrician, in his forties, described his own job as 'a challenge. When you get something like an I.B.M. machine to install and you have to figure it out on your own from a blue-print – to see it finally operating is a real satisfaction – it's sort of creative. You never get bored with it because its always something new.' Nevertheless, this craftsman would prefer that his son become a bookkeeper than enter a skilled trade where he might experience the same satisfaction as does his father: 'I sure have had some dirty jobs in my life and I wouldn't want him to have to handle some of the dirt I have had to handle – I'd like to see him in a job where he could at least keep clean.' This means that, in contrast to the findings of earlier studies, I am not able to find any clear-cut relationship between occupational dissatisfaction on the part of parents and high aspirations for their children.[23] The fact that 85 per cent of the craft sample were at least 'quite satisfied' with their jobs does not blind them to certain disagreeable features of those jobs; features which their own children will avoid in a white collar occupation.

It remains to determine whether or not the high aspirations expressed by the large majority of our sample for their children are realised. Ideally this would require some form of follow-up study, an enterprise clearly beyond the scope of the present investigation. However we are able to gain important clues as to the level of realism underlying parental desires by examining the educational and occupational achievements of those children of respondents who have already left full-time education and embarked upon a career.

Information regarding such achievement is shown in Table 19. It is

Table 19. *Children's educational and occupational achievements*

	Bricklayers and Masons		Cabinet makers and Carpenters		Electricians		Toolmakers		Total Craft		Clerks		Managers	
	Son	Daughter	Son	Daughter	Son	Daughter	Son	Daughter	Son	Daughter	Son	Daughter	Son	Daughter
Level of schooling attained	*Cumulative percentage*													
College graduate	31	22	20	17	32	—	18	19	26	15	18	23	66	25
Some college	31	44	35	25	37	10	43	33	37	28	30	29	66	37
High school graduate	69	67	85	92	91	70	94	81	86	79	81	94	89	75
Total number	13	9	20	12	22	10	16	21	71	52	16	17	9	8
Occupation*	*Percentage*													
Professional and managerial	11	11	28	17	37		42	8	31	33	40	43	78	25
Clerical and sales workers	11								8	50	13	57	—	75
Father's skilled craft	22	22	11		26	21	17		19	—	—	—	—	—
Other skilled craft	22		22		21	16	33		24	18	20	—	11	—
Non-skilled workers	33		22		16		—		18	18	27	—	11	—
Total per cent	100	100	100	100	100	100	100	100	100	100	100	100	100	100
Total number	9		18		19		12		58	28	15	7	9	4

*Children *currently* in full-time employment: housewives and servicemen omitted.

evident that a substantial discrepancy exists between the hopes expressed by those of my respondents with children still in school and the standards achieved by those offspring who have entered upon full-time employment. And it must be emphasised that this discrepancy exists for both the craft and clerical samples. 86 per cent of those craftsmen with sons still in school expressed the desire that those children would gain at least a B.A. degree. In the case of the clerks in a similar position, the proportion was 95 per cent. And yet if one looks at those sons of clerks and craftsmen who have completed their schooling, the fact is that only 18 per cent of the former and 26 per cent of the latter have in fact graduated from college. The disparity is no less striking when the educational aspirations and achievements of daughters are compared. (It can be suggested that the achievements of the children of managers are more nearly in keeping with the aspirations expressed by members of this latter grouping, but numbers are too small to argue this with certainty.)

However, while the educational aspirations expressed by many respondents must be regarded as unrealistic, it would seem that their hopes for the types of jobs their children might enter are more akin to reality. For two fifths of craftsmen's sons now working are employed in the kind of work situation so many of their parents desire: that of the office worker. Indeed only one-fifth of their offspring are engaged in jobs that can be taken to represent downward mobility. As a group the craftsmen would seem to be at least as successful as clerks in realising their parental ambitions. Nevertheless, that success, especially with regard to educational achievements, can only be regarded as limited. The question that remains to be answered is why this should be so.

On the surface, at least, it does not appear that this discrepancy can be explained by simply regarding these aspirations as lacking in authenticity or sincerity. For example 63 per cent of craftsmen with sons in elementary or high school were members of a Parent-Teacher Association. The proportion of those with daughters in a similar situation was identical. In addition the large majority of these P.T.A. members would seem to take membership seriously: of those parents with sons in school 50 per cent reported that they attended meetings frequently, while a further 34 per cent were able to go along at least 'occasionally'. Only 9 per cent admitted to 'never' attending association meetings. The figures for those blue collar members with daughters still in school were not dissimilar.[24]

Unfortunately, however, I have no information as to the *nature* or *content* of that participation. This is an important omission as other of my data suggest dissociation on the part of our clerks and craftsmen from the institution of higher education. As has been shown elsewhere in this chapter these people have positive views and techniques of child rearing and exhibit a genuine concern for the success of their children. And yet the extent to which they seem able to translate that concern into action in the realm of formal education would appear to be limited. For example, respondents expressing the desire that one or more of their children go to college were asked how strongly they felt about this. Over 80 per cent of each occupational grouping said they wanted this to happen 'very strongly'. Furthermore 68 per cent of the craftsmen and 74 per cent of the clerks said that they were already setting money aside especially to pay for a college education. However, the amount of money saved was, in the majority of cases, woefully inadequate. Of those craftsmen feeling 'very strongly' that their son or daughter should have a college education, only one quarter had total savings amounting to more than $5,000. Over half of the blue collar parents in this group had amassed less than $1,500. This was the case whether the child was in the sixth, ninth or twelfth grade. Thus a toolmaker with his only son in the eleventh grade 'very strongly' wanted him to go to an Ivy League college and yet had total savings of less than $1,000. If anything the amount of saving by clerical workers was below that of the various blue collar categories. And, as would be expected, the level of realism of both these categories stands in stark contrast to that evidenced by the highly paid managers in the sample. Of those respondents wanting 'very strongly' their children to go to college 85 per cent had savings of above $5,000, while over half exceeded the $10,000 level.

One explanation of this lack of financial planning on the part of the clerks and craftsmen might simply be the fact that these people cannot afford to save. While such an argument might be persuasive in the case of the lower paid clerical workers it is unconvincing when applied to skilled craftsmen, especially the toolmakers and electricians. And further doubt is cast upon this as an explanation upon examination of the pattern of responses to a question in which respondents were asked: 'If you were suddenly given a $2,000 bonus tomorrow, what would you do with the additional money?' Of those clerks and craftsmen specifically stating that they 'very strongly' wanted their child or children to go to college only 11 per cent and 14 per cent respectively said that they would put this $2,000 towards the costs of college fees and expenses. Indeed only 32 per cent and 40 per sent of the two groups said they would save this sum at all. The majorities of both said they would spend the money immediately, most usually on a house (or improving the existing one), car or vacation.[25] Thus a clerk who 'very strongly' wanted his son to go to college and become a doctor said that he would spend his $2,000 on a new car. The son was in his final year of high school and the father had total savings of less than $1,500. Similarly, an electrician with a daughter in a similar situation whom he 'very strongly' wanted to gain a B.A. degree, said he would spend $2,000 on a car for that daughter and a colour television for himself. He also had total savings of less than $1,500.

Again, I do not interpret these responses in terms of a lack of sincerity on the part of these people. There is no evidence to suggest that they are not quite serious in expressing high educational aspirations for their children. Rather it appears that these people are operating in a situation which is almost completely isolated from the sphere of higher education: their life experiences and values have not prepared them to adopt a role conducive to putting a son or a daughter through college. It is not that they are *unwilling* to save, it is that their position in society almost prevents them gaining access to information regarding how much, and how, one needs to save. And perhaps the greatest barrier to respondents' children successfully completing a university course is the fact that they themselves have not been exposed to such institutions. Not one of the skilled craftsmen I interviewed was a college graduate and only 8 per cent had undergone any formal education after graduating from high school. More important, 55 per cent of the total craft group (72 per cent in the case of the bricklayers and masons) had not graduated from high school. For the clerks the comparable figure was 25 per cent. Three members of this grouping were college graduates while an additional eleven (32 per cent in total) had undergone formal training, usually at a business college, after leaving high school. In direct contrast 82 per cent of the managers had attended college or university while 45 per cent had gained at least a B.A. degree. Identical differentials exist in the educational attainments of respondents' wives. Given the educational experiences of these people it is not difficult to explain why they should appear less able than managers to translate their hopes into action: having never been exposed to the higher educational system they are less than prepared to operate in relation to that system.[26] This is neither a new nor a startling finding: researchers have been pointing out ways in which the family acts as a barrier to educational mobility for a good many years. Nevertheless, given our concern with changes in class structure, it is a fact that needs to be emphasised. For not until the circle is broken will this crucial and inherited aspect of social stratification gain fluidity.

Conclusion

It would appear that a combination of stability and change characterises the family structure and patterns of child rearing of the contemporary American skilled craftsman. On the one hand, the majority of these men are the heads of families of relatively small size, cherishing hopes for the educational and occupational success of their children. On the other, they continue to be involved in frequent, albeit restricted, interaction with extended kin while rearing these same children to be conformers rather than innovators. The situation pertaining in a large number of those families headed by a clerical worker is not dissimilar. And perhaps most important, if the managers' families can be taken as representative of those of the middle class then this latter term can have little relevance in any analysis of blue collar and lower level white collar family units. Differences remain, and they are differences that are qualitative at the same time as they are quantitative. And as I have tried to argue, they are rooted in the distinct positions craftsmen, clerks and managers occupy in the social structure, especially those having to do with occupational situation. To the extent therefore, that people in these three types of occupation continue to occupy radically differing positions in the division of labour we may expect them to head families of distinctive form and socialise their offspring in particular ways. We may also expect blue collar families to continue exercising a conservative influence upon class structure, almost irrespective of the verbalised aspirations of these parents for the worldly success of their children.

4   The Organisation of Life Style

'It's a family street. There are white people, cops and firemen – all working class people with families – no roughnecks. Its handy for church, stores and the city.'

'We play cards – visit each others homes: eat, drink, jibber-jabber – jobs, job opportunities (we build all kinds of buildings). The women talk about kids and maybe looking for jobs. We eat – beer, pickles, olives, little necks, crabs, shrimp.

It is with regard to changes in the life style of the affluent American worker that speculations concerning the blurring of class lines have been most abundant, most strident and indeed most plausible. Popular writers, journalists, administrators and social scientists have all pointed to the rapid and substantial post-war increases in the earnings of large numbers of blue collar workers and gone on to claim that this has led to the universal adoption of middle class life styles. While *Business Week* published an article entitled 'Worker loses his class identity', *Fortune* magazine trumpeted the arrival of the 'all-American class', going on to claim that 'The United States is becoming a one-class market of prosperous middle-income people'.[1] Perhaps more soberly, sociologists, among them Mayer, Lenski, and Wilensky, attempted to demonstrate that 'a large part of the working class shares a "white collar" style of life'; that the standards of the middle class were 'permeating the working class more and more with each passing year' and that, as a result, there was emerging 'a new middle mass, a population, that increasingly shares common values, beliefs and tastes'.[2] Finally, as if to demonstrate its hand was indeed upon the pulse of the nation, the United States government declared: 'The wage-earner's way of life is well-nigh indistinguishable from that of his salaried co-citizens. Their homes, their cars, their baby-sitters, the style of clothes their wife and children wear, the food they eat, the bank where they establish credit, their days off, the education of their children, their church – all these are alike, and are becoming more nearly identical.'[3] It is the task of the present chapter to assess the validity of these claims.

The Home and the Neighbourhood

The home and the area in which it is located have for long been regarded as symbolic of class position. For Warner, 'house type' and 'dwelling area' were two of the four components of his Index of Status Character-istics, while home ownership was one of the most important factors distinguishing the lower middle class from what he called the upper–lower class.[4] Kahl, writing some years later, assigned the same significance to home ownership as a distinctive feature of lower middle class life: 'Home ownership is respectable, and is a symbol of stability and of family sol-idarity.'[5] Writing more recently, perhaps the most vigorous proponent of the thesis of *embourgeoisement* in the United States, Kurt Mayer has laid great stress upon the fact that 'higher wages of recent years have enabled working men to buy their own houses and to furnish them like those of white collar people'.[6]

If indeed it were possible to regard a high incidence of home-ownership on the part of skilled craftsmen as evidence of the breaking down of class lines, then this would be the position we should have to take. For in terms of numbers of owner-occupiers as well as quality of housing, it is apparent that, as a group, the skilled workers I interviewed are in a position sup-erior to that occupied by the lower level non-manual workers. As Table 20 shows, around three fifths of the craft group own their own homes, a figure slightly higher than is found in the case of clerks and, as would be expected, substantially lower than is found within the managerial category. Similarly, the value of blue collar housing is, on the whole, higher than that of the clerks. (Respondents were asked to estimate the sum they could hope to realise for their houses at the time of the study.) For example, 66 per cent of craft home-owners judged the value of their homes to be above $15,000 while only 51 per cent of the clerks did likewise. In addition 8 per cent of this former group owned homes whose present value they estimated to be above $25,000. Not one of the clerks fell into this category, while,

Table 20. *Housing and home-ownership*

	Brick layers and Masons	Cabinet makers and Carpenters	Electricians	Toolmakers	Total Craft	Clerks	Managers
	Percentage						
Home-owners	47	59	68	63	61	55	79
Total number	35	49	56	54	194	44	38
Value of housing (home-owners only)							
less than $10,000	19	4	8	10	8	4	1
$10,000–$12,495	24	15	5	13	13	32	3
$12,500–$14,995	13	11	16	10	13	13	7
$15,000–$17,495	19	22	24	31	25	17	10
$17,500–$19,995	13	22	31	16	22	21	24
$20,000 and up	12	26	16	20	19	13	55
Total per cent	100	100	100	100	100	100	100
Total number	16	27	37	31	111	24	29

as might have been expected, 41 per cent of the home-owning managers did so. Conversely, the proportion of clerks owning homes worth less than $12,500 is substantially higher than the percentage of craftsmen in a similar situation.[7] Again the bricklayers and masons appeared to be the most disadvantaged of the various occupational groupings. This is the case both in terms of the numbers of bricklayers and masons owning their own homes and with regard to the value of those houses.

Respondents, whether or not they already owned their own homes, were asked whether, in principle, they preferred to own or rent a place to live. They were requested to give reasons for their answers. The reasons go a long way toward explaining the relatively high level of home-ownership evidenced by the blue collar workers. As would be expected the overwhelming majority of all three major occupational groups said that they would prefer to own their own home rather than rent accommodation. Their explanations can be grouped into three categories: economic, the chance to gain increased freedom and/or privacy, enhanced prestige or status.[8] Many individuals gave more than one reason. But it is amongst those respondents who gave only a single argument for preferring to own their own house that the sharpest differences between craftsmen and white collar workers emerge. For 47 per cent of the total craft group explained their preference for home-ownership solely in terms of the fact that this gave them increased freedom or privacy. And the freedom that was uppermost in their minds was freedom from subjection to the rule of a landlord. Phrases like 'you can go as you want, do as you please – no one on your back'; 'you can make all the noise you want and there's no landlord to stop you'; 'Friction with landlords about children makes you want to own your own home'; 'I'm my own boss'; 'Can do as I please...I prize freedom' were repeated time and time again by these skilled blue collar workers, virtually every one of whom had rented at some time since marriage. In total over three quarters of the blue collar sample described the advantages of home-ownership at least partially in these terms. In contrast, while such reasons were mentioned by an identical proportion of the clerks, they were far more likely to give them in conjunction with one or more other inducements, usually economic. Thus a lower grade civil servant saw the advantages in owning his own home as 'security, privacy, freedom', while another explained 'privacy, I'm my own boss – no one can tell me to do anything. I like to think of it as an investment.' Indeed the words 'equity' and 'privacy' were the two appearing most often in responses of white collar workers to this question. Nevertheless only 24 per cent of this latter grouping explained their preference for home-ownership *solely* in terms of the independence and privacy that results.

The same is true for the managers: while only 18 per cent regarded increased freedom as the sole benefit of being an owner-occupier, a further 50 per cent gave this as one of the advantages of being in this situation. In addition, it was this group that placed the greatest emphasis on the long and short term economic gains that could be enjoyed through owning property. Indeed, 70 per cent gave financial reasons for owning rather than renting. The comparable proportions of clerks and craftsmen were 59 per cent and 36 per cent respectively. Similarly, only 18 per cent of the former and 13 per cent of the latter mentioned the prestige or status that might accrue to the owner-occupier as opposed to the renter. To be sure the wife of an electrician who had explained his preference in economic and privacy terms, added: 'you are building up equity all the time – it raises you socially too', while several respondents referred to 'the pride of ownership' or 'the prestige of owning'. But such viewpoints were few and far between.

Again it is apparent that we should make abundantly clear the distinction between a particular behavioural pattern and the symbolic significance attached to that pattern. In this case it is evident that blue collar workers, in owning their own houses, are behaving in a way that superficially could be described as middle class. It is equally evident that their reasons for buying could not be so labelled. Craftsmen wish to own their own houses not so as to symbolise their new found position in American society, but because by doing so they gain a measure of freedom and privacy that is not possible when living in a rented apartment. The majority have not even become sufficiently 'middle class' in outlook to consider or acknowledge the added economic bonus that is also the lot of the home-owner. It is their neglect of this advantage of home-ownership that sets the blue collar workers off from the clerks, and especially, the managers.

An identical picture emerges if one looks at the type of district in which craftsmen have bought or are buying houses, as well as the kinds of qualities they look for in an ideal neighbourhood. For home-ownership would not seem to be linked either with a move to the suburbs or to one or other of the higher status areas of Providence. Instead it is clear that for craftsmen *and* clerks alike, residence in an established middle class neighbourhood is not a goal towards which many aspire. This is not to say that where one lives is seen as being unimportant. The opposite is the case. But those neighbourhood characteristics that are most highly valued are not ones that can be regarded as middle class.

Only 19 per cent of the total craft category did not live within the city of Providence in 1967. More than 90 per cent of the bricklayers and masons and the cabinet makers and carpenters lived within the city limits, as did over 70 per cent of the electricians and toolmakers. The rush to the suburbs has not occurred. Neither is it in evidence amongst the clerical workers, 78 per cent of whom are city dwellers. The majority of those blue and lower level white collar workers not residing within Providence city limits were located in either Cranston or Warwick, areas adjacent to the city and to the south and south west. In contrast, only 57 per cent of the managers lived

Table 21. *Social ranking of area of residence*

	Providence total population	Brick-layers and Masons	Cabinet makers and Carpenters	Electricians	Toolmakers	Total Craft	Clerks	Managers
	Percentage							
High I	8	—	2	—	2	1	7	16
II	8	3	16	9	2	8	7	21
III	16	28	22	19	33	26	31	44
IV	37	49	36	45	46	43	35	8
Low V	30	20	20	25	13	20	20	11
Total per cent	100	100	100	100	100	100	100	100
Total number		35	48	55	52	190	44	38

within the boundaries of Providence and indeed one quarter had houses considerably removed from the city and its environs.

Goldstein and Mayer have developed an Index of Social Rank for all the census tracts of Rhode Island, based on the occupation, income and education of people living in those tracts in 1960.[9] The scores composing this index have been standardised to a range 0–100. The higher the score, the better the rank of the tract. Table 21 shows the proportions of the various occupational groups living within each quintile of the social rank index. The same information is also presented for the city of Providence.[10]

Compared to the total population of Providence, craftsmen would appear to be in a slightly superior situation. But the difference is not great and is mainly confined to the lower two quintiles of the ranking. Clerks and craftsmen alike are clustered in areas having a social rank score of between 20 and 60 with a larger proportion of clerks than of craftsmen located nearer the upper of these two limits. 45 per cent of clerical workers live in areas falling within the top three quintiles of the ranking, while only 35 per cent of the manual workers are in this favoured position. Again the managers occupy a superior situation with over one third living in neighbourhoods falling within the upper two quintiles of the scale. In general terms, then, clerks and craftsmen alike live within the city of Providence, and within the same parts of that city.[11] Overwhelmingly these people are located in a belt encompassing the north west and south of the metropolitan area, and disregarding the central city. Only seven craftsmen and four clerks were found in the fashionable East Side of the city, the locale of a significant proportion of the managers in my sample. This means that affluent craftsmen especially were not living in the higher status neighbourhoods of the city that economically were within their grasp.[12] The relationship between income and Index of Social Rank, while positive, was very weak, 32 per cent of craftsmen earning below $9,000 per annum lived in areas scoring less than 30. The comparable proportion of those earning above $9,000 was 33 per cent. Similarly, 31 per cent of the more affluent blue collar workers lived in areas scoring in excess of 50, a position enjoyed by 23 per cent of the less affluent. The situation is almost identical in the case of the clerks. Conversely, there is a very strong relationship between home-ownership and value of housing on the one hand, and income on the other. But this correlation can only be interpreted in the light or our earlier discussion. To be sure the large majorities of all three groups are buying houses when they are economically able and are allowing the nature of housing to be determined by their income. But for craftsmen especially, affluence enables the purchase of a large house or a more convenient one. It is not seen as being sufficient reason for a move to a middle class locale. And in the light of the respondent's analyses of the advantages and disadvantages of their present neighbourhoods, this is not surprising.

Table 22 shows clearly that within the clerical and craft groups the three features of present neighbourhood valued most highly are proximity to facilities such as schools, recreation areas, shops, or churches, friendly and pleasant neighbours, and a measure of freedom from noise or overcrowding. Of those people who had fault to find with their present residential area, noise from traffic or children were the two features mentioned most often by all four of the blue collar groups. Analysis of other features of the neighbourhood that might be highly valued again shows a situation of little difference between clerks and craftsmen, but a substantial gap separating the two white collar groups. For example, half of the managerial category valued the place where they presently lived either because of its suburban or its middle class character. Phrases like 'they're higher in-

Table 22. *Positive characteristics of present neighbourhood*

	Bricklayers and Masons	Cabinet makers and Carpenters	Electricians	Toolmakers	Total Craft	Clerks	Managers
	Percentage						
Convenience for various facilities	28	51	45	54	46	52	60
Quiet	40	24	41	44	38	45	39
Friendly and decent neighbours	51	35	48	33	41	20	11
Suburban character	—	6	16	7	8	7	24
Middle class character	3	2	—	6	3	14	36
Traditional reasons	11	10	11	2	8	4	3
Other	26	20	22	11	19	23	8
Total number	35	49	56	54	194	44	38

come people here'; 'people are in a higher bracket'; 'a nice class of people'; 'there's a better class of people here'; and finally, 'there are nice people living here – respectable people – a rabbi and a minister' demonstrate a conscious awareness of that which I have already demonstrated: the residential segregation of this upper level group from both clerks and craftsmen. Indeed two managers described the area where they lived in similar, but in *negative* terms: one earning over $14,000 a year and in his late thirties complained that he was living in a 'middle class Irish-American-Italian ghetto', while another, a suburban resident described the 'heavy concentration of wealth' which meant that 'our kids are growing up in a fairyland that doesn't represent the real world'.

Such complaints did not play a prominent role in descriptions of neighbourhood put forward by the clerks and skilled craftsmen. But this does not mean that these people were oblivious to the social structure of the areas in which they lived. The reverse is the case. Indeed, 20 per cent of this former group and 9 per cent of the latter voiced fears that the area in which they were presently living was deteriorating. The following comments, all made by respondents identifying with the working class are indicative of the nature of these fears:

> A carpenter:
> 'It was nice when the housing project was not here. Better class of people – all Irish – before. Now just riff-raff – unwed mothers, grass widows. They are getting everything for nothing. The kids – coloured – are pretty rough.'

> An electrician:
> 'Type of people who are coming in – no control over their children – they run loose and dirty. They don't keep up their property – upkeep is poor.'

> A toolmaker:
> 'Well ... these neighbours are low class – don't take care of their children properly.'

> A toolmaker:
> 'Class of people getting below me. They scream at their kids – peace and quiet all gone.'

> A clerk:
> 'The people across the street are vulgar.'

It is evident that these responses do not represent dislike of a move away from middle classness, but from stability and respectability. Discussion of the positive features of present neighbourhood lends weight to this interpretation. For, rather than relishing the presence of high status or income neighbours (as did a number of managers) craftsmen especially were concerned that the people amongst whom they lived should be friendly and that they should be 'pleasant' as well as 'decent'. Consider the following characterisations:

> A cabinet maker:
> 'It's a cleaner neighbourhood, the houses are painted and kept up – neater looking yards.'

> A mason:
> 'Neighbours are pleasant . . . take good care of their property.'

> A clerk:
> 'Quiet most of the time, friendly neighbours, generally nice people. Its a place where people generally help each other out.'

> An electrician:
> 'Because it's quiet here. . .many times at night I take a stroll. . . Close to city, neighbours are nice. It isn't a neighbourhood where you have a lot of ganging and commotion. We've never had any scandal up through here – riots and all that.'

> A bricklayer:
> 'It's a family street. There are white people, cops and firemen all working class people with families – no roughnecks. Its handy to churches and stores in the city.'

Neighbourhood descriptions such as these stand in contrast to the more prestige-oriented comments of the managers, many of which had almost an air of clinical detachment. To be sure they reflect a set of values pertaining to the ideal neighbourhood setting, but values that are in no sense pale reflections of those of the established middle class.

Leisure Time and Leisure Activities

Membership in organisations
The image of America as being a nation of 'joiners' dates back at least to the writings of de Tocqueville. Wirth saw the 'enormous multiplication of voluntary associations' as being a central feature of the urban way of life, while by 1927 Charles and Mary Beard felt able to claim: 'It was a rare American who was not a member of four or five societies.'[13] More recently a number of sociologists have demonstrated clearly that while large numbers of Americans do belong to one or more voluntary associations, 'joining' is by no means spread uniformly throughout the whole population. Rather, at least until the present time, membership of such

societies or organisations has been primarily a prerogative of the middle class. For the large proportion of blue collar workers, the kinds of services and satisfactions derived from membership in voluntary organisation have instead been provided by neighbourhood or extended family ties.[14]

It is difficult to draw an unequivocal picture of the organisational involvements of the craftsmen that are the subject of this research: while the proportion belonging to, and active in various clubs and associations is greater than that found in earlier studies, a gap remains between the level of joining of blue and white collar workers. Clues as to why this should be the case are provided by examination of some of the characteristics of those blue collar employees who are members of one or more voluntary associations. Income, age, education and ethnicity exact little or no effect on membership levels. Indeed the only variable that would appear to be linked with 'joining' is contact with the middle class via the working wife. 67 per cent of skilled craftsmen with a wife currently in the white collar labour force belonged to an organisation. Amongst those manual workers whose wives were also in manual occupations the figure was 39 per cent. Again the sub-sample of managers demonstrate their separateness from both clerks and craftsmen: over one third of the former occupational group belong to at least three formal organisations, a proportion not approximated by any of the other occupational categories in this study.

Table 23. *Husband's participation in organisations*

	Brick-layers and Masons	Cabinet makers and Carpenters	Elec-tricians	Tool-makers	Total Craft	Clerks	Managers
	Percentage						
Number of organisational memberships							
None	66	49	38	48	47	34	21
One	25	33	43	32	35	34	18
Two	6	10	13	3	8	19	24
Three	3	8	6	17	10	13	37
Total per cent	100	100	100	100	100	100	100
Type of organisation							
Church, religious	6	12	9	9	9	18	29
Veterans, military, patriotic	3	8	20	13	12	16	5
Lodges, fraternal	—	18	28	23	20	28	32
Sports, hobby	3	12	15	21	14	12	16
Civic, charity	18	14	11	17	14	7	61
Other	15	12	4	8	11	31	35
Total number	35	49	56	54	194	44	38
Office holders							
	17	28	11	28	21	28	43
Total number	28	25	12	35	100	29	30

This separateness is also evident in respect of the *types* of organisation to which these people belong. And nowhere is this more apparent than in that traditional middle class pursuit, involvement in civic and charity organisations. For, as Table 23 shows, three fifths of the managers are involved in one or more of this type of organisation. The numbers of clerks and craftsmen behaving similarly are very small. For example, not one belonged to a Planned Parenthood Association, or was linked with the organisation of the United Fund. Similarly, the vast majority of members of neighbourhood associations were drawn from the ranks of the managers as were, not surprisingly, those individuals willing to pay the high membership fees demanded by country and town clubs. A production manager interviewed belonged to a Hunt Club (the most prestigious country club in the area), the most prestigious town club in the city, an additional town club, and a golf club as well as being involved with Planned Parenthood. His wife belonged to the same country and golf clubs, worked with Planned Parenthood and was an active member of the Providence Art Club.

In all three occupational groupings Moose stood alongside Lions, Buffaloes and Elks. Surprisingly, Masons were no less prevalent in the craft than in the managerial categories. Rod and gun clubs and bowling associations were the most popular sporting organisations. Given the ethnic composition of Rhode Island the low level of membership in ethnic or national organisations is surprising. Equally, it is a crucially important finding in any study of changes in the American class structure. To be sure, several of the fraternal organisations and lodges in Providence have ethnic connotations, the Knights of Columbus being the obvious example. But the type of ethnic organisation that played such an important role in the immigrant communities of the North East in the earlier decades of the century would now seem to be irrelevant to the way of life enjoyed by the clerks and affluent craftsmen that are the focus of this study. One clerk belonged to the Sons of Irish Kings and the Shamrock Society of North Providence (the only time these organisations were ever mentioned); one of the two craftsmen belonging to the Sons of Italy laughed when he reported this as he was an Irish-American. Similarly the sole representative of the Sons of St. Patrick that we found had a father and paternal grandfather who were born in Yugoslavia. In total, only eight individuals out of a total sample size of 276 belonged to traditional ethnic organisations.

There are also important differences between the three major occupational categories in terms of degree of involvement within these various organisations, clubs and societies. Patterns of attendance within the managerial group are at a much higher level than those found within either the craft or clerical categories. Of those managers belonging to one or more organisations, around one third go to at least four meetings per month. The corresponding figures for the clerks and craftsmen are 9 per cent and 14 per cent. Similarly, 34 per cent of the blue collar organisational members do not attend any meetings at all in an average month. For the managers the figure is 17 per cent while amongst the lower level white collar workers it is 24 per cent. Finally, one third of the craftsmen and 46 per cent of the clerks who are members of a club or organisation attend meetings, on average, no more than once a month. It would seem that membership need not be linked with active participation. Given this, it is perhaps surprising that lower level non-manual and manual workers are represented to any extent within the executive of the organisations to which they do belong. But for at least two of the craft groups this is the case, as is again shown in Table 23. Indeed several skilled workers were concerned with the running of more than one voluntary association: one toolmaker was either president, chairman or committee man of four societies. Nonetheless, it is within the managerial group that we find the highest proportion of leaders: of the 13 managers who are officially connected with the running of an organisation, all but three hold office in at least two such groupings.

The pattern of organisational involvements of respondents' wives does little to alter the picture that has emerged so far. Indeed, if we consider the formal participation of the clerks and craftsmen as being on the low side, then we must regard that of their wives as being definitely muted. No fewer than 65 per cent of craft wives and 61 of clerical spouses did not belong to a single voluntary association or society. Amongst the managerial families the corresponding figure was 32 per cent. Again the significant gap is that separating the wives of managers from those of clerks and craftsmen. Over one third of this former group belonged to two or more organisations. For these latter categories the proportions were 8 per cent and 14 per cent. Of those wives that did belong to one or more organisations church-related associations of one kind or another were the most numerous. Within the managerial group, and to a lesser extent in the case of the clerical category, charitable and civic societies played a secondary role – Planned Parenthood being the organisation mentioned most often. As would be expected, it was among the managerial wives that were found the few individuals who were members of 'cultural seminars', the Providence Art Club or the College Hill Gardening Club. Similarly it was this group that provided the most regular participants in societies' meetings or functions. 40 per cent of those managerial wives who belonged to one or more organisations attended meetings at least twice a month. For the wives of clerks and craftsmen the comparable figures were 18 per cent and 23 per cent. The majority of members within these latter groups attended, on average, one meeting per month.

Informal social interaction

It would be difficult to characterise the blue collar workers in the sample as avid 'joiners'. The same is true, albeit to a lesser extent, of the clerks. And

Table 24. *Frequency of social activity, non-related friends*

	Brick-layers and Masons	Cabinet makers and Carpenters	Electricians	Toolmakers	Total Craft	Clerks	Managers
	Cumulative percentage						
Twice a week	17	16	18	26	19	12	10
Once a week	60	38	46	58	50	43	29
Once a fortnight	63	50	55	65	58	59	63
Once a month	80	80	75	85	80	70	79
A few times a year	94	100	95	91	95	86	95
Never	6	—	5	9	5	14	5
Total per cent	100	100	100	100	100	100	100
Total number	35	49	56	54	194	44	38

yet it would be a mistake to regard these people either as 'privatised' or as socially isolated. I have already shown in chapter 3 that the majority of clerks and craftsmen alike are engaged in frequent interaction with kin. In addition, as Table 24 makes apparent, not only do these people have large numbers of friends but they also spend time with those friends both regularly and frequently. Indeed, it is abundantly clear that the large majority of both blue and white collar workers are involved in meaningful and highly active social circles. Around half of the total craft group get together with non-related friends at least once a week while around three fifths of each of the main occupational categories spend leisure time with friends at least once a fortnight. Further, it is within the blue collar groups that we find the largest numbers of people engaging in what migh be regarded as intensive sociability: one fifth of the craftsmen spend time with non-related friends at least twice a week, while 7 per cent of the total reported sharing leisure time with friends on at least three out of every seven days. The only variable appearing to exert any influence on degree of sociability was ethnicity. Comparison of craftsmen whose paternal grandfathers were born in Italy with those who were at least third generation Americans demonstrated a tendency for the latter grouping to spend more time with non-related friends. While not substantial, this finding is in accord with data presented earlier and showing Italian-American respondents to be enjoying a comparatively high level of interaction with kin. Although family-centredness would seem an inappropriate concept in any description of these people, it is nevertheless evident that the home does play a central role in their social lives. Indeed, it is not overstating the case to say that for the large majority of these blue and white collar workers, the home is *the* focus of social life. The truck driver, interviewed in a study conducted less than ten years earlier, who remarked 'It don't make any sense, this rushing around to everybody's house', would find few kindred spirits in my own sample. For 69 per cent of the total craft group, when asked what they did when they got together with friends, talked about activities that took place within the context of each other's homes. In the case of the toolmakers and the cabinet makers and carpenters, the proportion approached three quarters, while in the case of the electricians it was a little over three fifths. Less surprisingly, 70 per cent of the clerks and 75 per cent of the managers entertained and were entertained by their friends in each other's homes. The kinds of things that are done on these social occasions are, with almost unbroken regularity, the same: they 'talk, drink and eat'; 'have a few beers'; 'have pastry and coffee'; 'chew the fat'; 'pass the evening by'; 'have a big gab session'. Watching television with friends was mentioned by only 8 per cent of the skilled craftsmen and 5 per cent of the clerks. The need to be entertained would seem to be little developed. Perhaps, as one toolmaker remarked, 'conversations are trivial – ridiculous'. Nonetheless, a fellow toolmaker was undoubtedly wrong when he replied: 'talk to each other – a lost art these days'. Whether or not it be art, it most certainly is not lost.

The only specific activity mentioned to any extent by the blue and white collar workers was card playing. 23 per cent of the total craft group and 18 per cent of the clerks mentioned that they sometimes or often played cards with friends in each other's houses, perhaps gambling for pennies. It would seem that a variety of games are played, but bridge was not once instanced by either a craftsman or a clerk. This was not the case with the managerial category, several of whom said they got together with other couples specifically to play bridge. This latter point is of some significance: the impression is strong that the large amount of mutual visiting between couples within the craftsmen and clerical categories is of a non-formal nature. While managers talked about 'visiting each other's homes' and 'being invited to each other's homes', blue collar and lower level clerical workers tended to talk in terms of 'we go there and they come here' or simply launched into a description of what went on during a typical social evening, without bothering first to point out that this entailed mutual visiting. Certainly I came upon as many instances of visiting with relatives being of a formal or semi-formal nature, as we did of visiting with non-related friends. This does not mean that such visiting can be viewed as being extremely casual or superficial. Rather, it is clear that access to each others homes is seen by the large majority of the people I interviewed as being a normal and straightforward situation. It is something that is enjoyed and valued, but it is a commonplace nonetheless. If the blue collar home ever was a place reserved exclusively for one's family and kin, this would no longer seem to be the case.

Similarly, it is evident that the large majority of both blue and white collar workers enjoy their leisure activities *as couples*. To the extent respondents reported doing things exclusively in the company of other men, these were normally *in addition* to the activities they might enjoy with their wives. It was not unusual for a craftsman to play golf or visit a tavern with one or two friends, as well as getting together with them and their wives of an evening to sit around and chat, or in some cases go out to a restaurant, bowling or a picnic. Only three craftsmen and one clerk discussed their leisure time in terms that excluded their wives. (The activities in these cases involved watching a ball game on T.V. or going to the club or bar for a beer.) Again this is important, as it runs directly counter to the picture that has been built up of the American working class during the last forty years. Nonetheless, this is not to say that there are no differences between the clerks and craftsmen on the one hand and the managers on the other. For while clerks and craftsmen certainly spend the large part of their leisure time in the company of their wives, this takes place within fairly narrow limits and is limited mainly to mutual visiting in each other's houses or going out for a meal or a picnic in the summer. The managers, on the other hand, give a much clearer impression of entering into a wider variety of leisure pursuits in the company of their wives and other couples. A development manager in his early fifties and earning above $15,000 a year described the social life of him and his wife: 'We visit homes, often for dinner, often play bridge afterwards. We play husband and wife golf with other couples, then have dinner, or tennis with other couples.' Other managers talked about 'attending various functions' with their wives, weekend trips to New York, the theatre in Boston, sailing in Narragansett Bay and so on. Despite the fact that clerks and craftsmen alike are spending a good deal of time in the homes of non-related friends, and spending that time with their wives, descriptions of social life such as those immediately above stand in stark contrast to the 'we just sit around a chat' comment which was so typical of the majority of the blue collar and clerical workers I interviewed.[15]

The exception to this situation is in the numbers of skilled workers having both relatives and friends to dinner. Again, until the present time the dinner party has been confined very much to the middle class. In describing the social life of a group of blue collar families in the late 1950s Komarovsky stated unambiguously: 'We have not heard of a single dinner party; the men may go out to bring pizza for late evening refreshments, but only relatives have meals together.'[16] As Table 25 shows, this is not the case amongst this particular group of affluent craftsmen. To be sure, relatives continue to be overrepresented as dinner guests but this cannot detract from the fact that the large majority of skilled craftsmen are inviting non-relatives into their homes for dinner and that this is a radical departure from what has traditionally been working class practice. Of the 194 craftsmen in the sample only 29 said that they never had non-related friends to dinner while almost half either had friends over to eat more than relations or the two groups about equally.

Table 25. *Guests for dinner*

	Brick-layers and Masons	Cabinet makers and Car-penters	Elec-tricians	Tool-makers	Total Craft	Clerks	Managers
	Percentage						
Amount of entertaining							
Ever entertain people to dinner	91	98	93	85	92	84	89
Mean number of invitations per annum	6	7	9	9	9	9	9
Total number	35	49	56	54	194	44	38
Relationship to dinner guests							
Guests more often relations	59	50	48	57	53	46	21
Guests more often friends	13	25	8	13	15	35	47
Guests, relations and friends equally	28	25	44	30	33	19	32
Total per cent	100	100	100	100	100	100	100
Total number	32	48	52	46	178	37	34

Nonetheless, it would be dangerous to view these changes as the whole-sale adoption of a middle class behavioural pattern. Rather, it would appear that having people over for dinner is seen as an extension of simply spending an evening with them. The ritual of an imaginative menu, seating arrangements and the shimmering of candles (electric or otherwise) seems absent. Instead, the corollary of spending time with friends in each other's houses is that one eats with them. They may often take place with other things, such as playing cards or watching television. Dinner, in other words, will be part of an evening rather than the evening. It was often not until after the second or third probe, for example, that a respondent mentioned that they would have a meal with their friends. It would certainly not appear to signify a notable occasion. The clerk who explained '... can always tell when we've got company here – there's an empty refrigerator!' illustrates this clearly. As such, the nature of the blue collar 'dinner party' remains different from that of the established middle class dinner party. In addition, relatives continue to play a relatively minor role in the guest lists of our managerial sample. It is evident that, in certain ways, the patterns of having people over for dinner are different in all three occupational groups.

The media
The reading public has never been representative of American society. In general the middle classes have read books and magizines to a much great-

er extent than have members of the working class and, more important, they have viewed those books and magazines from a very different perspective. Reading, in other words, has not been merely a pleasant way of passing the time, but has been seen as a valuable way of learning about, and therefore coming to terms with, the environment. This has been the case for both fiction and non-fiction.[17] An analysis of the reading patterns of my own respondents suggests that, while these differences remain, it would be difficult to characterise the clerical sample as purveyors of 'high culture'. In fact exactly one half of this latter group reported spending some time reading a book 'in a normal week'. Just over one third of the total craft group were book readers thus defined. Not surprisingly education exerts an important role, almost every book reader in these two occupational categories having completed a high school education. The wives of these men are very much alike in their reading habits: 49 per cent of blue collar wives and 45 per cent of the spouses of clerks found time to read a book for some part of each week. Once again, both groups are set apart from the managers, 70 per cent of whom (and of their wives) were book readers in terms of this criterion. This pattern is reinforced if one looks at the numbers of individuals in each occupational category owning a public library card and using that card. 20 per cent of the craftsmen in the sample and 25 per cent of the clerks possess a library card. In the case of their wives the figures are 28 per cent and 29 per cent respectively. And even these cards are not used at all frequently. Of the 11 clerks owning a library card 8 used it no more than once every three months, if at all. Similarly 67 per cent of the blue collar card carriers visited the library no more than four times a year. Not so the managers: around half of this group and their wives were members of the public library. And perhaps more impressive, nearly half of the managers and three quarters of their wives who belonged to the local library used that library at least once a month.

In terms of exposure to books, then, something of the traditional pattern has emerged: while clerks do seem to spend more time reading a book than do skilled blue collar workers, the difference is not overly large, and certainly not as great as that separating clerks and craftsmen from managers. This is certainly the case if we look at the *kinds* of books these people were reading at the time they were interviewed.[18] With few exceptions clerks and craftsmen alike (and their wives) were reading fiction rather than non-fiction, and fiction that can be regarded as 'light' rather than 'classic'. The few examples of non-fiction were primarily books on the late President Kennedy, war, bloodshed, or mayhem. *Profiles in Courage, P.T. 109, Death of a President, A Thousand Days, The Making of a President,* had been read by a good number of these people, while *In Cold Blood, The Longest Day, The Green Berets, Seven Days in May* ran a close second. But all of these titles were outdistanced by *Valley of the Dolls, Hawaii, Hotel* (for one toolmaker 'the greatest story ever told') or 'All the books by Harold Robbins'. There were a handful of deviants: an electrician with a grammar school education was reading *Ulysses*; another had just finished *1984* and *Animal Farm* while a clerk was reading *Sons and Lovers* ('I don't know the author'). But these people were rare. Overwhelmingly the kinds of books blue collar and lower level white collar workers were reading can be regarded as 'light fiction' of the sort sold by every drugstore on every street corner.

The managers also bought books at the local drug store but such purchases did not exhaust their literary tastes. To be sure managers read *Valley of the Dolls* and *The Spy Who Came In From the Cold* but they also read *Parkinson's Law, Understanding Media*, Churchill's *The Great Years*, or Draper's *Abuse of Power*. Similarly their wives read *Sand Pebbles, The Fixer* or *Taipan* as well as they read Harrington's *The Other America* or Caplovitz's *The Poor Pay More*. It is this that sets these lower level captains of industry off from the other blue and white collar workers in the sample: they read more and they read differently.

A similar, although less decisive picture emerges from a glance at the magazine subscriptions of my respondents. Table 26 lists the proportions of each occupational group subscribing to at least one magazine within the categories I have delineated. Perhaps the first thing that should be pointed out is the surprisingly large number of individuals within all occupational groups subscribing to at least one magazine. Only 13 per cent of craftsmen, 18 per cent of clerks and 5 per cent of managers did not have a subscription to at least one publication. Indeed, almost exactly half of the clerical and craft groups and over 60 per cent of the managers had standing orders for at least three magazines. (One member of this latter grouping took ten periodicals, while several read more than five.)

Table 26. *Subscriptions to magazines*

	Brick-layers and Masons	Cabinet makers and Carpenters	Electricians	Toolmakers	Total Craft	Clerks	Managers
	Percentage						
Reader's Digest	23	16	16	33	22	30	29
Life	23	47	30	33	34	27	37
Look, Saturday Evening Post	23	32	32	26	29	23	21
Newsweek, Time	9	20	9	11	13	20	40
Home & Household	9	20	18	15	16	12	24
Women's	24	36	31	31	32	41	34
Men's Hobby	9	26	26	18	22	5	13
Other	26	26	30	35	31	28	33
Total number	35	49	56	54	194	44	38

In the case of clerks and craftsmen the two most popular magazines were those which were the most widely distributed throughout the United States – *Reader's Digest* and *Life.* This latter magazine was the one most read by the managers, followed by *Time*, which outnumbered subscriptions to *Newsweek* by two to one. Within the craft and clerical groups the reverse was the case. It is these two news magazines, and those that I have classified as 'home and household' that once again, set off the managerial group from the clerks and craftsmen. Few homes within these two groups had either of these types of magazine coming into them. And this is surprising. In a consumer oriented society such as the United States it is worthy of note that only 12 per cent of a sample of clerical workers express an interest in the style of life exemplified in magazines such as *Better Homes and Gardens* or *American Home.* Correspondingly, the only type of magazine that would appear to differentiate blue collar from white collar groups are those devoted to male hobbies, especially those concerned with 'do-it-yourself' such as *Popular Mechanix, Workbench* or *Mechanix Illustrated.* But despite the fact that subscriptions to such magazines are more numerous among the blue collar members of the sample, the important thing is they are not *that* numerous: such periodicals are going into no more than one quarter of the homes within any one craft group. For the manual workers as a whole, almost 80 per cent of blue collar respondents do not receive a single journal of this type. And yet it is these home workshop or car repair magazines that have in the recent past been linked inseparably with working class males. Shostak only recently suggested that such publications have 'refined a formula for lasting appeal to male blue-collarites anxious to hold their own with the gadgetry and mechanical aspects of modern life'.[19] *Popular Mechanix* was clearly appealing to what it saw as working class self-imagery in an advertisement published in the *New York Times* the year before this study was carried out. In this full-page advertisement the kind of men that read *Popular Mechanix* were depicted thus:

> They'd rather look at a picture of auto racing Champion Dan
> Gurney in a G.T. than go shopping for a dress with their wives.
> They'd rather buy a boat than take a cruise. They'd rather
> build a summer house than spend a month at the Greenbriar.
> They'd rather paint the house than the town. They'd rather
> have a new outboard than wall-to-wall carpeting.[20]

If the level of subscriptions to do-it-yourself and home-workshop magazines can be regarded as an indicator, and much of the evidence discussed elsewhere would suggest that it can, it is clear that for the overwhelming majority of the blue collar workers in this particular sample, the description above is irrelevant. The contemporary skilled craftsmen evidences no more desire to adopt the rugged, oaken, frontier-building image depicted here than does the modern clerk hanker for a green eyeshade, a celluloid collar and his very own roll-top desk. At the risk of being repetitious we cannot, and must not, regard 'blue-collarites' as an undifferentiated mass. If *Popular Mechanix*'s image of its readership applies to any sectors of the working class in the latter part of the twentieth century it does not apply to electricians, toolmakers, bricklayers or carpenters.

While books and magazines do play an important role in the lives of large numbers of the sample, it is a role which is undoubtedly secondary to that of television. Indeed, within only a few years of its appearance television took up more American leisure time than any other activity.[21] Blue collar workers were no exception: when television sets began to be widely distributed after the Second World War it was the working class that took them into their homes more readily and more swiftly than did families within the upper echelons of the class structure. Indeed a study conducted around that time in New Haven, Connecticut (in which the investigators distinguished six social strata) found that over three quarters of the families within the two lower classes had television sets; the comparable figure for the upper class being 25 per cent.[22] It is indeed an excellent example of Lockwood's dictum: 'a washing machine is a washing machine is a washing machine'. Status considerations aside, as a comparatively cheap, reliable and exciting form of entertainment television has no equal. Small wonder then that Berger found almost half of his sample of automobile workers were spending more than 16 hours a week watching television, while amongst the 58 blue collar families studied in depth by Komarovsky television was rated by both husbands and wives as being their most enjoyable leisure time activity.[23] Of my own respondents, only 12 craftsmen, one clerk and three managers claimed that they did not watch television and were therefore unable to name their three favourite television programmes or shows. Many homes contained more than one television set and over one fifth of the craftsmen and managers possessed a colour television, while an additional 51 per cent of the former and 37 per cent of the latter expected to get one within the next two or three years. In the case of the clerks the comparable proportions were 14 per cent and 52 per cent respectively. Television clearly plays an important role in the use of leisure time.

Table 27 shows the proportions within each occupational group mentioning a particular type of television programme as being at least one of their three favourite shows. The results are not in accord with what has been forwarded as the established pattern of class viewing. For until the present time, not only have manual workers differed from non-manual workers in terms of viewing-time but also in terms of choice of programme. Television, for the blue collar worker '. . . actually helps drain off emotion and strain produced during the day. An avenue of escape from all that is or may be burdensome. TV is pursued primarily for pleasure and for enjoyment.'[24] As such Westerns and sports coverage have been seen as the

Table 27. *Favourite television programmes*

	Brick-layers and Masons	Cabinet makers and Carpenters	Electricians	Toolmakers	Total Craft	Clerks	Managers
	Percentage						
News, documentaries	15	20	23	27	22	26	51
Sports	24	11	25	31	23	46	26
Variety, musicals	58	44	62	46	52	49	46
Adventure	24	31	21	25	25	28	20
Drama	45	33	33	31	35	16	23
Westerns	30	29	31	21	27	32	23
Comedy	15	24	21	23	21	16	17
Movies	18	20	15	15	17	9	6
Other	21	22	29	29	26	19	34
Total number	33	45	52	52	182	43	35

staple diet of the blue collar viewer: the same man that would rather look at a picture of Dan Gurney than go shopping for a dress with his wife is far more able to identify with the Virginian or a lineman in the Green Bay Packers than he is with the Man from Uncle or Harrison Salisbury. The middle class, on the other hand, have been seen as using television in the same way as they use other media: not only as a form of non-demanding relaxation but also as a way of coming to understand, and therefore to grips with, the environment.

Given this situation, the patterns of viewing shown in Table 27 are as surprising as they are supportive of my general thesis. For if one fact stands out, it is that these skilled craftsmen do not rate sports programmes and Westerns very highly. Only around one quarter of the total craft group mentioned a Western or a sports show as being one of their three favourite programmes, a figure that was exceeded in both cases by the lower level clerical employees. Indeed, it is clearly for the clerks that sports programmes have a special importance, second only to musical and variety programmes. Several of these people mentioned more than one sports programme with their top three. 'Baseball, football and fights' was the swift reply from one white collar afficionado when asked 'what are your three favourite TV shows?' Overwhelmingly, the blue collar workers seem to select programmes that do not demand involvement on their part, that are relaxing and amusing. They choose, in other words, variety and musical programmes: shows like the Dean Martin Show, Ed Sullivan or Andy Williams; drama as could be found in The Fugitive, Perry Mason or Twilight Zone; adventure as it happens in Mission Impossible, Secret Agent or Star Trek. But these are not programmes that set them apart from lower level clerical workers. Indeed, perhaps the remarkable thing is the general degree of similarity in the general pattern of viewing on the part of these two occupational groups.

The pattern of viewing evidenced by managers contains fewer surprises. Clearly television is also used to a large extent by the group as a form of relaxation. But what separates them from the other members in the sample is their use of television as a news and information medium. One half of the managers included a news or documentary programme within their lists of three favourite programmes. As would be expected Huntley – Brinkley led the field in terms of popularity, but Meet the Press, The David Suskind Show (a topical discussion programme), Walter Cronkite and C.B.S. Report were also watched regularly by a large proportion of these people.

Conclusion

As a result of the foregoing discussion three points should be stressed regarding the styles of life enjoyed by this sample of blue and white collar workers. First, statements regarding the disappearance of identifiable working and middle class life styles must be treated with a good deal of caution. Differences remain. Whether these differences will wither away in the future I am not in a position to predict. But grounds for scepticism are provided by my second point, which is that the life styles of the three major occupational groups form something of an integrated pattern. For example, the low levels or organisational involvements found within these craft and clerical groups can only be understood insofar as it is realised that they go hand in hand with high levels of informal social interaction both within the extended family and within friendship groups. Similarly, the degree of organisational commitment exhibited by the managerial sample must be viewed as part of a life style where frequent and informal interaction with related and non-related friends is not at a premium. Finally, in those instances where skilled blue collar workers at least *appear* to have adopted features of a middle class life style, care must be taken to differentiate between the behavioural or consumption pattern and the meaning attached to it by the actors involved. Thus buying a home, or a colour television, or having friends round for 'dinner' are all activities that superficially could be described as 'middle class'. And yet the data indicate clearly that this is not the case. Rather, they can be viewed simply as extensions of established behavioural patterns made possible by factors such as affluence or improved occupational conditions. Certainly, the findings prevent us from accepting notions relating to the collapse of class boundaries. Equally it is evident that these craftsmen are behaving in ways that cannot be regarded as symptomatic of the traditional American working class, while the clerks are not enjoying a style of life that can be viewed as representative of the established middle class.

5   Political Behaviour and Attitudes

'My father was a Democrat and also my grandfather – because of Franklin D. Roosevelt. I guess it was just kind of bred into me.'

'The average people (support the Democratic party) – the working class. Sometimes nationality has a lot to do with it, and sometimes religion goes into it. Most of the Catholics seem to support it.'

'They (the Democrats) are more in tune with the working man. But things are changing, and sometimes I split the ticket, even if basically I consider myself a Democrat.'

'I vote both ways – pick the best man. I belong to C.O.P.E., an organisation attached to the union. They advise us about the candidates.'

The relationship between social class and political behaviour in American society is too well known to require documentation.[1] In general terms the bases of support for the Democratic party have been located within the manual sectors of the occupational structure, while those of the Republican party have been found in the non-manual groups. As recently as 1963 Alford, after extensive examination of the literature, could find no evidence of decline, either in the extent or patterning of class voting in the United States.[2] Four years earlier that doyen of American political sociology, Seymour Martin Lipset, had felt justified in writing: 'Such factors as occupational status, income, and the class character of the district in which people live probably distinguish the support of the two major parties more clearly now than at any other period in American history since the Civil War.'[3]

Given this situation, if a process of structural change is occurring in the middle ranges of the American class structure, we should expect to see this reflected in the political behaviour and attitudes of skilled craftsmen and/or lower level clerical workers. In particular we are interested in the possibility of a decline in support for, and identification with, the Democratic party on the part of the affluent skilled workers in the sample; or, alternatively, a tendency towards dissociation from the Republican party by the clerks that I interviewed.

Party Identification and Voting Behaviour

The political loyalties of the sample are shown in Table 28. They represent a blend of the expected and unanticipated. Support for the Republican party is minimal throughout the entire sample, *including* the managers. Nevertheless, this latter grouping remains distinct: over one half of their number see themselves as independents, while only one quarter feel able to support the Democratic party. Significantly, and in contrast to the findings of earlier studies, the clerks provide the largest block of support for the Democrats, three fifths of them identifying with this party. But, without doubt, the most significant feature of Table 28 is the number of blue collar workers who reject the label of Democrat, and who prefer to be considered as independents. Indeed, in the case of the toolmakers, independents constitute a larger grouping than do Democrats. Even among the bricklayers, the most staunchly Democratic, over one third refused to be identified with either of the established parties.

Furthermore, few of the large number of independents within any of the occupational groupings admit to having *become* disassociated from either the Democrats or the Republicans; the large majority claiming that they have never been attached to a particular party. As Table 29 shows, within the craft and clerical occupational categories, only the electricians have a proportion larger than one fifth admitting to ever having switched political allegiance. Approximately one third of the managers have done likewise. But even this latter figure is lower than one would have predicted, given the fact that approximately one half of this group come from blue collar backgrounds, and have therefore experienced a substantial degree of upward mobility.

This means, then, that I am not able to explain the high level of verbalised independence on the part of the craftsmen I interviewed by reference to their changing position in American society, and I certainly cannot use this to account for any move towards the Republican camp. In-

Table 28. *General political affiliation* (I)

	Brick-layers and Masons	Cabinet makers and Carpenters	Electricians	Tool makers	Total Craft	Clerks	Managers
	Percentage						
Democrat	60	47	50	41	48	61	26
Republican	3	8	4	11	7	9	13
Independent	37	41	45	46	43	30	56
D.K./Unwilling to say	—	4	1	2	2	—	5
Total per cent	100	100	100	100	100	100	100
Total number	35	49	56	54	194	44	38

Table 29.   *Stability of political affiliation*

	Brick-layers and Masons	Cabinet makers and Carpenters	Electricians	Tool makers	Total Craft	Clerks	Managers
	Percentage						
Have never changed affiliation	94	78	71	81	80	93	63
Have changed affiliation	6	18	27	17	18	7	32
No response	—	4	2	2	2	—	5
Total per cent	100	100	100	100	100	100	100
Total number	35	49	56	54	194	44	38

deed, of the 34 craftsmen who had changed political preference at some time in their lives, *only two* had moved in the direction of the G.O.P., while 16 had become Democrats. One of these people – a bricklayer in his twenties whose parents were Democrats – who *had* changed political affiliation in favour of the Republicans, explained simply: 'I just knew a lot of politicans who were Republicans, so I voted for them.' In the rest of his interview, on specific political questions, this respondent did not give the impression of any coherent rejection of Democratic ideas and corresponding adoption of a Republican philosophy. Although too young to vote in the 1960 presidential election he had not voted in 1964 either, and said he was 'not very interested' in politics. In addition he took definite non-Republican stands on several of the opinion-attitude questions – wanting to see Medicare extended to the whole population, supporting workers as opposed to employers in industrial disputes, and seeing himself as a 'dove' on the Vietnamese war. This was not the case with the other craftsmen who had switched support from the Democratic to the Republican party. This man, an electrician, in his late twenties and earning between $9,000 and $10,000 a year, explained his change of loyalties in terms of 'the income bracket I got into...as far as money is concerned the Republicans can manage it better. The Republicans is the better party. They are more conservative, watch how money is spent.' However, this was the *only* instance of 'political *embourgeoisement*' that I found, if indeed this was the case. For it is interesting to note that in the previous two Presidential elections this affluent Republican craftsman had voted for Kennedy and Johnson.

Regarding movement to the Democratic party, of the 16 craftsmen, now Democrats, who have entertained other loyalties, 14 said that they switched back and forth regularly, depending on particular candidates or issues. The other two both came from Republican homes, and had themselves identified with that party for a time. The first subject simply changed to the Democrats because 'this state is Democratic – there are fringe benefits I would like to get, so I support the Democrats...I was a Republican but they have poor candidates.' (The 'fringe' benefits in question included getting a distinctive number plate for his car, gaining help in getting his son into West Point and getting traffic tickets 'fixed'.) The other respondent, in his early fifties and the son of a police officer, had rejected his father's Republicanism for class linked reasons: 'in the depression when jobs were scarce I got work through the Democrats. I've voted that way ever since.'

Similar results emerge upon examination of those individuals who have rejected one or other of the major parties in order to become independents. Again, the numbers here are very small. Of the total sample of 194 craftsmen only 16 had in their political lives become independents. Of these, 11 had not done so for any positive reason, but so that they could switch back and forth, split their tickets and so on. An electrician in his early thirties commented: 'I have split my ticket sometimes, I just don't go in and pull the Democratic lever, I screen out a few people.' The remainder had forsaken their old party because they no longer liked some aspect of its policies or performance, or its candidates. But *not one* of these people had become independent because he now saw the Democratic party as no longer representing his economic or class interests.

While the importance of the relatively large numbers of independents must not be minimised, it would be a mistake simply to accept such identification at face value. It is comparatively easy to verbalise a measure of aloofness from a particular party, but still behave and think as one of its members. A serious attempt was made, therefore, to ascertain the extent to which these people were really prepared to judge each political issue or candidate on its own merits. To this end, I attempted to 'persuade' individuals who had identified themselves as independents to 'admit' that one or other of the main parties 'came closer to (their) interests'. The results of this persuasion are shown in Table 30. It is clear that when 'pushed' to side with one or other of the major parties the largest single proportion of all the blue collar groups, as well as of the clerks, opt for the Democrats. The toolmakers, who have the greatest number of indepen-

Table 30. *Political party that comes closest to interests of independents*

	Brick-layers and Masons	Cabinet makers and Carpenters	Elec-tricians	Tool makers	Total Craft	Clerks	Managers
	Percentage						
Democrat	46	50	52	56	51	46	33
Republican	23	25	20	20	22	15	48
'Pure' independent	31	25	28	24	27	39	19
Total per cent	100	100	100	100	100	100	100
Total number	13	20	25	25	83	13	21

dents, compensate for this by having the largest segment of those independents subsequently identifying with the Democrats. In contrast, among the
managers, almost half of those claiming independence now identify with
the Republican party.

In order to get an overall picture of the political allegiances of the
sample, as well as the strengths of those allegiances, it is useful to combine
Tables 28 and 30 into a single table. Table 31 shows the party leanings of
both those subjects initially claiming party loyalty and those regarding
themselves as independents but admitting that one or other of the main
parties 'comes closer to their interests'.

It is evident that the Democratic inclinations of the majority of the
craftsmen and clerks cannot remain in doubt. Even though large numbers
of manual respondents prefer to think of themselves as independents, they
are not prepared, when pushed, to reject the Democratic party and identify with the Republicans. The same is true of the clerks who are (with the
exception of the bricklayers and masons) the most intensely Democratic
and the least independent of any of the occupational categories in the
sample. In contrast, among the clerks and craftsmen, the amount of support the Republicans seem able to amass never exceeds 20 per cent. Again
it is the managers who stand alone, with about two fifths of their number in
favour of this latter party.

The extent of the support given to the Democrats is portrayed dramatically by an examination of the voting behaviour of respondents in the
1960 and 1964 Presidential elections, the two preceding the time of the
interviews. See Table 32. One of the most striking features of the data pre-

Table 31. *General political affiliation* (II)

	Brick-layers and Masons	Cabinet marked and Carpenters	Elec-tricians	Tool makers	Total Craft	Clerks	Managers
	Percentage						
'Pure' Democrat	60	47	50	41	48	61	26
'Independent' Democrat	17	21	24	26	23	14	19
Total Democrat	77	68	74	67	71	75	45
'Pure' Republican	3	8	4	11	7	9	13
'Independent' Republican	9	11	9	9	9	5	28
Total Republican	12	19	13	20	16	14	41
'Pure' Independent	11	13	13	13	13	11	14
Total per cent	100	100	100	100	100	100	100
Total number	35	47	55	53	190	44	36

Table 32.   *Proportion voting and choice of candidate in two Presidential elections*

	Brick- layers and Masons	Cabinet makers and Car- penters	Elec- tricians	Tool makers	Total Craft	Clerks	Managers
	Percentage						
1960: Kennedy versus Nixon							
Proportion voting	69	80	91	87	83	95	89
Total number	35	49	56	54	194	44	38
Kennedy	92	77	88	74	82	76	74
Nixon	4	18	6	23	13	14	21
*Total per cent	96	95	94	97	95	90	95
Total number	24	39	51	47	161	42	34
1964: Johnson versus Goldwater							
Proportion voting	74	84	95	89	86	95	97
Total number	35	49	56	54	194	44	38
Johnson	88	83	81	75	81	74	73
Goldwater	8	10	13	15	12	17	22
*Total per cent	96	93	94	90	93	91	95
Total number	25	41	53	48	167	42	37

* Totals do not add to 100 per cent: a small number of respondents refused to say for whom they voted.

sented in the table is the high number of all occupational groups voting in both elections. In 1960, with the single exception of the bricklayers and masons, at least 80 per cent of each group went to the polls. In 1964 the proportion was never lower than three quarters of any occupational group. With regard to choice of candidate in these two elections, the findings are those one would predict, given the political preferences revealed earlier in this section. Indeed, in all cases, the proportion voting for either Kennedy or Johnson is higher than the proportion claiming to be either 'pure' or 'independent' Democrats. It would seem that in both of these elections, the majority of 'pure' independents voted for the Democratic candidate. Within the managerial group it is clear that even individuals expressing Republican loyalties nonetheless voted against their party's representative in these two elections. Finally, an interesting aspect of these voting data is the stability of the vote between the two elections. Given the closeness of the 1960 presidential election and the unpopularity of Goldwater four years later, I would have expected there to have been an appreciably larger vote for Nixon than for Goldwater. As can be seen in Table 32, however, this was not the case.

Perceptions of Party Support

Having documented a continuing high level of support (albeit qualified) for the Democratic party and its candidates, let us look first at some of the reasons respondents gave in explanation of their own political allegiances, and secondly, at their perceptions of the bases of party support generally.

As Table 33 makes apparent, within the clerical and craft groupings, the single most important reason 'pure' Democrats gave for their choice of party was that they still see themselves as average or working or common men, and they still see the Democratic party as representing the interests of such people. Perhaps most significant is the fact that the largest group to put forward this class oriented explanation is the clerks, who, it will be remembered, contained in their ranks the largest proportion of 'pure' Democrats. Thus, a computer clerk in his late twenties and earning around $7,000 a year commented: 'I believe the Democratic party is for the working man – for the white collar worker like me,' while a clerk 25 years his senior, and earning less, felt the Democratic party was 'representative of people in the lower middle or lower classes'.[4] Similar reasoning underlies many of the comments made by craftsmen, although in some cases a higher degree of class consciousness is exhibited, especially by the older men. An electrician in his sixties and earning between $11,000 and $12,000, explained: 'I think mainly it is because they try to do more for us – for the working people – they get jobs – there is more construction when they are in.' An electrician between 55 and 59 years old, earning between $8,000 and $9,000 a year, agreed: 'suppose mainly we always considered it the party of the working man and for labour – my family did. They used to say they are for the poor man – they are more for the union man.' Finally, a bricklayer in his later thirties, and earning between $6,000 and $7,000 a year explained: 'Democrats do more for the working man – when they are in you always have jobs. There is plenty of work for the ones who want to work. I think they do more for us than the Republicans.'

Table 33. *Reasons for Democratic party support ('pure' Democrats only)*

	Brick- layers and Masons	Cabinet makers and Car- penters	Elec- tricians	Tool makers	Total Craft	Clerks	Managers
Party for the working man	35	55	40	32	40	67	33
Traditional reasons	20	14	28	41	26	26	11
Policies and/ or performance	35	18	24	14	22	15	33
Other	15	27	20	18	20	22	27
Total number	20	22	25	22	89	27	9

A considerable number of blue and white collar workers also explained their allegiance to the Democratic party in terms of family background: having been reared in homes where one or both parents were Democrats, they had come to adopt the same political standpoint. (Such explanations are classified as 'traditional reasons' in Table 33.) There is a certain amount of overlap between class and traditional explanations: several respondents giving class oriented reasons for supporting the Democratic party and mentioning that they had learned this from their parents. Despite experiencing large increases in standard of living, these skilled craftsmen are still able to remain loyal to values leaned in the early part of their lives. A toolmaker in his late twenties and earning over $10,000 a year explained: 'I was brought up to be a Democrat, my parents were Democrat, I just stayed with the Democratic party.' Similarly, a clerk who was the same age but earning half the income, and whose father is a custodian, said simply 'family tradition, I guess'.

Finally, it would appear that significant numbers of the sample support the Democratic party because of a liking for its policies and/or for its performance (or in some cases, a dislike for those of the Republicans). Again there is a degree of overlap with the class oriented category of explanation, as several respondents clearly considered policy to be in line with their own interests. Several respondents remembered or mentioned Roosevelt and the depression, seeing the Democratic party very much as the saviour of the situation, and not being able to forgive the Republicans for having brought that situation about. A clerk in his early fifties commented: 'I lived through a depression and the Republicans were in charge then, I still bear the scars.' A bricklayer of the same age remarked: 'I remember the rough times during the Republican administration – Hoover – and since then I have always been Democratic, never voted Republican.' But memories of Roosevelt are by no means the only reasons people gave for supporting the policies of the Democratic party. The Republicans' attitude towards trade unionism was mentioned more than once, whilst many craftsmen especially were aware of the benefits they had gained from the economic boom of the 1960s. For example, a young highly paid electrician thought the Johnson administration was 'doing a good job, more people are working, more schools, less poverty'. The fact that there are more jobs when the Democrats are in office is, of course, particularly important to trades such as bricklayer or carpenter, the building industry being far less stable than, for example, toolmaking.

The reasons given by over two fifths of the total sample for identifying themselves as independents are, with monotonous regularity, the same: 'I vote for the man not the party.'[5] It would seem that, for an increasing number of the electorate, ticket splitting is becoming the order of the day: while, as we have seen, the sympathies of these people are clearly with the Democratic party, they are not prepared to give it blanket support. The point is made dramatically by the response of a toolmaker in his sixties and earning over $13,000 a year, who does consider himself to be a 'pure' Democrat because they are 'more in tune with the working man, but things are changing and sometimes I split the ticket even if basically I consider myself a Democrat'. Furthermore, several independents made the distinction between national and state politics, appearing to retain a certain level of loyalty to the Democratic party at the national, but not at the local, level. At the time of the study, Rhode Island was governed by John Chaffee, a liberal and popular Republican. An electrician in his fifties who had voted for both Kennedy and Johnson commented: 'at one time the Democrats always favoured labour, the Republicans are coming up good now, I like the Republicans in the State now, I'll split my ticket'. Apparently the unions also are not entirely aloof from this movement toward ticket splitting. An electrician who is an independent explained: 'I vote both ways, – pick the best man. I belong to C.O.P.E., an organisation attached to the union. They advise us about the candidates.'

In addition to asking respondents why they *personally* supported a particular party, I was able to gain further information as to their perceptions of the bases of the two parties by asking them what kind of people, *in general*, they thought favoured these parties. Their responses with regard to the Democratic party are shown in Table 34. It is evident that not only 'pure' Democrats see a link between that party and the American working class. And again, the clerks (the group with the highest proportion of Democrats) had the largest number describing Democratic party supporters in these terms. A clerk in his early fifties commented: 'Apparently from the way the country has been going the last few years I would say the

Table 34. *Perceived bases of support for Democratic party*

	Brick-layers and Masons	Cabinet makers and Carpenters	Elec-tricians	Tool-makers	Total Craft	Clerks	Managers
	Percentage						
Working/ working class people	49	68	55	49	55	70	40
Average/middle class people	14	17	11	13	14	11	14
Poor people	17	4	12	15	12	9	3
Trade union members	9	11	9	15	11	5	29
All kinds of people	9	8	11	9	9	11	20
D.K./Other	17	22	18	9	16	9	14
Total number	35	47	56	53	191	44	35

common people like you and I support it – big business men, a great many, but not as many as back the Republican party.' Similarly a Republican-leaning independent who voted for Goldwater and who was an electrician, commented: 'The working class – not white collar – the blue uniform type'; while a classic 'vote for the man not the party' carpenter in his early forties replied: 'The working man truthfully or the blue collar man. Since the Roosevelt era I believe the working man is Democratic.' On the other hand, very few respondents in any of the occupational groups saw the poor as having strong ties with the Democratic party. This fits in with what we would expect, given the general identification the majority of the sample had with this party. Neither did many of the craft or clerical groups see any great link between the trade union movement and the Democratic party. Several of the managers mentioned 'Organised labour or the unions', but even here not more than 29 per cent said they thought these were the kinds of people supporting the party in general.

A number of respondents, again the managers in particular, thought they could detect a change in the bases of support for the Democratic party – a change I have not been able to document. A Republican manager in his early fifties replied: 'the working man, lower income people, union type of member – although I think it's changed a lot in recent years – but the basic factors are there, although some high level management support the Democrats today'. In similar terms a Republican executive in his sixties replied: 'traditionally people who felt the Federal Government should do more – also gave the impression of catering to the less well-to-do, but this has changed a lot in the last few years'. Finally, a Democrat in his late fifties replied: 'today it's hard to say – you can't say just the working people, there's been a change in the political thinking of working people'. It would seem that the thesis of *embourgeoisement* is not prevalent among sociologists alone.

Turning now to characterisations of the kind of people that in general

Table 35. *Perceived basis of support for the Republican party*

	Brick-layers and Masons	Cabinet makers and Car-penters	Elec-tricians	Tool-makers	Total Craft	Clerks	Managers
	Percentage						
Wealthy class/ people	60	53	45	45	50	68	40
Business men/ professional people	17	21	39	34	29	23	31
All kinds of people	11	11	9	11	10	14	17
D.K./Other	20	23	23	24	23	9	20
Total number	35	47	56	53	191	44	35

support the Republican party, as Table 35 makes apparent, the largest single proportion of each occupational group simply equates that party with wealth. In the words of a middle-aged electrician earning over $13,000 a year, and classifying himself as a Democrat: 'the opposite (of workers) – what do you call them – capitalists or some goddam thing – business people, people with money.' Another middle-aged Democrat electrician replied: 'dyed in the wool money people – businessmen, factory or mill owners, people who want to hold down wage increases.' Closely linked with this identification of wealth with the Republican party is the awareness of its close ties with business men. For many crafts-men and clerks, and indeed, for over one quarter of managers, the Repub-lican party is the party of big business. A Democrat clerk regarded it as supported by 'big business men for the most part – big business and more or less agricultural areas. The industrial people, unless you have a popular figure like Eisenhower, won't support them,' while an independent brick-layer in his sixties remarked 'cigar smokers – it's the businessmen'.

In conclusion, I have been able to find no evidence of any significant move toward the Republican party on behalf of the affluent craftsmen in the sample. Admittedly, large numbers began by identifying themselves politically as independent, but when asked which of the two major parties came closest to their interests, and when voting in national elections, their Democratic sympathies are evident. Similarly, and in contrast to the find-ings of studies conducted earlier and elsewhere in the United States, the amount of support for the G.O.P. among the clerical workers is minimal. Furthermore, this high level of commitment to the Democratic party and its candidates exists despite the fact that these clerks and craftsmen alike are in situations which contemporary writers have come to regard as con-ducive to Republicanism.

For example, two of the most long standing generalisations regarding political behaviour have to do with the high positive correlations that exist between income and voting behaviour, and education and voting behaviour.[6] And yet within my own sample neither affluence nor educa-tion was related to political ideology or voting behaviour within *any* of the three major occupational groups.[7] Similarly, in the late 1950s, such differing analysts of American society as Lipset and Bendix and Vance Packard were suggesting that the greater incidence of home-ownership found among blue collar workers would lead to a gradual abandonment of the Democratic party on the part of these people. While the latter, in his own particular style, felt content to claim: 'Nothing makes a person a Re-publican faster than acquiring a mortgage,' Lipset and Bendix suggested that in the United States (and perhaps also in Britain and Australia) high-ly paid skilled workers were given more real opportunities to adopt middle class consumption patterns and aspire to middle class status generally, and that 'on assuming a middle class consumption pattern they also adopt the voting pattern of the middle class'.[8] Again, my own data lend no support to this view. The question that remains therefore is why despite affluence, comparatively high levels of education and taxation, and a materially comfortable life the skilled craftsmen and lower level clerks 'persist in obdurately sticking to what others believe is a lower class habit'.[9] It is to this question that we now turn.

The Bases of Party Support

It is a commonplace to state that political ideologies and behaviour are learned, and that much of that learning takes place relatively early in life within the family unit. Indeed, it has recently been claimed that 'the child's political world begins to take shape well before he even enters elementary school', a view in accord with Hyman's assertion that 'foremost among agencies of socialisation into politics is the family'.[10] This latter statement was made on the basis of an exhaustive review of a large number of studies on the development of political attitudes. Nonetheless, this same writer was quick to point out that in cases where children were upwardly mobile relative to their parents, the possibility existed for the rejection of parental teaching, and the adoption of the new membership group's political perspectives. On the other hand, downwardly mobile children were much more likely to adhere to political values leaned in the home, retaining their parents as the more prestigous reference group.[11]

Clearly these findings are of significance for this study, especially those having to do with the interplay of socialisation and mobility in influencing political behaviour. Of the 38 clerks who could tell us their parents' political leanings, 32 came from Democratic homes. Of these 32, 72 per cent were themselves 'pure' Democrats while 25 per cent were independents. Only one clerk whose parents had been Democrats was himself a Republican. Six clerks came from Republican backgrounds: three had adopted their parents' political party, one had changed to the Democrats and two were independents.

It would seem then, that the high level of Democratic party identification found amongst the clerks must be associated with the fact that the very large majority were exposed to party supporters and beliefs during childhood and adolescence within the family unit. This, despite the fact that 37 of the 44 clerks I interviewed came from manual backgrounds, and could therefore be regarded as having experienced 'upward' mobility (accepting the relevance of the manual/non-manual line).[12] As already pointed out, previous research has suggested that upward mobility is often linked with a diminution of parental influence. In this instance, however, I would suggest that the reason this influence has not been weakened in this case of 'upward mobility' is that it has not been *experienced* as such by the clerks themselves. As will be seen in the next chapter, the large majority do not see colour of collar as being a relevant criterion of social class. Indeed only 12 per cent of the clerks considered themselves to be in a higher class than skilled craftsmen, while 28 per cent regarded such people as their class superiors.

The history of immigration into Providence and Rhode Island has been outlined in chapter 1. In general terms, two parallel trends have taken place in the region, trends that have by no means been limited to Rhode Island but to a large extent have been witnessed in all the six New England states. First, drastic changes have occurred in the ethnic composition of Rhode Island in the last one hundred years. Secondly, and more recently, the Democratic party has emerged and subsequently come to dominate political life in these Eastern states. Since the middle of the nineteenth century the population of Rhode Island has moved from one that was almost entirely Yankee to one that consists overwhelmingly of Catholic foreign stock. In 1850, 148,000 people lived in Rhode Island, of whom 84 per cent were native born Americans. Fifty years later the population had almost tripled in size, but now contained a third who had been born abroad. By 1930 nearly two thirds of the state's population were either foreign-born, or of foreign-born parents. There were two great waves of immigration: the Irish who began to flock into Rhode Island in the middle of the nineteenth century, and the Italians who were arriving in large numbers at the turn of the century. In between these two peaks, significant numbers of French-Canadians, Swedes and Portuguese also arrived. The greater majority were from Catholic countries. The impact of these two waves of immigration is evident when one discovers that in 1967 only about 16 per cent of the population of Rhode Island were Protestants, while 80 per cent were Catholic.

Politically, until very recent times, Providence, like the rest of New England, has had a long history of Republican domination. It was not until the present century that the Democratic party in Rhode Island was anything more than a very minor second party, and not really until the 1920 elections that it began to make inroads into Republican strongholds. At the present time, with several notable exceptions, Providence can be regarded as a solidly Democratic city in a Democratic state. In the 1964 presidential election, Johnson polled 86 per cent of the vote in Providence. Two years later the Democrat candidate for mayor was re-elected with 67 per cent of the vote. In both houses of the Rhode Island General Assembly in 1967–8, Democrats outnumbered Republicans by a majority of two to one.

These two parallel trends are not unrelated. Indeed, the rise to power of the Democratic party can be explained largely by the fact that it was, and has remained, successful in winning the support of the majority of newly arrived minority ethnic groups. There are a variety of reasons why this has been so. One of the most important of these is the fact that from the early days of large scale immigration into Providence and Rhode Island, the Democrats went out of their way to enlist the support of the newcomers. The arrival of large numbers of Irish after the famine of 1842 generated bitter hostility amongst the Protestant native-born population. Anti-Catholic, anti-foreigner parties emerged and flourished briefly, the most notable of which was the Know Nothings. As a result, immigrants were 'practically driven into the ranks of the Democratic Party'.[13] According to these authors, the anti-Catholic nature of this hostility led immigrants to view the Democratic party in both political *and* religious terms.

During this first influx, the battle to extend the right to vote to all residents of Rhode Island began in earnest. The two main groups of people excluded from the ballot were non-property owners and the foreign-born. As might be expected, the minority party, the Democrats, put their full weight behind the protest of these two groups. As also might be expected, the Republicans and the Whigs entered into battle on the side of law, order and the status quo. Gradually over a period of one hundred years the electoral laws were relaxed, until in 1928 the vote was given to any United States citizen who had lived in a city for two years. The Democratic party had won a battle for the oppressed and earned itself a significant block of new voters at the same time. It was around this time that the rise of the Democratic party in Rhode Island became meteoric and in 1930, for the first time in its history, the Democrats won control of both branches of the Providence City Council (the Yankee establishment having 'held out' longer in Rhode Island than in any other of the New England states).

Another important reason for the development of this link between the Democrats and minority ethnic groups has to do with the economic position of these new arrivals. Almost all of them went into occupations which were not only manual, but also at the lower end of the manual scale. Given the increasingly liberal position adopted by the Democratic party, it was not surprising that it should be chosen by the majority of the immigrants purely for class or economic reasons. These ethnic groups can thus be seen as a particular example of a more general phenomenon: namely, the tendency of lower level socio-economic groups to support the Democratic party, seeing it as the party that will do most to advance their own interests, primarily economic ones.

Finally, a less important, but still relevant, explanation of the links between religion and ethnicity and political behaviour lies in the possible similarities in the ideologies of a particular political party and those of a particular ethnic group. Alford has pointed out that the 'very notion of the separation of Church and State is against traditional Catholic stands', which provides a compelling reason for Catholics to side against the traditionally Protestant Republican party.[14] Similarly, in a study of various referenda elections in seven major American cities between 1956 and 1963, Wilson and Banfield found that in economic interest group terms, ethnic minorities acted 'irrationally'.[15] That is to say, affluent Protestants and Jews supported proposals which they would pay for and not use, while various ethnic groups voted against these same proposals, even though they would benefit from them while not contributing to their funding. This apparent paradox the authors explain by reference to the 'cultural belief systems' of these groups. More specifically, Protestants and Jews were far more likely to equate their own interests with those of the community, while the ethnic groups concerned tended to see themselves and their families as being in, but not of, the community as a whole. These differences were rooted in the belief systems of the various religious or ethnic minorities and manifested themselves in attitudes towards specific political issues.

These then are some of the reasons why an affinity developed between the Catholic ethnic minorities and the Democratic party in Rhode Island. The question that now arises is whether ethnicity still exerts such an effect – whether it is 'preventing' affluent craftsmen from adopting middle class political behaviour patterns at the same time as maintaining a 'working class political ethic' within the lower ranges of the white collar population. There is little doubt that it was still exerting a considerable effect after the Second World War. Stedman and Stedman obtained a rank order correlation of 0.88 between Democratic percentage of the two party vote in 1948 and the percentage of total population who were foreign-born for towns and cities in Rhode Island.[16] At that time Providence had the fourth highest Democratic vote in the state (66.4 per cent). More recently, however, students of Rhode Island politics have begun to differ in their evaluations of the situation. Lockard worte in 1959: 'The traditional ties of New England's ethnic minorities with the Democratic party are less significant now than they were a generation ago. The upward social and economic mobility of ethnic minority people has resulted in some desertion from the Democratic party.'[17] In other words, Lockard sees New England ethnic groups as being well on the way to what Dahl has called 'political assimilation'.* If this is the case, my concern with the potential effect of ethnic factors is misplaced.

Regrettably, much of my own analysis must be confined to the religious

---

* Dahl has in fact hypothesised that any ethnic group passes through three stages on its way to political assimilation, during which time ethnic influences decline in importance and socio-economic variables come to take their place as the crucial determinants of political behaviour. In the first stage, immigrants are almost entirely blue collar as well as being 'low in status, income and affluence'. As such they are politically homogeneous and are drawn towards left wing parties. The second stage is reached when a significant number of the ethnic groups have been mobile into white collar occupations and correspondingly have gained positions of influence. Ethnicity, however, is still a relevant basis for solidarity. Finally, in the third stage the particular group has become, occupationally, highly heterogeneous with large numbers in both the middle and upper class. Ethnicity has become correspondingly irrelevant and 'political attitudes and loyalties have become a function of socio-economic characteristics'. In the light of this developmental schema, Dahl then presents an impressionistic picture as to when the five major ethnic groups in New Haven – the object of his study – went through these three stages. According to this survey, the Irish reached the point of total assimilation in 1930 and the Italians in 1950. See Robert A. Dahl, *Who Governs?: Democracy and Power in an American City* (New Haven, Conn., 1961), pp. 34–6.

Table 36. *General political affiliation, by religion*

	Craftsmen	Clerks	Managers
	Percentage		
Protestants			
Democrat	19	*14*	9
Republican	28	*43*	36
Independent	53	*43*	55
Total per cent	100	*100*	100
Total number	32	*7*	11
Catholics			
Democrat	56	70	38
Republican	1	3	5
Independent	43	27	48
Total per cent	100	100	100
Total number	151	37	21

dimension of ethnicity, involving a comparison between Catholics and Protestants. This is simply because of the small numbers in each ethnic group within the sample, with the single exception of the Italians.

The data presented in Table 36 leave little room for doubt that what 'pure' support there is for the Republican party comes almost entirely from the Protestant sector of the sample. Amazingly, of the entire Catholic craft group of 151 people, only two were initially prepared to say that they considered themselves Republicans. Although the actual numbers in the Protestant group are small, they are sufficiently large within the total craft group to enable comparison. That comparison is striking. Amongst these Protestant skilled workers, only 19 per cent considered themselves to be Democrats, against the 28 per cent identifying with the Republican party. Similarly, although there has been some movement towards 'verbalised independence' among Catholics, the proportion of Protestants doing so is larger in every occupational group. Finally, it is interesting to note the extent to which religion seems to exert an influence even within the upper middle class. In a group of 21 Catholic managers, only one considered himself to be a Republican, while nearly two fifths identified themselves as Democrats.

This pattern of overwhelming support for the Democratic party, and a corresponding disinterest in the Republican party by Catholic voters does not change when independents are asked to say which party comes 'closer to their interests'. Catholic craftsmen initially calling themselves independents moved over to the Democratic rather than the Republican party by a margin of over three to one. Similar results hold true in the case of both white collar Catholic groups. Yet the exact reverse is the case amongst the Protestant members of the sample. In these groups the majority of independents who were prepared to identify with one of the major parties opted, *in all cases*, for the Republicans. Again one can see the interplay of class and religious variables. Although Protestant craftsmen opted for the Republican party by a margin of five to three, this is a much smaller ratio than that found in the two white collar groups, especially the managers.

The relationship between religion and political choice is highlighted if one looks at the way these people voted in the 1960 and 1964 presidential elections. Indeed, its importance is heightened further by the candidacy of Kennedy, himself a Catholic, in the earlier contest. The voting patterns in this 1960 election go even beyond what one would predict, given the link between the Catholic community and the Democratic party. In every Catholic occupational group, including both non-manual groups, the proportion voting for Kennedy was above 90 per cent. This means, of course, that in all groups religion outweighed other sources of influence and that some individuals who regarded themselves as Republicans crossed party lines to support a Catholic Democrat. For example, in the managerial group, out of the 15 Catholics who told us how they voted in 1960 only one person supported Nixon, the other 14 throwing their support behind a fellow Catholic. Amongst the Protestant sample, support for Kennedy was slighter. Protestant craftsmen were in fact split evenly over the 1960 race with equal numbers supporting Kennedy and Nixon. Similarly, of the six Protestant clerks reporting their choice of voting in 1960, five supported Nixon. This is surprising, given the general picture that has emerged of clerks being solid Democratic supporters. It may well be the fact that the majority (37 of the 44) of clerks are Catholics which effectively prevents any adoption of middle class political behaviour. When this 'barrier' is removed, i.e. in the case of Protestants, clerks vote for the establishment party.[18]

In conclusion, the data show unambiguously that Catholicism is strongly linked with a tendency to support the Democratic party and its candidates, rather than the Republican party and its representatives. Given the religious composition of New England, Catholicism thus emerges as perhaps one of the most important factors considered so far in explaining the maintenance of manual support for this party, despite the newly acquired affluence of those workers, as well as helping to account for the disinterest shown in the G.O.P. by the lower level clerical employees.

In addition to analysing the relevance of religion for political behaviour, I was able to gain some clues as to the importance of ethnicity *per se*, although only in the case of the Italians, because of the even smaller numbers involved in other minority groups. Ethnic background was ascertained by asking where the respondent's grandfather (on his father's side) was born. This means that third generation Americans were not, for these purposes, regarded as members of an ethnic group. Table 37 shows the ethnic composition of the sample using this definition. Given the history of immigration to Providence, this is probably what one would have ex-

Table 37. *Ethnic background (by place of birth of paternal grandfather)*

	Craftsmen	Clerks	Managers
	Percentage		
U.S.A.	16	21	24
Eire	4	9	21
England	5	7	8
Canada	3	16	3
Italy	49	40	18
Eastern Europe	7	—	16
Other/D.K.	16	7	10
Total per cent	100	100	100
Total number	194	44	38

pected. Not a large number of Italians have 'reached' managerial status, and correspondingly few Irish are 'still' in blue collar occupations. The ethnic make-up of Rhode Island is clearly underscored by the fact that only one quarter of the managers have paternal grandparents born in the United States. Outside of New England this figure would be substantially higher.

Limited though the numbers are, the pattern of political differences between respondents of Italian derivation on the one hand, and at least second generation Americans on the other, seems clear (see Table 38). In all cases the Italians are more prone to support the Democratic party than the native-born Americans, while being prepared to identify with the Republicans to a minimal extent. It is evident that the data do not bear out Dahl's assertion regarding the political assimilation of ethnic minorities. Some clues as to why this should be the case may be gleaned from the writings of Wolfinger and Parenti, two political scientists who have carried out research in Newhaven, Connecticut.[19] Wolfinger set himself the task of explaining why, in contrast to the rest of the North East, there should be

Table 38. *General political affiliation, by ethnicity*

	Craftsmen	Clerks	Managers
	Percentage		
Paternal grandfather American			
Democrat	37	45	45
Republican	20	33	33
Independent	43	22	22
Total per cent	100	100	100
Total number	30	9	9
Paternal grandfather Italian			
Democrat	50	71	50
Republican	1	6	—
Independent	49	24	50
Total per cent	100	100	100
Total number	94	17	6

such a high level of Italian Republicanism in Newhaven, and why this link appears to be as strong today as in the earlier part of the century. The specific explanation is couched largely in terms of factors peculiar to New-haven, and these do not really concern us. But relevant to my findings is the explanation Wolfinger produces for his own data, which he calls the 'mobilisation theory of ethnic voting'. The most important aspect of this theory centres around the emergence of leadership within an ethnic group, which is itself dependent on the emergence of a middle class within that group. This assumes that there is already some developed *and structured* link between a particular party and a particular ethnic group – as in Rhode Island – in which case, 'ethnic voting will be greatest when the ethnic group has produced a middle class i.e. in the second and third generations, not in the first'.[20] Given the early identification of a group with one party, and the mobilisation of latent support for that party by middle class leadership, this support will, for Wolfinger, go on a long time after ethnic conscious-ness has faded. My own findings are certainly in accord with this con-tention.

Michael Parenti has attempted to explain the persistence of ethnic fac-tors in political behaviour from a somewhat different standpoint. His thesis revolves around the distinction between assimilation and accultura-tion, and, following from this, a negation of Dahl's and Wolfinger's assumption that assimilation is taking place. For Parenti, while minorities have undoubtedly adopted many of the cultural aspects of American life, in *social structural* terms there has been little breakdown of separateness. As such, discussion as to why, for example, the Italian- or Irish-Americans still identify with one particular party, despite absorption into the host society, is misguided, since it rests on a false assumption. Indeed, and very relevant to my own research, Parenti claims that occupational and finan-cial mobility may *enable* minority groups to institutionalise even further their political separateness from the rest of the society. 'In general terms the new "affluence", often cited as a conductor of great assimilation, may actually provide minorities with the financial and psychological where-withall for building even more elaborate parallel sub-societal structures, including those needed for political action.'[21]

There are, of course, great similarities between the ideas of Wolfinger and Parenti. The most important of these is that neither sees the emergence of a middle class or widespread affluence as detrimental to the main-tenance of ethnic consciousness, as does Dahl. Indeed, the reverse is the case. The main point of divergence between the two writers revolves around whether or not assimilation is taking place as fast as acculturation, or whether it is in fact taking place at all. At this time I am not able to say which of the alternatives is the case among Rhode Island minorities. But this is of little consequence for my present purposes. Whether assimilation and/or acculturation is taking place, the effects, in political terms, would appear to be identical. Ethnicity is still a crucial part of any discussion of political behaviour, and this is a finding of central importance for this discussion.

In the early part of the century, when class and ethnic lines of divergence tended to coalesce, with minority groups making up the bulk of the working class, and Yankees occupying most white collar positions, then ethnicity could be seen as militating against the adoption of middle class political beliefs by members of ethnic groups. However, increasingly as, for example, Italians achieve middle class status, *but still behave like Italians,* then this may be a most important factor making for the disappearance of any firm line between established middle class and traditional working class political loyalties. The continued Democratic allegiance of the middle class Irish in Newhaven is notorious. In 1959 only 20 per cent of the Newhaven Irish were still in manual occupations, yet 64 per cent, the highest proportion of any group in the city, voted Democratic. If this is the case elsewhere–and amongst the Italians in Providence in particular – then we have a good example of the 'proletarianisation' of one dimension of traditional middle class behaviour. As such, affluence has contributed to the breakdown between blue and white collar behaviour patterns but not in the way normally assumed. This, is of course, not so outrageous a finding. Several studies on the political consequences of upward and downward mobility show that the mobile tend to take with them the political ideologies of their parents. Indeed, we have shown this to be the case amongst the clerical workers in our sample. The important difference is that in the case of ethnicity, there do exist structural factors that will reinforce and maintain these 'imported' values.

Conclusion

It is evident that, despite the occupancy of differing positions in the division of labour, and differing levels of material welfare, we are unable to distinguish between skilled craftsmen and clerical workers with regard to political attitudes and behaviour. Furthermore, the reasons given by these people in explanation of the affinity with the Democratic party, and its candidates, are not difficult to understand. And the most important thing about these reasons is that none of them can be considered as representative of the established middle class. Instead respondents talk about the Democratic party being the party for the common man, about being brought up to be a Democrat, and about benefiting from Democratic policies or performance. And the performance in which they are most interested relates to a buoyant economy and to a plentiful supply of jobs for working men. In contrast, the managers provided the only sizeable number of people regarding the Republicans' party as coming closest to their interests, as well as the largest proportion of individuals who admitted to changing political allegiance during their political lives. Again, we are justified in treating these middle class respondents as a distinct and identifiable grouping.

Finally, for the first time in the analysis the importance of ethnic background as a determinant of behaviour and values was made evident. But it must again be stressed that much of what I am suggesting here can really only apply in the north east of the United States. Apart from the *numbers* of people of ethnic origin in this area, it is almost a commonplace that concern with national origins is much greater in the North East than in some other parts of the country. This is usually explained by reference to the stable class structure the immigrants found on arrival in New England. In contrast, other parts of the country, especially the West, had much more fluid systems of stratification. Newcomers therefore were not forced to be as inward looking as was the case in New England.

6   Perceptions of Class and Class Structure

'I think they (skilled craftsmen) are in a class by themselves. They usually stick together and have more in common.'

'I (a carpenter) might eat better – have steak twice a week where he (the clerk) has it once a week. We both might put $10 per week away. My earning power may be more than his but we would enjoy the same things and do the same things. It might be a strain on him financially.'

'Skilled plumbers live well. I see them wining and dining at the Biltmore. But just not in the same social class – business men stay on one side, workers on the other. They feel they're a better type.'

In the preceding chapters I have discussed in some detail what I regard as being the crucial aspects of the class situations of skilled craftsmen, clerical and managerial employees. I have also been able to contrast my findings with those of earlier studies, and thereby highlight the extent to which the positions occupied by these occupational groups in the American class structure are different from those existing in the past. In this chapter I am more concerned with what these changes have meant to the people that have experienced them. Particularly, I am interested in the way in which they now view American society. What kind of class structure is visualised, where its main lines of division fall, how many groupings or classes there are, in which one respondents place themselves, and others, what criteria of placement they use, are therefore some of the questions that will be asked. Most important will be an examination of how members of the three main occupational groups I interviewed see the relative positions of affluent blue collar workers and lower level clerical workers within the class structure. For, as has already been made clear, any discussion of changes in the middle ranges of class structure must ask how clerks and craftsmen now regard themselves *and* each other. Thus, if one can make the distinction between objective class placement of particular occupational groups in the American class structure, and subjective evaluations and placement, this chapter is concerned with the latter aspect.

Self-placement in Class Structure

In attempting to ascertain what picture, if any, respondents had of the American class structure I was initially concerned not to impose any pre-determined schema or classification upon them. Rather, I wanted to get them to talk in their own terms about the number of classes they thought there were in American society, and which one they and their family were in.

Of the total sample of 276 respondents, only seven refused to discuss class differences, insisting instead that everybody was equal, or that they didn't believe in social classes. A further group, whilst not denying the existence of inequalities, were unwilling or unable to say how many classes there were in America. The bulk of the sample, however, appeared to be quite comfortable in discussing both the number of social classes in American society and their names.

As is evident from a glance at Table 39, the vast majority of both crafts-men and clerks see the American stratification system as being composed of three social classes which they usually refer to as 'the rich', 'million-aires', 'upper class'; the 'average' or 'middle class', the 'in-betweens'; and finally the 'bottom', 'poor' or 'lower class'. The names assigned to these strata already give clear indication that these people are seeing social classes as being economically based. Very few respondents visualise society as being dichotomised in terms of 'them' and 'us', or 'rich and poor' – only seven per cent of the total craft group in fact, and one each of clerks and managers. In addition, only the managerial group had a signi-ficant number of respondents who saw society as comprising four or more classes. The difference between the two white collar groups is important, and is undoubtedly linked to the differential amount of career mobility

Table 39. *Perception of number of social classes in America*

	Brick-layers and Masons	Cabinet makers and Car-penters	Elec-tricians	Tool makers	Total Craft	Clerks	Managers
	Percentage						
Two	3	8	11	6	7	2	3
Three	68	66	79	78	73	75	55
Four or more	9	6	7	13	9	9	34*
Don't believe, don't know, other	20	20	3	3	11	14	8
Total per cent	100	100	100	100	100	100	100
Total number	35	49	56	54	194	44	38

*Includes six responses of five classes and one of six classes.

Table 40. *Social class identification*

	Brick-layers and Masons	Cabinet makers and Car-penters	Elec-tricians	Tool-makers	Total Craft	Clerks	Managers
	Percentage						
Upper middle	3	2	—	—	1	—	24
Middle	63	64	78	72	70	73	60
Average	14	12	7	9	10	2	8
Lower middle	—	4	2	6	3	2	3
Working	11	8	7	9	9	14	—
Lower	3	4	2	2	3	—	—
D.K./Other	6	6	4	2	4	9	5
Total per cent	100	100	100	100	100	100	100
Total number	35	49	56	54	194	44	38

inherent in the two occupations. This almost exclusive view of America as a three tier society is a view that appears to hold no matter which control variables are held constant. Age, income, home-ownership, education and so on all seem to be incapable of modifying the proportions of the various groups dividing America into three main classes.

Given this fact, it is not surprising that the majority of respondents see themselves as being placed in the middle of these three strata. As is shown in Table 40, fully four fifths of the total craft group and three quarters of the clerical group termed themselves as being in either the middle or the average class. For these people, America is a middle class society and they are part of that middle class. With the exception of the managers, grada-tions *within* the middle class are hardly mentioned. One bricklayer and one carpenter used the term upper middle class, while three toolmakers and two carpenters thought they were more in the lower middle class. But with the exception of these five craftsmen, the label 'middle' was seen as being sufficiently accurate. A little surprising is the small number of craftsmen who used the term working class – only 17 out of 194 did so. Interestingly enough, it is the clerks who have, by a slight margin, provided the largest proportion of working class identifiers – a not overly significant 14 per cent. It appears to be a term used by the older, less educated members of the sample. Three quarters of the craftsmen who called themselves work-ing class were over forty, as was every one of the clerks. Only two of the 17 craftsmen who used the term had completed high school.

To summarise, when no predetermined scheme is thrust upon them, but instead respondents were encouraged to discuss the American class structure using their own categories and terminology, the majority see it as being a three tiered system, and see themselves as being part of the middle tier. Only the college educated managers identified four or more social classes or made divisions within the middle class to any real extent.

Similarly, few members of the sample had a dichotomous picture of the stratification system.

In addition to being asked to comment upon social class in this unstructured way, respondents were also asked to place themselves in and indeed discuss the American class structure using Richard Centers' fourfold classification.[1] It is realised that from certain standpoints this is an unsatisfactory manner in which to investigate images of class structure. Clearly, if I were interested *solely* in building up an accurate picture of the way in which a group of people perceive patterned inequalities, the only valid way to do this would be in an unstructured depth interview. However, the central question of this part of the research was the way in which clerks and craftsmen placed themselves and each other in the stratification hierarchy. It was therefore considered that the advantages gained by imposing on respondents the additional distinction between the middle and the working class clearly outweighed the disadvantages of such action.[2] In the light of these conditions it was 'pointed out' to interviewees that 'some people think there are four social classes in the United States'. They were then asked which of these four classes they thought their families were in: the upper, the middle, the working or the lower class.

As is readily apparent from Table 41, almost every respondent chose either the middle class or the working class. Most of those who earlier had been unwilling or unable to say how many classes there were, now, with these 'clues' were prepared to identify with one or the other. Not a single person said he was in the lower class, and only two clerks and four managers identified with the upper class. One electrician – the only one in the sample – refused to place his family within this fourfold categorisation. Perhaps the most significant feature of this table is the large number of clerks who have placed themselves in the working class. Indeed, both the toolmakers and the electricians have larger proportions claiming to be middle class than have these lower level white collar workers. Mills claimed in the early 1950s that the psychology of white collar employees 'can often be understood as the psychology of prestige-striving'.[3] This

Table 41. *Social class identification using Centers's system of classification*

	Bricklayers and Masons	Cabinet makers and Carpenters	Electricians	Tool makers	Total Craft	Clerks	Managers
	Percentage						
Middle class	31	47	55	52	48	50	82
Working class	69	53	43	48	52	45	8
Total per cent	100	100	98	100	100	95	90
Total number	35	49	56	54	194	44	38

claim was certainly borne out by the results of Centers's research, conducted around the same time. Centers found a 'definite and sharp break' in the class identification of skilled craftsmen and lower level white collar workers. While 61 per cent of the clerical workers in his sample said they were in the middle class, only 26 per cent of skilled manual workers thought they were. Conversely, 71 per cent of the craft sample regarded themselves as working class, as against only 34 per cent of the clerical group.[4] However, as I have shown, the self-evaluations of the people I interviewed twenty years later were very different. The question that has to be answered is why this should be so. Subsequent discussion and analysis in this chapter, on, for example, the perceived bases of social class, should provide adequate explanation. It would, nonetheless, be instructive if some clues were provided at this point.

There are three variables or characteristics which, to varying degrees, appear to be most closely associated with middle class identification. These factors are home-ownership, affluence and the completion of a high school education.[5] We have already seen that in terms of each of these variables the traditional advantages enjoyed by clerks have been substantially eroded since 1945–7, when Centers conducted his own study. And as we shall see later in the chapter, blue and white collar workers alike are well aware of these changes. The toolmaker, a high school graduate, owning his own house and enjoying a comfortable standard of living, *knows* that he is in a more fortunate situation than many other manual and non-manual workers who are nevertheless by no means poor. He therefore feels able to place himself above them, in the middle class. Conversely, a proportion of clerical workers are cognisant of their declining position relative to both what they see as the established middle class and people who used to be less privileged than themselves, i.e. large numbers of blue collar workers. They therefore feel unable to regard themselves as the equals of either group, and identify instead with the working class.

Images of Class Structure

An important dimension of any individual's perception of class and class structure is his total *Gestalt* of that class structure. This means that not only is it important to find out how many social classes he sees as existing in a particular society, but also the relative sizes of the various social classes. By size is meant simply the proportion of the total population in each of the main groups identified. This is a vital aspect of any complete picture of class structure. Clearly it means something very different if an individual says he is middle class and sees the majority of the population as being in the middle class than if he identifies himself as being in the middle class which he regards as comprising only a small proportion of the population.

Crucial though this aspect of class awareness is, to the writer's knowledge, no one until now has attempted to study it systematically.

In this case each member of the sample was handed a card, divided by horizontal lines into 5 per cent steps, going from 0 per cent to 100 per cent. Respondents were simply then asked to draw lines across the card so as to represent the relative size of the four classes in Providence.[6] Using this procedure, it was hoped an image of class structure could be depicted on paper. Respondents were encouraged to take their time and 'practise' on a spare card first if necessary. The mean average images of class structure thus obtained are presented for the six occupational groups in Fig. 1. Perhaps the most important thing to emerge from these representations of class structure is the fact that in a sense these people subscribe to the crude popular assertion that 'We're all middle class now'. It will be remembered that before being forced to make the distinction between the middle and the working class, the large majority saw America as comprising three social classes. To be sure, the majority were then quite happy to differentiate within this middle class between the middle and working classes, but initially they distinguished only three social groupings. The image of American society behind this threefold and later fourfold classification is evident. It is a diamond shaped structure, with the bulk of the population being in one or the other of the middle two classes.

Despite seeing the majority of the population as being in the middle ranges of the class structure, white and blue collar workers alike are prepared to recognise the presence in American society of a lower or bottom class, and indeed place about one fifth of the population in that class. But this should not really be regarded as startling. At the time of the study the plight of large numbers of Americans was very much in the public eye. The Civil Rights movement had already reached its peak and was being supplemented by riots in the ghettos, including those of Providence and nearby Boston. President Johnson's War on Poverty was being waged, especially on television and in the newspapers, and migrant farm workers on the West Coast were beginning their struggle for union recognition. Under such circumstances it would have been difficult to deny the existence of a sizeable group of people under or below the established middle and working classes.[7] There is an equal recognition of the existence of an upper class although this is regarded unanimously as being significantly smaller than the lower class. The Kennedys were mentioned by several respondents as being symbols of life 'way up there' and clearly represented a style of life that respondents really had not the knowledge or experience to deal with or understand. They could discuss clearly their perceptions of both the middle and the working class, whatever their own identification. But the few clues I obtained pertaining to images of the upper class showed none of the detailed accuracy or understanding found in the descriptions of these central strata.

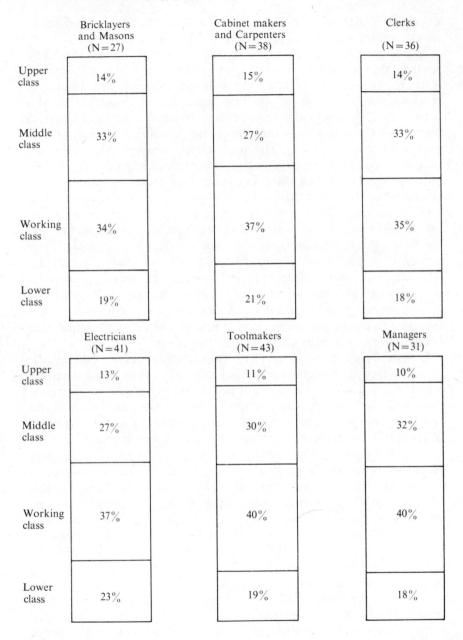

Fig. 1. *Mean images of class structure*

It is significant that there are no great qualitative differences in the images of class structure held by any of the occupational groups. Managers see the class structure in essentially the same way as toolmakers. These images of class structure do not change to any appreciable extent when factors such as age, education or 'exposure' to workers on the other side of the manual/non-manual line are controlled. There is a discernible tendency for affluent craftsmen and clerks to portray a slightly larger middle class, but this is at the expense of the upper and lower classes rather than the working class. That symbol of arrival in the middle class – home-ownership – appears to have no effect upon the way in which the society is viewed; nor does that traditional working class characteristic, trade union membership. Surprisingly, opportunities for promotion, attitudes towards promotion and interaction with workers wearing a different coloured collar also seem to bear no relationship to the way in which an individual views the stratification system. I had anticipated that the reverse would be the case.

However, there is a significant difference in the way class structure is depicted, depending upon whether the viewer regards himself as being middle or working class. Broadly speaking, although this is not as significant for middle class identifiers, individuals tend to regard the class in which they have placed themselves as being the largest one in the society. As Fig. 2 shows, both working class clerks and craftsmen paint pictures of the class structure in which the working class contains 14 per cent and 15 per cent more of the total population than the middle class. Amongst middle class identifiers this difference is not as large. Indeed, for middle class craftsmen the middle class is only fractionally bigger than the working class. But the trend is clear. In both the craft and the clerical groups, middle class identifiers depict a much larger middle class then do working class identifiers.

This tendency to view one's own class as being the largest in society is not difficult to explain. The individual develops his ideas about stratification largely through interaction with people with whom he comes into contact by virtue of his role set in society, most notably at work, but also in his wider family and the community. The majority of these people are going to be in a similar situation to the individual himself in terms of the criteria which he comes to learn are relevant in the ascription of class situation. Clearly he will also brush shoulders with individuals very different from himself, as well as learning about them from other sources such as the mass media. These other individuals will be crucial in influencing self-placement in the perceived hierarchy. Nonetheless, the majority of his contacts and experience will be with people similarly situated to himself. It is therefore relatively easy to understand why most respondents will think the class they are in contains the largest number of people. And this is especially so in the case of the majority of my own respondents. These men, located in a particular work situation, and possessing only a moderate education are not exposed to the full spectrum of class to the extent that the college educated professional might be. Bott has made this point clearly:

In brief the individual constructs his notions of social position

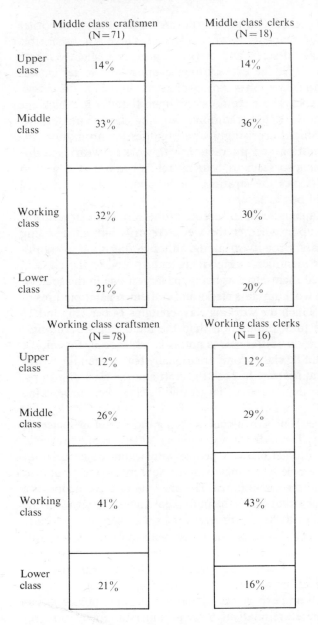

Fig. 2. *Mean images of class structure by social class*

and class from his own various and unconnected experiences of prestige and power and his imperfect knowledge of other people's... He creates his own model of the class structure and uses it as a rough-and-ready means of orienting himself in a society so complex that he cannot experience directly more than a very limited part of it.[8]

The main exception to this tendency to view one's own class as the largest is to be found in the managerial group, all of whom, apart from three individuals, consider themselves to be middle class, but who nevertheless see the middle class as being considerably smaller than the working class. Managers are clearly not in the socially indeterminate position of the clerks and craftsmen, but are subjectively and objectively middle class. There are two main reasons why managers should have this 'realistic' picture of the class structure which does not put their own class as numerically the largest. First, the educational level of the managerial group is significantly higher than for either of the other two main groups, clerks and craftsmen. This means that managers have read more, perhaps taken courses in areas that enable them to analyse class in a more sophisticated manner and generally be more informed than other respondents, who have to rely far more on their more limited experience. Secondly, in his work role, like the craftsmen the manager will interact largely with people in a situation similar to his own, but unlike the craftsmen he is, in most cases, going to be well aware that he and his peers are in a minority. In the work situation executive staff will outnumber other staff whether or not a line is drawn so as to regard clerks as equals or inferiors. In terms of power, income or education, it is going to be clear to the established middle class manager that he, and his peers, are in a situation that is superior, and yet numerically smaller than the rest of the labour force. It is therefore not difficult to understand why individuals in upper level administrative posts should not regard their own social class as being the largest in the society.

From the discussion so far it is evident that the large majority of people in the sample have reasonably clear ideas on class and class structure. A picture has emerged in which both manual and non-manual workers see the American class structure as a three tiered system, and see themselves as being part of the middle tier. Again, with few exceptions, respondents are willing to accept the distinction between a middle and a working class. Clerks and craftsmen have roughly equal proportions identifying with the middle and working class in this four tiered framework. Finally, the image of the American class structure that emerges when respondents are asked about the relative proportions of the population in these four classes most nearly approximates a diamond. The majority of the population are seen as being in either the working or middle class, although the former is seen as being the larger of the two.

The Bases of Social Class

In order to might gain some idea of the criteria and bases of social class being used by respondents (whether explicitly or implicitly), respondents were asked a number of questions designed to get them to describe typical working and middle class people, and the differences between them.[9] Their responses again indicate a high level of awareness of patterned inequality in American society, and go a long way toward explaining the image of class structure to which the majority subscribe. Most important, we are able to understand why only around one half of the craftsmen claim membership in the middle class and why a similar proportion of clerks did not feel able to do so. For the description of the working and middle classes portrayed in Table 42 makes it apparent that few of these blue collar and routine white collar employees view stratification in occupational terms. To be sure they depict middle and working class people in terms of occupationally related characteristics, but characteristics that apply equally to manual or non-manual workers. Thus, only 18 craftsmen and two clerks could be categorised as *'embourgeoisement* theorists', in that they described people in the working class as those not having a skilled trade. A toolmaker (who was also a functionalist) explained: 'they're not tradesmen – labourers – they do less important jobs'. A cabinet maker thought a typical working class person was 'one who has no trade...and has very little responsibility'. The fact that a skill, because of its rarity, brings protection from unemployment was also a consideration. A toolmaker, citing jewellery shop workers as an example of working class people, explained: 'less pay, numerous lay-offs', while another characterised this stratum as being made up of the 'labourer who goes from one job to another – unskilled'.

The only other criterion of working and middle class people couched in occupational terms is that equating the former with manual work and the latter with non-manual employment. This, of course, is the answer I was most looking for. But again, with the exception of the managerial group, only a small minority see colour of collar as being a crucial variable – 19 craftsmen and six clerks out of the total sample. Having to punch a time clock, and being paid by the hour were mentioned several times as indicative of membership in the working class. For a few, symbols clearly remain important. An electrician replied: 'works in a shop, gets splinters in his hand – wears a working man's clothes', while a clerk, in little doubt about his own position in the middle class answered: 'A person who works with his hands. A craftsman or manual labourer would automatically be in the working class...' Nevertheless, on this issue in general there is a fundamental difference between the two white collar groups in the sample. Whereas only 14 per cent of clerks saw the manual/non-manual line as differentiating the working from the middle class, 47 per cent of the managerial group did so. This was by far the single most important characteristic of the working class given by managers. Similarly, the only appreciable proportion of any one occupational group identifying the middle class with white collar occupations is found amongst the

Table 42. *Criterion used in describing typical working and middle class persons*

	Working class descriptions							Middle class descriptions						
	Brick-layers and Masons	Cabinet makers and Carpenters	Electricians	Tool makers	Total Craft	Clerks	Managers	Brick-layers and Masons	Cabinet makers and Carpenters	Electricians	Tool makers	Total Craft	Clerks	Managers
	Percentage							Percentage						
Income (specific and unspecific)	20	6	12	15	13	16	19	30	17	11	23	19	33	8
Education/education & income	20	21	20	23	20	34	16	28	23	28	24	26	32	36
Style of life	6	23	25	19	19	11	5	11	30	37	30	28	16	26
	46	50	57	57	52	61	40	69	70	76	77	73	81	70
Skilled/non-skilled line	6	13	9	9	9	5	5	3	6	4	6	5	—	3
Manual/non-manual line	11	6	9	13	10	14	47	11	8	4	9	8	11	24
Two classes the same	11	8	9	6	8	7	3	11	6	12	6	9	2	3
Anyone who works/other/D.K.	26	23	16	15	21	13	5	6	10	4	2	5	6	—
Total per cent	100	100	100	100	100	100	100	100	100	100	100	100	100	100
Total number	35	49	56	54	194	44	38	35	49	56	54	194	44	38

managers, a quarter of whom made this stipulation. (It is interesting that fewer managers described the working class in terms of occupation. It may well be that in discussion of the middle class, upper level administrators regard a white collar occupation as axiomatic and therefore less needful of mention.) Nonetheless, around one half of the managerial group portray the working class in terms of manual or blue collar work:

> 'A family who may have quite a nice income, but is likely to be a production worker in an industrial enterprise, as opposed to clerical or management. They don't belong to many social groups and may be satisfied with a public school education.'

> 'The only ones I know are those working for me. They work hard – long hours and often two jobs. Income – low; education – little. They depend on manual skills for their bread and butter.'

> 'As I say, hourly wage, union membership identify the working class. Salaried employees belong to the middle class – you have to start using more of your brain power than your physical powers.'

It is important to note that whereas a significant proportion of managers describe the working and middle classes in terms of criteria which place clerks securely in the latter category, few of the clerks realise their good fortune with anything like the clarity or certainty of their superiors. I would suggest that again, the reasons for this disparity can be traced back to the influence of the work situation. Managers are working with and often alongside lower level white collar workers, and yet in the majority of cases are physically and therefore socially separated from blue collar employees. Half of the managerial sample reported that they never came into contact with manual workers, and in those cases where contact was made it would appear to be of a fleeting and impersonal kind. Comments, such as 'Checking to see if a job is being done O.K.'; 'making the rounds'; 'in building a job and trouble with it, go and see what the trouble is' give a clear indication of the *content* of the limited interaction that does exist between the managerial sample and blue collar employees in the work situation. It is therefore perhaps not surprising that managers still regard the blue collar/white collar line of demarcation as having social significance. On the other hand, while clerks are in a situation in which they are provided with opportunities to interact with managerial or administrative personnel, it is by no means an interaction of equals. And as I have already suggested, decreasing opportunities for promotion and increasingly routinised work tasks are more and more placing the clerk in a situation not unlike that occupied by certain types of manual workers. Indeed, it is likely that many of the lower level white collar workers in the sample have personally experienced this change in their fortunes. In these terms it is not difficult to explain why such very small numbers of clerks see the manual/ non-manual line as having much significance in separating them socially from at least a section of the affluent blue collar labour force. I do not feel able, in other words, to accept Mills's prediction that the demotion of bookkeepers 'to the level of the clerical mass' is leading to 'status panic' on the part of these workers.

Instead the great majority of both blue and lower level white collar employees view the American class structure in terms of the distribution of either income or education, or with reference to a correlate of these two variables – style of life; i.e. classes are being discussed in a language that can be applied equally to clerical or to craft workers. And the portrayal found most frequently in the answers of both groups is in terms of income or income plus education. Turning first to portrayal of the working class, descriptions *solely* in educational terms are few – four per cent of craftsmen and nine per cent of clerks. But the prominence given to income *and* education as determinants of working class status are clear in the response of a toolmaker who regards himself as being working class. When asked to describe his own class this man replied: 'People in the lower income scale – little education, mostly manual or low pay white collar.' A mason was under no illusions about the importance of an income scale when he replied simply: 'People are judged by the amount they make.' The actual amount that is seen to be made by the working class varies considerably, although several respondents stipulated specific figures. The average is somewhere between $5,000 and $7,000 a year. A clerk who considers himself middle class thought that: 'Usually (maybe some of them do make more) most of them average in the neighbourhood of $5,000 per annum. Usually to have what they want they have to put their wives out to work.'

The phrase 'to have what they want' is important in understanding why over half of the clerical and craft groups discuss the characteristics of the working class in income, education and style of life terms. For it is style of life that is the fundamental component in their characterisations of social class. To be sure, the clerical group portrays the working class more in terms of income and education than do the craft groups. But to a large extent they are saying the same thing. In these middle ranges of the class structure income and education are being included not as ends in themselves, but as means to an end. That end is, of course, a particular style of life. This link may be 'spelt out' either crudely or in a sophisticated manner, as is demonstrated by the following images of the working class, all of which were made by people identifying with that grouping when confronted with Centers' classification:

A toolmaker:

'A person of moderate means, fairly comfortable, not really working for anything, yet not having everything he would like to have. High school education – maybe one or two years of college.'

An electrician:
'People of average education. Education tells a lot about a person. Of course there are exceptions. The working class has to keep working to have the things they want to have. The middle class can have these things without too much worry about where the money is going to come from...'

A clerk:
'Moderately educated (high school graduate). He is totally dependent on his salary. He would have a mortgaged home or rent. He would have two cars sometimes. No private schools, probably not an avid reader.'

All three of these quotes are linking education and income to style of life in a causal sequence. None of the stages in that sequence is limited to white collar occupations. A high school diploma is now a requirement for entry into both office jobs and craft apprenticeships, while if there is any difference between clerks and craftsmen in terms of income, home-ownership and so on, it is a difference which puts the latter group in the preferential position.

A very similar picture presents itself when the criteria used in describing the middle class are examined. Around three quarters of craftsmen, clerks and managers portray this group in terms of income, income plus education or style of life. The causal chain evident in images of the working class is replicated. Within this general pattern of similarity there are, however, some differences. As in the case of descriptions of the working class, clerks are more prone to analyse the middle class in terms of cause rather than effect, while craftsmen tend to see 'style of life' as being the single most important characteristic of the middle class. In all groups the proportion viewing the middle class as being based *solely* on educational criteria is negligible, but two thirds of the clerical group characterised the middle class in income or income plus educational terms, as opposed to 45 per cent of the craft groups doing likewise. Very few respondents specified a *particular* income as being representative of the middle class, but of those that did the majority quoted figures of over $8,000 a year. Significantly more craftsmen see education as being also important and are clearly aware of its relationship to income. Nonetheless, for a number of people in all three major occupational groups, income, and income alone is the determinant of class position. More than one respondent explained that 'You are *judged* by your income today. The better the job, the higher salary you have.' A clerk thought a middle class person was: 'a working class person with a larger income'. A manager agreed: 'Income tells the tale – there's an excellent income for those in the middle class,' while a toolmaker had no doubt that 'A man is always looked up to if he makes good money and can buy material things – that counts.' For another toolmaker, the fact that in the middle class the head of household earned a sufficiently high salary to support his family *by himself* was the crucial characteristic: 'Earns anywhere from $5,000 to $10,000 – has a little more – the wife doesn't have to work if she doesn't want to.'

In addition to the large numbers seeing social class purely in income terms, a substantial proportion was very much aware of the link between education and income, and was concerned that this link be made clear. Responses such as: 'Education is what counts today – your wages would be higher'; 'a person well educated gets more money and a job of respect and prestige'; 'a worker having more education is getting more money', all made by skilled craftsmen, demonstrate this clearly. Respondents mentioning education as a requirement for membership in the middle class were split about evenly between those specifying a certain level of attainment and those using terms such as 'a formal education', 'above average', 'well-educated' and so on. Some clues as to the meaning of these terms is given by the respondents who did specify. Of these, more than half stipulate 'college-educated' or 'some college'. The remainder all require at least high school graduation. No one seemed prepared to accept less than a high school graduation certificate for entry into the middle class.

However, although large numbers of craftsmen discuss the character of the middle class in these causal terms, the most frequent portrayal is in terms of style of life. And the extent of the detail sometimes given by these craftsmen could, in many instances have been culled from the pages of an undergraduate textbook in stratification. An electrician, when asked how he would describe a middle class person replied: 'Like me – goes to work for 37 hours, he has leisure time for camping and quahogging, he lives within his means. He doesn't do without some luxuries – has two cars, a home, a trailer.' If we construct an ideal type middle class style of life as seen by these affluent workers, home-ownership stands as perhaps being most important. It is certainly the characteristic of a middle class life style most often mentioned and several even give what they consider to be the value of a middle class home. For a clerk, a member of the middle class can, amongst other things, 'afford and maintain a home worth $15,000'. A toolmaker qualifies his statement:'...doesn't have to be an elaborate home', while a fellow toolmaker gives us a snapshot Warner would find it hard to improve: 'Anybody that has a good modern, well-kept home and grounds. Also educated – at least a high school graduate. At least $10,000 per annum. Has at least one car, a vacation – at least two weeks. His house is worth at least $20,000.' The requirement that the house should be in a 'decent neighbourhood' is also mentioned by more than one respondent.

One electrician described a middle class person simply as someone who 'lives in a fairly good section of the city'.

One important aspect of style of life hardly mentioned at all by the craft and clerical groups, but seen as being a crucial dimension of a middle class existence by the managerial group, is involvement in community affairs. 'Leaders, as relative to their status, in their community life' was the way one manager put it. Another said'. . . involved in community activities, civic or charitable – takes a leading part in it if possible'. This and other evidence suggests that the managerial group views the middle class in terms which sociologists are more apt to associate with the upper middle class. Compared to the craft and clerical groups, few (only three people), give solely economic criteria for membership in the middle class. Well over a third saw income *and* education as being the bases of membership in this grouping. However, the size of income is perhaps summed up in the phrase of one of them, 'financially successful', and the educational level is a college rather than the high school graduation most often cited by the clerks and craftsmen. In short the image of the middle class held by the managerial group, though couched in the same 'income, education and style of life' terms as the lower clerical and craft groups, is qualitatively different from that held by these two groups. And both images are rooted in the differing life experiences of the craft and clerical groups on the one hand and of the managers on the other.

This then is the picture of the working class drawn by the majority of skilled blue collar and lower level white collar subjects, although there are differences between middle class and working class identifiers. For example, 23 of the 24 craftsmen who regard the working class as comprising everybody who works for a living, i.e. without his own business or profession, think of themselves as working class. Similarly 17 of the 19 craftsmen equating the working class with manual work identified themselves as members of the working class. In contrast, the middle class identifiers downplay, almost to a point of insignificance, occupational factors and stress instead income and style of life. Indeed, 60 per cent of the middle class craft groups described the working class in these terms. As one would expect, none of those craftsmen who regard themselves as being middle class see colour of collar as being important, but a fifth did view the working class as being made up of individuals with no skill or trade. Clearly this legitimises their own claim to middle class status.

However, these differences between groups within the clerical and craft categories do little to detract from the general picture that has emerged from respondents' descriptions of the working and middle classes. With the exception of the managerial category these people are seeing the bases of class divisions in terms of education, income, and a resulting style of life. For craftsmen and clerks alike, a white collar or any other *occupational* characteristic is relevant in the ascription of class position only insofar as it is linked to these other factors. By itself it is powerless.[10] This interpretation is augmented by the fact that income and education were chosen most frequently when respondents were handed a list of variables on a card, and asked which one it was most important to know, in deciding to which social class a person belonged. Indeed, 65 per cent of the total craft group chose one or other of these two factors, as did 78 per cent of the clerical *and* managerial groups. Occupation was chosen by only 11 per cent of the blue collar sample, seven per cent of the lower level white collar category and 16 per cent of the managers. In a study of changes in the middle ranges of the American class structure, this finding is of enormous importance. For, to the extent that both clerks and craftsmen have come to view social class in terms that do not *automatically* place the former in a superior position to the latter, then a major barrier to change is no longer present.

Finally, the impression is strong that both craft and clerical workers are far more aware of class differences in the middle ranges of the class structure than previous research had led one to believe would be the case. Berger, for example, found amongst his sample of 100 primarily non-skilled blue collar workers that 'the hierarchy of class which is meaningful to these workers is not a conceptual framework that applies to society as a whole, but one that is limited rather to *what is possible for them*'[11] (italics in original). While, as has already been pointed out, the respondents of my sample could not visualise the upper class at all coherently and in this sense approximate Berger's workers, they were not as blinkered with regard to the middle ranges of the stratification system. This included in many cases sophisticated discussions of a class that was seen as beyond their own possibilities, and applied to both middle and working class identifiers.

There are several reasons for this increased level of sophistication. First, the sample are all craftsmen and, as such, many of them come into contact frequently with a wider range of people than Berger's auto-workers. Toolmakers deal with non-skilled help, draughtsmen, customers and managers. Carpenters work in a variety of environments, as do bricklayers, and electricians. Many of their contacts will be members of the lower and upper middle class. Secondly, the level of education of these skilled workers is higher. Thirdly, in the ten years that separates the two studies, the influence of the mass media has increased. Its role in increasing awareness cannot perhaps be entirely discounted.

The Class Situation of Clerks and Craftsmen

In addition to being asked about the American class structure in general, and the middle and working classes in particular, members of the sample were also questioned on the positions of various occupational groups. At the risk of repetition this was felt necessary in order to force respondents to discuss the blue collar/white collar line. I considered it quite possible (as was indeed the case) that subjects might discuss in detail their conceptions of class, without reference to this traditional line of demarcation. On the one hand, this could mean that it is considered irrelevant, or, on the other, it could mean simply that it is considered important, but is subsumed under, or implicit in, portrayals in style of life or other terms. In order to determine which of these alternatives was in fact the case, attention was therefore purposely focused on the relative class situations of skilled blue collar workers and lower level clerical employees. To this end, respondents were asked whether they thought that 'Nowadays, skilled craftsmen are doing better than men who work in offices.' The meaning of the phrase 'doing better' was left to the respondent to interpret. There was almost complete unanimity on this issue. And nearly all respondents did think that craftsmen were 'doing better' than clerks. In only one occupational group – that of the bricklayers and masons – did the proportion responding in the affirmative fall below 90 per cent. This means that there is no significant difference between the craft groups as a whole and either of the white collar groups. And almost to a man these people interpreted the phrase 'doing better' in economic terms. A manager commented: 'White collar jobs are a dime a dozen at $100 a week – all trades pay a lot better than that.' A clerk explained: 'Going back a long way a white collar worker is underpaid. They regard us as overhead – we don't produce.' But perhaps the most ironic remark, given the traditional difference social scientists have emphasised in comparing the market situation of blue collar and white collar workers, is that of a carpenter: 'It might be about even. A manager in a store might make about the same as I do, but I bet he puts in more hours.'

Large numbers of respondents went further and, taking the higher incomes of craftsmen as a given, explained why craftsmen were now doing better – i.e. earning more – than clerks. There were three main sets of reasons they gave to account for this: first, the ability of trade unions to gain higher incomes for blue collar workers, given the fact that few clerks are unionised; secondly, the greater demand for skilled craftsmen; finally, functionalists in the sample were persuaded that as skilled craftsmen took longer to train, and thus possessed greater skills than white collar workers, they deserved higher rewards. In the words of a cabinet maker: 'They have a trade and need more knowledge. A skilled craftsman could work in an office in one year, but it couldn't work the other way.' Clearly in the minds of many of the people we interviewed the traditional market advantages of clerks over craftsmen are no more. Illuminating is the fact that the tone of the comments is not one of incredulity or awareness of sudden change. A situation is being described as it is seen, and has been seen, for some time. As a toolmaker observes: 'Craftsmen are in demand – there are a lot of automated machines for the office worker.' It's the white collar worker who is being most affected by automation, not the aristocracy of labour.

There is a degree of awareness among both white and blue collar workers of the disadvantages white collar workers have suffered as a result of not becoming unionised. A toolmaker explained: 'They (skilled craftsmen) are better organised than office workers – they are at the mercy of employers,' while another commented: 'The office man hasn't bettered himself by joining labour organisations.'[12]

Thus the majority of each of the occupational categories see the craftsmen as doing better than the clerk; they interpret this in economic terms and large numbers are happy to give causal reasons why this should be so. That majority were then invited to translate their evaluation of the relative economic positions of the two groups into class terms. They were asked: 'So would you say skilled craftsmen and office workers are now in the same social class or not?' The pattern of answers to this question is presented in Table 43. Again they are unambiguous. Amongst the four craft groups between 69 per cent and 84 per cent of those who thought craftsmen were doing better than clerks regarded members of these two occupational groups as now being in the same social class. 68 per cent of the managers and 50 per cent of the clerks thought likewise. At first sight this latter figure appears low. However, it is explained when one looks at the proportions of clerks who consider craftsmen to be in a *higher* class than themselves: over a quarter think this is the case. Indeed, amongst both the clerical and the craft group those considering craftsmen to be in a higher class than clerks outnumber those who consider the opposite to be true – by a majority of three to one amongst craftsmen and two to one amongst clerks.

Again I received responses that, in terms of the situation in the earlier part of this century, seem ironical. Several people thought that I was wondering whether clerks were coming up to craftsmen, rather than vice versa. A manager explained: 'The last barrier has been removed – that of union participation.' An electrician who considered craftsmen to be in a

Table 43. *Perceived class situation of craftsmen and clerks*

	Brick-layers and Masons	Cabinet makers and Car-penters	Elec-tricians	Tool makers	Total Craft	Clerks	Managers
	Percentage						
Craftsmen in higher class	12	14	21	22	18	28	6
Both in same class	84	77	69	70	74	50	68
Craftsmen in lower class	—	7	8	6	6	12	20
D.K.	4	2	2	2	2	10	6
Total per cent	100	100	100	100	100	100	100
Total number	26	44	52	49	171	40	35

higher social class than clerks was nonetheless aware that there could be exceptions: 'A man in an office gets less money – but he could invest money and so have as much income as a craftsman. Then he would be in the same social class – otherwise, no.' An equally liberal bricklayer proclaimed: 'I know I don't feel superior to office workers.' It is only on this aspect of the discussion that there seems to be a difference between managers and the other two occupational groups: 20 per cent consider craftsmen to be in a lower class than white collar workers. This is in keeping with some of the findings reported above. Managers would appear to be the only people to whom the blue collar/white collar line still has significant meaning, albeit to a minority.[13]

To summarise, we have seen that over nine tenths of the craft group and over three quarters of both white collar groups consider craftsmen to be either in the same social class or a higher social class than clerical workers. Out of the 246 respondents who considered craftsmen to be doing better than clerical workers, only 22 thought that craftsmen were still in a subordinate position to clerks in class terms. Perhaps even more significant here is the fact that of the 27 respondents who earlier said they did not think craftsmen were doing better than clerks, only nine regarded the two groups as being in different social classes. All nine of these people were themselves craftsmen. The remainder (apart from the uncommitted) all regarded craftsmen and clerks as being in the same social class. Not one of the seven clerks or managers who thought craftsmen were not yet doing better than clerks, placed them in different social classes. Clearly, for the majority of these respondents, the blue collar/white collar distinction has minimal social significance.[14]

The Class Situation of Skilled and Non-skilled Workers

For reasons similar to those enumerated at the beginning of the previous section, it was also considered desirable to focus analysis purposefully on the comparative class situation of skilled and non-skilled workers. In particular, I was anxious to ascertain whether or not clerks and craftsmen were seen as belonging to a class superior to that occupied by non-skilled blue collar workers, or whether at this level also occupation was viewed as relatively unimportant in its own right. In order to determine which of these alternatives is in fact the case, respondents were asked whether or not they thought it true that 'nowadays *some* semi-skilled and unskilled workers are doing as well as skilled craftsmen. . .' Despite the qualified nature of this question, the pattern of responses was very different from that elicited earlier in the comparison of clerical workers and craftsmen. In only one of the four craft groups did a majority consider some non-skilled workers to be in as fortunate a situation as craftsmen. For the craft group as a whole, nearly three fifths do not think that this is the case. Over half of

Table 44. *Perceived class situation of craftsmen and non-skilled workers*

	Brick-layers and Masons	Cabinet makers and Carpenters	Electricians	Tool makers	Total Craft	Clerks	Managers
	Percentage						
In same class	51	62	42	45	50	33	58
Not in same class	43	36	54	53	47	60	42
D.K.	6	2	4	2	3	7	—
Total per cent	100	100	100	100	100	100	100
Total number	35	48	35	51	189	42	38

the managerial group thought likewise, while two thirds of the clerical group gave this response. This last finding is important, as up to now, clerks have been the most liberal group in their inclusion of skilled craftsmen in the middle class. Clearly however, their generosity stops at the level of semi- and unskilled workers.

The halt is evident if one looks at Table 44. All interviewees were asked whether or not they thought skilled and non-skilled manual workers were in the same social class. By a comfortable margin the clerks have the smallest proportion of any occupational group viewing members of these two occupational categories as social equals. Once again, toolmakers and electricians have similar views which set them off, to an extent, from the other two craft groups. Interestingly, it is the managerial category which has the largest proportion regarding craftsmen and other manual workers as being in the same social class. As these people have consistently laid the greatest stress on the continuing relevance of the blue collar/white collar line, this finding cannot be regarded as unexpected.

Finally, the large proportion who did not consider non-skilled workers to be the social equals of craftsmen were asked why they thought this was the case. The main reasons offered are shown in Table 45. As can be seen, the most important reasons given by both craftsmen and clerks are again economic, with the response couched either in income or style of life terms. A toolmaker commented: 'Skilled help will make much more money and use it to belittle the unskilled workers,' while another (showing an awareness of the interactional nature of social class discussed later in this chapter) replied: 'Well, they (craftsmen) earn more and can afford to go better places – meet and socialise with a higher class of people.' The higher standard of general education and/or training received by skilled craftsmen was also regarded as important. Indeed, three fifths of the clerical group gave lack of education as being a factor in the maintenance of a class differential between skilled and non-skilled workers. For the craft group, the corresponding proportion was 45 per cent. A toolmaker explained: 'You can't say people digging ditches belong to the same class

Table 45. *Reasons why craftsmen are judged to be in a higher social class than other manual workers*

	Brick-layers and Masons	Cabinet makers and Car-penters	Elec-tricians	Tool makers	Total Craft	Clerks	Managers
	Percentage						
Higher income/ style of life	47	64	57	34	49	40	19
Higher income and education	33	12	33	36	30	32	25
Higher education/ training	13	24	7	19	15	28	25
Prestige difference, other	7	—	3	11	6	—	31
Total per cent	100	100	100	100	100	100	100
Total number	15	17	30	27	89	25	16

as skilled help – they don't have to have any education at all.' A carpenter agreed: '. . . because of the years of training behind them. They have some education and can be accepted.'

Thus the same picture emerges of social class divisions being determined by differences of education, income and style of life. To the extent that education is discussed, it is usually seen as a means to an end – a higher income. But this is not always the case. An electrician, for example, gave as the reason for non-skilled workers being excluded from the same social class as skilled craftsmen the lack of education of the former, adding 'their (the non-skilled) characters and living habits are different'; while a manager thought that 'in his thinking' the craftsman was 'superior to the unskilled'.

Class Consciousness

In addition to determining the ways in which the sample viewed the American class structure, as well as their perception of the bases of social differentiation, I was also concerned with finding out something about their level of class consciousness. This term is taken to include the extent to which the people I talked to feel strongly that they are members of one particular class, that this class may, as a group, have goals or interests which may be different from those of other classes, and finally, that as a result, the relationship between classes may be one of conflict. Class consciousness was therefore studied from two main perspectives. First, by using a series of questions designed to test certain of its dimensions without referring to social class specifically, but centring on the relationship between management and workers. Secondly, by investigating the level and intensity of union membership, as well as the way in which unions and the union movement, the traditional vehicle of class consciousness, are generally viewed.

Management and the worker

The most detailed of this former group of questions was one that has been posed in one form or another in several studies. Respondents were asked: 'Do you think it is more realistic to look at a large firm somewhat like a football team, with each person doing his bit towards the success of the enterprise, or is it more realistic to see it composed of two *opposed* parts, managers on the one side and workers on the other?' In general the pattern of replies to this question does not indicate anything approaching a high level of class consciousness. Around three quarters of the total sample did consider a large firm to be like a football team. Moreover, there was little difference between the blue and white collar groups on this issue. 72 per cent of the total craft group gave this response as compared to 82 per cent of the clerical group and 74 per cent of the managerial group. Within the craft group the proportion of 'footballers' varied from 67 per cent (cabinet makers and carpenters) to 75 per cent (electricians). This means that not more than one quarter of any of the six major occupational groups sub-scribed to a view of a large firm that involved management and workers in opposition.

Furthermore, in examining the reasons given by respondents in jus-tification of their particular views of the structure of a large firm, one is struck by the almost complete absence of ideological responses. Class conscious answers, either pro-management or pro-worker, are few and far between. Rather, of those respondents who considered it more realis-tic to look at a large firm as if it were a football team, the great majority gave as their reason the fact that simply this was the only way a firm could get things done. A clerk, who, judging by his answers to other questions, clearly does not identify with management, explained: 'That's the way we work. We can't work without the help of management, and management can't work without our help.' An electrician clarifies this further: 'If the boss doesn't make any money, you won't either, so you have to work to-gether.' In fact, 71 per cent of the total craft group regarding a firm as a football team gave this kind of pragmatic response, as did 83 per cent of the clerical group and 96 per cent of the managerial group. For these people, to discuss a firm in terms of conflict relationship between management and workers is silly and meaningless. The large firm and teamwork are, by definition, inseparable. Finally, the majority of the remainder of the 'foot-ballers' based their view on the fact that, from their experience, firms *do* work harmoniously. Responses such as 'The success of our company is proof' given by a clerk; or 'I've been working with the company so many years and we've been almost like a family and have all tried to see that the company goes ahead' proffered by a toolmaker, are examples of straight-forward and almost atheoretical answers that result simply from personal experience.

On the other hand, those respondents who regard it as more realistic to view a large firm as comprising two opposed parts gave two main reasons for holding this view. The largest number again answered in this way be-cause, from their experience, this was the situation in large companies. Thus an electrician replied: 'Our company has no trouble at all. Through the intervention of unions for the workers we get higher pay and higher benefits. They take our side and management field for their side. Each side may compromise – we get satisfied.' For this man, the analogy of a football team has some validity, but there are *two* teams, one for manage-ment and one for workers. This man is aware of a dichotomy, but he sees it as a fair instrumental bargaining relationship between equals, as in any commercial relationship. And the use of phrases like 'management field for their side' gives little indication of the perception of structured conflict or exploitation. This is not to say that none of the affluent workers studied exhibited such feelings. A toolmaker, for example, commented: 'If management want to take advantage of us, they do. Years ago kids worked and died for management,' while a cabinet maker exclaimed bitterly: 'When they (the other side) need you, they're good, when they don't, then the hell with you.' But only a small number of individuals per-ceived the structure of a factory in pro-worker class conscious terms. Of the total sample of 193 craftsmen, only 15 gave explanations that I could categorise as exhibiting class consciousness – an awareness of differential interests and a feeling that one side was on the offensive, while the other was forced to organise to defend itself. No clerks or managers gave this kind of explanation.

The second question simply asked respondents: 'In general do you think that working people are usually fairly and squarely treated by their employers, or that employers sometimes take advantage of them?' The patterns of answers to this question is shown in Table 46. Again, in general, the skilled craft group does not exhibit anything approaching a high level of awareness of possible structural differences between employers and emplyees. In response to this fairly 'mild' inquiry, less than 30 per cent of the total craft group thought that employers even *sometimes* take advan-tage of working people. There is however greater variation within the craft group than on the previous question. Toolmakers, the factory work-ers in the sample, are the odd ones out. Almost half of the group do think that employees are sometimes taken advantage of. But this is the only craft group where the figure is over the 30 per cent mark. As would also be expected there is a substantial difference between the managers, and the clerks and craftsmen. Only five managers were prepared to say that em-ployers are not always completely 'fair'. There were slight differences bet-

Table 46.   *Perception of whether or not working people are usually fairly treated by their employers*

	Brick-layers and Masons	Cabinet makers and Car-penters	Elec-tricians	Tool makers	Total Craft	Clerks	Managers
	Percentage						
Working people fairly treated	78	62	63	46	61	66	71
Employers sometimes take advantage	11	22	24	48	28	23	13
Depends on situation/D.K.	11	16	13	6	11	11	16
Total per cent	100	100	100	100	100	100	100
Total number	35	49	55	54	193	44	38

ween the total craft group and the clerical group, but they are not sociologically significant.

Finally, the third question inquired: 'In strikes and disputes between working people and employers, do you usually side with the workers or with the employers?' Clearly in a question such as this one would expect very few craftsmen or clerks to side with employers. I was, however, most interested to finding out what proportion of the skilled sample would be prepared to, as it were, give *carte blanche* support to the workers, and conversely, what proportion would refuse, giving instead a qualified answer, backing workers in certain situations, and employers in others. In fact, as Table 47 makes evident, only seven craftsmen reported that they identified with employers in time of conflict. More significant however is the

Table 47.   *Whether or not workers or employers are supported in strikes and disputes*

	Brick-layers and Masons	Cabinet makers and Car-penters	Elec-tricians	Tool makers	Total Craft	Clerks	Managers
	Percentage						
Workers	48	43	38	48	44	34	8
Employers	3	4	4	4	4	9	24
Neither/It depends	49	53	58	48	52	57	68
Total per cent	100	100	100	100	100	100	100
Total number	35	49	55	54	193	44	38

fact that over half of the craft group, and a slightly higher proportion of clerks were *not* prepared to side with workers in an unqualified way. This is not the kind of finding one would expect in cases where skilled craftsmen had a clear concept of their manual class status, of their situational ties to blue collar workers generally. As it is, 44 per cent of skilled craftsmen are prepared to give *carte blanche* support to workers as opposed to employers or managers. For the clerical group the proportion is smaller, although the figure is far nearer that of the craftsmen than that of the managers. This latter group, as would be expected, is the only one to give any sizeable amount of unqualified support to employers.

Cross-tabulation of responses to one of these three measures of class consciousness by another, gives added weight to the picture built up from examination of responses to the three questions separately. Those who view a large firm more as football team than composed of two opposing parts are more likely, for example, to refuse to side with one camp or the other when asked whether they usually support management or workers. This means that only 25 of the 195 craftsmen regard large firms as comprising two opposed parts *and* are prepared to side with workers in industrial disputes, as it means that only one quarter of craftsmen think employers sometimes take advantage of working people *and* side with workers in periods of industrial strife. On the other hand, 75 craftsmen regard a football team as a fitting analogy of a large firm *and* refuse to automatically side with the workers in an industrial dispute, while 95 craftsmen regard a large firm like a football team and think that in general, working people are fairly and squarely treated. Only 21 craftsmen did not think a modern firm was like a football team as well as thinking that employers sometimes take advantage of their workpeople.

In summary, the level of class consciousness, as measured by these three questions, is very low within all three major occupational categories. Such factors as income, or proximity to white or blue collar employees in the work situation can make little difference to what is a fairly uniform pattern. The only exception to this is the effect of trade union membership. In the final question, the only one where craftsmen are, to an extent, divided, 56 per cent of union members said they usually sided with workers, as against only 20 per cent of the non-union group. In the other two questions, the pattern was such that union membership had little effect on response.

Trade unions

Although the situation is changing, traditionally both membership in, and support for, trade unions has been almost exclusively limited to manual workers. 'Show me two white collar workers on a picket line... and I'll organise the entire working class,' Samuel Gompers, one-time president of the A.F.L. once remarked.[15] As such, the ways in which re-

Table 48.   *Trade union membership and attendance at meetings*

	Brick-layer and Masons	Cabinet makers and Carpenters	Elec-tricians	Tool makers	Total Craft	Clerks	Managers
	Percentage						
Membership level	74	61	59	50	60	18	12
Total number	35	49	56	54	194	44	38
Regularity of attendance							
Often	57	23	55	30	42	12	—
Sometimes	31	30	21	45	31	25	100
Rarely	8	30	12	18	17	51	—
Never	4	17	12	7	10	12	—
Total per cent	100	100	100	100	100	100	100
Total number	26	30	33	27	116	8	4

spondents relate to the union movement provide important clues as to their general level of class consciousness. As can be seen in Table 48, by no means all of the blue collar workers interviewed belong to a union. Indeed, for the craft group as a whole, 40 per cent do not belong to a union, while for the toolmakers, this proportion rises to one half. It is clear then, that where union membership is not obligatory, as in closed shops, a large proportion of craftsmen elect not to join. The high level of membership found amongst the bricklayers is largely due to the structure of employment within the building industry which, as we have seen, is one of inherent instability. In this situation the union becomes very important in acting as a clearing house for jobs, or information about jobs and conditions generally. In addition, within the building trades the differential between union and non-union rates is considerable, providing an additional incentive for membership. In my sample, for example, 93 per cent of bricklayers and masons earning a family income of above $10,000 a year belonged to the union. Amongst those earning less than this figure the proportion was 62 per cent. In contrast, for the toolmakers there was virtually no difference between the two groups. A fairly large proportion of toolmakers also work in smaller owner-run firms where there is a greater tendency for unionism to be viewed as 'unnecessary'.

While the majority of the blue collar sample are members of a union, this cannot be regarded as a clear measure of identification with this working class organisation. Undoubtedly many people do work in closed shops, or experience pressure from workmates or friends to join the union when they have little personal commitment. Attendance at union meetings does, however, come closer to measuring interest in, and perhaps identification with, the union movement. Accordingly, those subjects who did belong to unions were asked whether they attended union meetings 'often, sometimes, rarely or never'. Responses to this question reveal a fairly high level of union participation. Again the bricklayers' and masons' group have a much higher proportion of members who attended meetings 'often' than have the other occupational groups, but over half of the union electricians also show this level of commitment. For the craft group as a whole, nearly three quarters of those who belonged to a union attended meetings 'often' or 'sometimes'. Only 10 per cent reported that they never went to union meetings.

Thus the picture emerging so far is one suggesting that while by no means all craftsmen belong to a trade union, those that do exhibit a fairly high level of commitment to that union. It is not, however, sufficient to demonstrate simply that somewhat less than half of the affluent workers I talked to take an active part in the union movement. In terms of our overriding consideration, that of class consciousness, it is also important that we explore the way in which these people view their union, and un-ionism generally. To this end *all* respondents were asked what they saw as being the prime purpose of trade unions. The categorised responses to this question are presented in Table 49. They are not difficult to interpret. For the majority of craftsmen as well as for the majority of both white collar occupational groups the purpose of trade unions is seen purely and simply as an instrumental and *personal* one. Over half of the respondents do not discuss the functions of trade unions in terms of advancing or protecting the interests of any collectivity or group as a whole, they certainly do not envisage the role of trade unions as being one of engagement in any form of class struggle, and least of all do they see the trade union movement as having anything to do with changing society. Instead, unions are there

Table 49. *Perception of the main purpose of trade unions*

	Brick-layers and Masons	Cabinet makers andCar-penters	Elec-tricians	Tool makers	Total Craft	Clerks	Managers
	Percentage						
Purely instrumental	69	48	48	54	54	60	59
Awareness of links to working class	9	18	16	21	16	18	22
Awareness of links in class conflict terms	11	20	23	19	19	8	—
Hostile/critical descriptions	8	6	4	6	6	7	11
Other	3	8	9	—	5	7	8
Total per cent	100	100	100	100	100	100	100
Total number	35	49	56	52	192	39	37

to increase the wages, the vacations, the working conditions or whatever of the *individual* worker. In the same way as he will bargain with the car salesman to get the best deal he can on a new car, his union will bargain with his employers to get the best deal it can for union members. As such the relationship between union and employers is a commercial one. It is a conflict relationship only insofar as any commercial relationship is a conflict one, and it is questioning the existing form of social structure only as much as the man buying a new car is questioning the concept of a money economy.

A carpenter who is not a member of a union has no illusions about working class solidarity. He sees the main purpose of unions as being to 'make better wages and benefits for the working man. Sometimes I wonder why I don't join it. I would have more benefits working for the union.' A toolmaker, clearly not over-anxious to stand united with his non-skilled brother replies: 'Recognition of your skill so that you're adequately paid and protected. America has progressed by it – the worker has been elevated socially, financially. Can now afford better – send his children to schools.' While another toolmaker, rather than fight for his class interests, sees unions as existing in order to 'improve working conditions on the whole, management and employee relationships, wages, job security'. Original unionists did not, one suspects, conceive of unions as existing in order to improve management – employee relations.

The impression that the majority of blue and white collar respondents conceive of trade unions essentially in instrumental and individualistic terms is reinforced by the pattern of responses to a further question. This was: 'Suppose there is a section of the country where very few workers are unionised. A drive is started to unionise the companies there. People all over the country are asked to give money to support the drive. Some people think they should give money, others think they shouldn't. How do you think you would feel about this? (This would be in addition to any union dues you might have paid.)' Here, I was concerned with finding out whether or not the worker sees unionism as only being relevant at the local level, where it directly affects him, or whether he sees it as being a national movement of which he is a part. In fact, for both union and non-union members, the former of these alternatives is the case. Only around one third of craft union members said they would give money, while for men who were not union members the figure was only 13 per cent. Amusingly, one quarter of both the clerical and managerial groups said they would subscribe, as perhaps they would to any deserving charity or occupational association. Further evidence, perhaps, for the picture that portrays the majority of respondents as viewing the trade union movement essentially in classless terms.

The fact that the majority of both union members and non-members see unions in this non-ideological, personal manner does not of course mean that no one in the sample is aware of the possibilities of unions being linked to a particular class, or even of unions being engaged in the class struggle. Indeed, as Table 49 shows, the only other picture of unions that emerged was one that described them in these terms. Thus, a number of all three occupational categories saw managers or owners and workers as com-comprising two different and separate groupings with unions representing one of these groupings. Key words that came up in this characterisation of unions were 'fair' and 'rights'. Respondents saw unions as existing to obtain a fair share of the profits, a fair wage, or to protect the rights of the workers. Comments such as 'to see that the working class shares in the profits'; 'to make sure the men are fairly treated and paid a fair wage' are indicative of this viewpoint. The minority, in other words, appears well aware of a structural division within industry and of the place of unions in that structure – unions are working for workers generally or for 'the working man'. Such a conceptualisation demonstrates, above all, the awareness of *groups*, but does *not* appear to recognise the possibility of endemic conflict between these groups, or the possibility of one group having to protect itself against the other.

However, 19 per cent of the total craft group do view unions within such a framework. Responses such as 'unions prevent exploitation of the worker'; 'working man without a union would be slave help'; 'they keep the manufacturers in line; if not, they'll push you all over the place' are illustrative. Nonetheless, as I have said, views such as these are definitely in the minority. By a margin of two to one those blue collar workers exhibiting this degree of class consciousness are the older members of the sample, i.e. between 45 and 65, and are themselves union members. Of the 197 craftsmen interviewed, only 37 gave answers that could be categorised in this way, as against the 102 who saw unions in individualist, instrumental terms. Equally important is the fact that not one manager, and only three clerks took this 'minority' view of unions.[16]

We have seen that the majority of skilled craftsmen do belong to a union, and the majority of union members attend union meetings at least 'sometimes'. However, their concept of the function of unions is very different from the traditional one. In general, they do not seem to see unions as having anything to do with the interests of a particular grouping or class, and even less to do with any form of conflict or struggle. Instead, unions are rather like a professional association, to gain as much for their individual members as possible, in the context of a commercial bargaining relationship between equals – union and management. This instrumental view of the role of trade unions in American society, plus the way in which the large firm, and employer – worker relationships are perceived (as discussed earlier in the chapter) leave little room for doubt that the level of class consciousness amongst these affluent craftsmen and white collar workers is minimal.

Conclusion

It is evident that the large majority of the people I interviewed possess a clear image of the American class structure, and of their own place within that structure. The ways in which typical middle and working class individuals were described, as well as the general refusal to distinguish between the class situation of clerks and craftsmen, give clear indication that the bases or criteria of social class placement are seen as being education, income and style of life – often referred to in terms of a causal chain. Similarly, the concepts of power and conflict are virtually absent from the models or images of class structure posited. While there is separation between the various social classes, and while one is superior to another, this superiority is seen in terms of a higher standard of living, or a better income.[17] The notion of competing interests and a resulting antagonism and perhaps organisation, appears to be irrelevant and meaningless. Indeed, increasingly we have been led to the conclusion that the class structure is not viewed as being qualitatively different from any other structure of groups in society. The married and the unmarried, the rural and the urban, the young and the old, tend to live differently, with little intermixing, and yet they are not *by definition* viewed as having competing interests or antogonistic relations. In the same way respondents view social classes as being separated, one from another, by differences in income, education or style of life. But this separation in no way involves enmity or the exercise of power. As such being working class means that one has a certain style of life, and spends one's time with individuals in a like situation. It assumes nothing about the way in which one should therefore relate to the middle class. Indeed the question does not arise.

Nonetheless, I am arguing that many of these affluent workers are seeing social class in *interactional* terms. Such a suggestion is at odds with the 'desocialised' perception of class structure held by Lockwood's ideal typical 'privatised worker'. In this perception, status, based solely on the possession of material goods, is a continuum along which virtually the whole population is strung out. One can move up or down this continuum simply by increasing or decreasing one's income and therefore material possessions. Because for a variety of reasons the contemporary worker has become inward looking, and because the possession of goods is such a fluid determinant, the modern affluent worker does not regard prestige as being a phenomenon that manifests itself in group relations. It is 'not seen in terms of the association of status equals sharing a similar style of life'. The relational dimension of class and the concomitant existence of boundaries between classes is not therefore regarded as being anything to do with prestige or style of life.[18]

In certain respects we have found these skilled affluent workers and indeed clerical workers to exhibit many of the characteristics enumerated by

Lockwood as being symptomatic of the privatised worker. However, this neglecting or ignoring of the group characteristic of social stratification does not appear to be one of them. Unfortunately, the interview schedule did not contain any questions directly related to this dimension of social class. Nevertheless, despite this omission, 45 per cent of the total craft group and around two thirds of the clerical and managerial groups, in their discussion of the bases of social class, referred *explicitly* to the fact that social class has to do with the *interaction* of individuals in a like situation. The following comments are representative:

> An electrician:
> 'They (craftsmen and clerks) belong to the same churches, clubs, organisations – play golf.'

> An electrician:
> 'The run of the mill office worker isn't qualified to associate with higher-ups than him – so he has no choice but to socialise with craftsmen.'

> A mason:
> 'Surely – they (craftsmen and clerks) run around together – they all accept each other as equals.'

> A clerk:
> 'As a rule the man in the office wouldn't associate with a craftsman.'

> A toolmaker:
> 'They marry office workers – as a general feeling of identity between them (craftsmen and clerks) – the same general outlook and desires.'

> A carpenter:
> 'We fraternise together – they (clerks) don't look down their nose at us any more – they go to the same organisations, live in the same neighbourhoods, drive the same cars, their kids go to the same schools.'

> A manager:
> 'A middle class person is one who has a responsible position, good income, nice home life, nice people to associate with'.

I am suggesting, in other words, that the affluent craftsmen we talked to, as well as the clerks and managers, were *aware* of social class. But they were not *conscious* of it in the Marxian sense of the term.

7   The Web of Associations

It would be difficult to overemphasise the importance of the relational component of class position. While changes in life chances, value and behavioural patterns may comprise a necessary condition for the breakdown of class differentials they are not themselves a sufficient condition for such structural change. It is also necessary that individuals finding themselves in a new class situation are *accepted* as equals by the existing members of that class, in both formal and informal interaction. We have seen, in the previous chapter, that the large number of clerks and craftsmen now regard themselves as members of the same social class: physical labour is no longer perceived as a 'disqualification' from social intercourse. It remains to determine if, *in reality*, these people are social equals: whether, *as a group*, they intermingle freely, and whether, *as a group*, they can be distinguished from others within the class structure. I hope to do this by focusing first on patterns of interaction, and secondly, on the content of that interaction.

Patterns of Interaction

In order to gain some idea of the extent to which blue and white collar workers were associating freely with one another, respondents were asked to report the occupations of the five people with whom they spent most time socially. Few were unable or unwilling to do this. Comments such as those received by Berger, in his study of automobile workers – 'we're not much on socialising' or 'I don't think it pays to have a lot of friends' were few and far between.[1] Instead, around one third of each occupational group were able to account for five friends with whom they spent time socially, while only 19 per cent of the total craft group, 16 per cent of clerks and 24 per cent of managers, could not refer to at least three such people.

The extent to which clerks, craftsmen and managers do treat one another as social equals can best be tested by measuring the extent to which their patterns of friendship interaction are similar. I have used as a measure of similarity, or rather dissimilarity, an index of dissimilarity applied in a number of other studies concerned with similar problems.[2] It involves in this case taking the sum of positive percentage differences between the friendship choices of each pair of the occupational groups. If their friendship choices are identical in composition the index has a value of 0. If there are no overlaps the value is 100. It must be emphasised that while we can interpret indices of dissimilarity relatively, we cannot regard them as representing absolute differences. We can say, for example, that the pattern of association of group A is more similar to that of group B than it is to that of group C. But we are not able to measure these relative differences exactly. Finally, this statistical technique is in no way concerned with the *content* of patterns of interaction. It merely enables us to determine the extent to which these patterns of interaction between two or more occupational groups are similar, no matter what these patterns might be; it is their content that I discuss in the following section.

In Table 50 are shown the indices of dissimilarity of the patterns of association in which members of the six occupational categories are involved. The contents of that table are clear and unambiguous: the four craft groups are clustered together at the lower end of the scale, separated by a considerable distance from the clerks, who themselves exhibit an interactional pattern clearly distinct from that of managers. The two occupational groupings exhibiting the most nearly identical patterns of interaction are the bricklayers and electricians. The former of these two groups and carpenters are the two craft categories who have the least similar friendship patterns, but the difference is still small (19.7), and nowhere as large as that separating carpenters from clerks (31.0).

More interesting than these simple comparisons, however, is the treatment of the data in such a way as to examine the extent and nature of the *structuring* of the dissimilarities of patterns of association. Are they, for example, ordered in a way which could be meaningfully related to a stratification hierarchy? A first approach entails the use of Coombs' unfolding technique.[3] This is a means of exposing the regularities in preference choices of individuals, or, as in this case, groups of individuals. If one takes similarity of patterns of association as analogous to preference,

Table 50.   *Indices of dissimilarity in patterns of association*

	Brick-layers	Elec-tricians	Tool-makers	Car-penters	Clerks	Managers
1 Bricklayers	—					
2 Electricians	9.0	—				
3 Toolmakers	15.4	9.7	—			
4 Carpenters	19.7	16.2	11.8	—		
5 Clerks	44.5	37.5	31.8	31.0	—	
6 Managers	58.5	51.3	44.8	43.9	29.6	—

Table 51. *Rank orderings of similarities between patterns of association*

	1st choice	2nd choice	3rd choice	4th choice	5th choice
1 Bricklayers	Electricians	Toolmakers	Carpenters	Clerks	Managers
2 Electricians	Bricklayers	Toolmakers	Carpenters	Clerks	Managers
3 Toolmakers	Electricians	Carpenters	Bricklayers	Clerks	Managers
4 Carpenters	Toolmakers	Electricians	Bricklayers	Clerks	Managers
5 Clerks	Managers	Carpenters	Toolmakers	Electricians	Bricklayers
6 Managers	Clerks	Carpenters	Toolmakers	Electricians	Bricklayers

then from the figures in Table 50 can be constructed the patterns of ranked
'choice' for each occupation of all other occupational groups. Table 51
gives these results. The patterns are consistent with ranging the groups
along a *single* dimension. The ordering along that dimension is bricklayers, electricians, toolmakers, carpenters, clerks and finally managers.
We have also one further piece of information: because carpenters 'prefer'
bricklayers to clerks the gap between carpenters and clerks is potentially
the largest anywhere on the dimension. Only the gap between clerks and
managers, about which we have no information by this method, could be
larger. *The separation of manual and non-manual occupations is therefore
very distinct.*

While unidimensional unfolding has told us something of the structuring of similarities of friendship patterns, it has also been wasteful of
information. As I have already made clear, we are not able to use the indices of dissimilarity as absolute measures of distance, but if we accept that
they are in the correct order, then they can be used for a more rigorous
analysis using multidimensional scaling. The problem is to find a space
with sufficient dimensions to represent the ordered distances among points
(the occupational groups) in the data and to place the points in that space.
Using the numbers against occupations in Table 50 the rank ordering of
distances between all occupations is shown in Table 52.

Table 52. *Rank ordering of inter-point distances between patterns of
association*

Basic distances	Solution distances	Basic distances	Solution distances	Basic distances	Solution distances
1 – 2	5.00	1 – 4	18.00	4 – 6	37.90
2 – 3	6.00	5 – 6	18.02	1 – 5	38.00
3 – 4	7.00	4 – 5	20.00	3 – 6	44.89
1 – 3	11.00	3 – 5	27.00	2 – 6	50.88
2 – 4	13.00	2 – 5	33.00	1 – 6	55.87

Table 53. *The positioning of patterns of association in two dimensional space*

	1st co-ordinate	2nd co-ordinate
Point 1 (Bricklayers)	-21.312	-0.467
Point 2 (Electricians)	-16.312	-0.467
Point 3 (Toolmakers)	-10.312	-0.467
Point 4 (Carpenters)	-3.312	-0.467
Point 5 (Clerks)	$+16.688$	-0.467
Point 6 (Managers)	$+34.488$	$+2.333$
Per cent of variance	99.72	0.28

This set of ordered distances is no longer completely compatible with a single dimension.[4] The distances can, however, be represented in two dimensions where the second dimension is very small indeed; so small that it may be regarded as insignificant. A possible set of positions of the points in two dimension is given in Table 53. Again, it is evident that the patterns of association of the four craft groups are analogous and can be clearly distinguished from those of either clerks or managers. In addition, the latter two white collar categories cannot be regarded as a homogeneous group: their friendship patterns in turn are easily separable. This means that while blue and white collar workers alike may *see* each other as social equals, in *relational* terms they remain isolated. Despite substantial gains on the part of skilled craftsmen and a movement away from the established middle class on the part of lower level clerical workers, it is not sociologically meaningful to regard these people as members of the same social class. This must be regarded as perhaps my most important finding.

The Content of Interaction

Table 54 shows, in two ways, the extent to which blue and white collar workers alike recruit their friends from only a limited sector of the division of labour: first with regard to the occupational distribution of the total number of friends mentioned; secondly in terms of the occupational spread *within* respondents' friendship sets. In that part of Table 54 devoted to the make-up of friendship sets, I have included all respondents who reported having at least one friend with whom they spent time socially. Thus the category 'all friends manual workers' includes respondents with perhaps only two friends as well as those reporting five friends, all of whom were blue collar workers. Similarly, the category 'majority of friends non-manual workers' contains individuals who have four white and one blue collar friend, in addition to those who may fraternise with two people in non-manual occupations and one who works with his hands.

The content of the dissimilar patterns of friendship enjoyed by clerks,

Table 54. *Occupations of friends*

	Brick-layers and Masons	Cabinet makers and Car-penters	Elec-tricians	Tool makers	Total Craft	Clerks	Managers
	Percentage						
Total number of friends							
Non-manual workers	20	37	26	34	30	63	86
Skilled craftsmen	55	43	53	48	49	17	8
Other manual workers	25	20	21	18	21	20	6
Total per cent	100	100	100	100	100	100	100
Total number	124	178	203	190	695	157	138
Friendship sets							
All friends manual workers	46	31	35	38	37	7	3
Majority of friends manual workers	37	27	39	25	32	21	3
Friends manual & non-manual workers equally	14	10	13	8	11	12	8
Majority of friends non-manual workers		16	9	17	11	30	24
All friends non-manual workers	3	16	4	12	9	30	62
Total per cent	100	100	100	100	100	100	100
Total number	35	49	54	52	190	43	37
Mean number of friends							
	3.54	3.63	3.76	3.65	3.66	3.65	3.73

craftsmen, and managers is evident. Overwhelmingly blue collar workers chose other blue collar employees as friends, while clerks and managers remain similarly isolated. Within the four craft groups between 63 per cent and 80 per cent of the total number of friends mentioned were also manual workers. And these figures in themselves do not exhaust the degree of particularism shown by the craft workers in their choice of friends. For of considerable importance is the fact that skilled workers would not appear to choose friends randomly from within the traditional working class, i.e. from the total population of blue collar workers. Instead, by a margin of considerably more than two to one leisure time companions are selected only from within the ranks of the skilled. Furthermore, it would be dangerous to assume that such people are recruited from within an individual's own particular skill or trade. Instead, the evidence is clear that we are witnessing the operation of class as well as occupational pressures.

For example, an electrician identified his leisure time companions (none of whom were relatives) as being a mechanic, a plumber, a tinsmith, an electrician and a machinist. As would be expected, such catholic tastes were not found among all craft respondents. One cabinet maker, for example, fraternised with eight other cabinet makers, none of whom were relatives, while his social life looks positively meagre alongside that of the electrician who relaxed with a maintenance man in a power plant, a claims clerk and an armoured car driver (all of whom were brothers-in law) and fifteen electricians, none of whom were related. Nonetheless, such men are the exception: the majority of craft respondents spend their leisure time with other skilled men from a variety of trades. It would seem that while both Mayer and Lenski were wrong in their support of the thesis of *embourgeoisement* they were only too right in emphasising that sociologists must begin to focus their attention on divisions *within* the working class.

To the extent that craftsmen do chose non-craft friends however, the likelihood would seem to be that they spend time with white collar rather than non-skilled blue collar companions. This should not be regarded as surprising: it will be remembered that almost half of the manual respondents considered non-skilled workers to be in a class lower than that occupied by skilled craftsmen. This pattern is especially predominant in the case of the toolmakers, and cabinet makers and carpenters. Within both of these occupational groups one third of the total number of friends mentioned were white collar workers, and not necessarily low level white collar workers at that. Thus a toolmaker numbered among his friends, again none of whom were related, a newspaper pressman, a foreman, two executives and an engineer. Not to be outdone, a fellow toolmaker reported as his friends a record analyist working for the state, a factory foreman, a chartered accountant, a master plumber and a percussionist with the Rhode Island symphony orchestra. Unskilled manual workers are relatively rare, the one exception being in the case of the bricklayers and masons, several of whom cited non-craft construction workers among their friends. Again the importance of differential work situation is demonstrated.

The distinction between skilled and unskilled manual work does not appear to be as relevant in the eyes of clerks as it does in those of craftsmen. In those cases where clerks had chosen friends from the other side of the blue collar/white collar line, they would appear to spend time with skilled and unskilled workers in about equal proportions. Thus one clerk counted a banker, a lawyer, a truck driver, a barber and a construction worker amongst his leisure time companions, while occupations such as fireman, policeman, and other service occupations were in evidence. Nonetheless, in general clerks seem to spend their leisure time with people who are also in the lower echelons of the white collar hierarchy – other office workers, shipping clerks, expeditors, estimators, railroad inspectors, salesmen – as well as with people that can be categorised as members of the semi-professions: social workers, computer programmers, real estate or insurance agents. Leisure time companions who were drawn from upper level management or from the professions were, in most cases, conspicuous by their absence.

This is, however, not the situation with regard to the managerial group in the sample. Again, the picture that has emerged throughout the analysis – that of the disassociation of managers from craftsmen and clerks alike – is apparent. As a group these upper level white collar workers were able to muster a total of only 19 blue collar friends. Indeed, as far as friendship is concerned, over 60 per cent of them were completely isolated from any form of contact with manual workers. Instead occupations such as doctor, lawyer, stock broker, banker, teacher and professor figure in the friendship sets of these people with monotonous regularity. Perhaps the most politically liberal manager I interviewed spent leisure time with two lawyers, a university professor and a stockbroker. Of the total number of 119 white collar friends possessed by the managerial group only six were lower clerical workers and only nine were salesmen of whatever kind. The picture is unambiguous; first, individuals in the upper reaches of the white collar hierarchy remain as isolated from lower level clerical workers as they do from people who work with their hands; secondly, the changes experienced by clerks and craftsmen in the post-war years have not led to a fusing of the two groups outside of the work situation.

One of the most obvious explanations of this latter situation would involve reference to the extended family structure typical of what has been the traditional working class. The supreme influence exerted by the family upon every aspect of working class life has, until at least the present time, been a commonplace. Furthermore, as I have shown in chapter 3, manual and non-manual respondents alike continue to be involved in frequent interaction with kin. Given the fact that overwhelmingly the clerks and craftsmen in the sample are from working class backgrounds, it follows that if the extended family continues to exert an influence in the latter half of the twentieth century, than the leisure time companions of skilled craftsmen might well be recruited largely from the blue collar labour force. This would also help to explain why the clerks I interviewed are, in this sense, the most liberal of the various occupational groupings – mixing more with blue collar workers than do craftsmen with white collar employees. (It will be remembered that 37 of the 44 clerks in the study are from manual backgrounds.)

In this particular case however, reference to extended family networks cannot explain the nature of the patterns of association I have found among these craftsmen, clerks or managers. For within these occupational groupings relatives play only a minor part in friendship sets. For the craft group as a whole, only 25 per cent of the total number of leisure time companions are relatives. For the clerks and managers the comparable figures are 20 per cent and 16 per cent respectively. Within the craft category, bricklayers and masons are the group having the largest proportion (30 per cent) of relatives amongst their leisure time companions, while the lowest figure (22 per cent) is to be found within both the tool-makers and the cabinet makers and carpenters.

Not only do relatives comprise a fraction of leisure time companions, they are by no means evenly distributed throughout the sample. Indeed, with the exception of two of the craft groups, over half of the respondents did not name a single relative as being one of the people with whom they spent most time socially. The composition of friendship sets, in terms of relatives versus non-relatives is shown below in Table 55. The contents of this table can only be described as startling. That kin should play such a relatively minor part in the social lives of a large group of manual workers runs counter to the picture built up over the last forty years, a picture that is the summation of a large number of empirical investigations. In the present study, not only do the friendship sets of such a large number of craftsmen contain no relatives at all, but the majority of those who do spend leisure time with kin could only name one such person. Indeed, for the craft group as a whole slightly less than one quarter referred to two or more relatives as being leisure time companions.

Table 55. *Relatives and non-relatives in friendship sets*

	Brick-layers and Mason	Cabinet makers and Carpenters	Electricians	Tool-makers	Total Craft	Clerks	Managers
	Percentage						
All companions non-relatives	37	53	32	52	43	58	62
Majority of companions non-relatives	37	29	46	23	34	28	19
Companions relatives and non-relatives equally	9	8	7	11	9	2	11
Majority of companions relatives	11	6	6	10	8	7	8
All companions relatives	6	4	9	4	6	5	—
Total per cent	100	100	100	100	100	100	100
Total number	35	49	54	52	190	43	37

Table 56. *Occupations of related and non-related friends*

	Brick-layers and Masons	Cabinet makers and Carpenters	Elec-tricians	Tool-makers	Total Craft	Clerks	Managers
	Percentage						
Blue collar friends							
Friends	73	84	73	81	78	80	68
Relatives	27	16	27	19	22	20	32
Total per cent	100	100	100	100	100	100	100
Total number	99	111	150	126	486	56	19
White collar friends							
Friends	60	68	71	73	70	81	86
Relatives	40	32	29	27	30	19	14
Total per cent	100	100	100	100	100	100	100
Total number	25	66	52	64	207	97	118

In the case of the two white collar groups the proportions were even smaller.*

On the other hand, kinship *is* associated with the existence of friendship circles involving people wearing a different colour collar to oneself. Information regarding this relationship is presented in Table 56. In other words, the fact that managers and craftsmen do intermingle with people on the other side of the blue collar/white collar line can be partially explained by the fact that blood ties already exist. However two points should be made: first, this is not the case within the clerical group, where kinship would seem to exert no influence on choice of companion; secondly, even within the craft groups, familial influence would not seem to be particularly strong: the fact remains that 70 per cent of the white collar friends of craftsmen are *not* relatives. It is apparent, therefore, that kinship exerts only a minor influence on the patterns of friendship enjoyed by affluent manual and non-manual workers alike.

---

* At first glance the low number of relatives mentioned as leisure time companions is puzzling, given the fact I have already demonstrated that clerks and craftsmen alike see kinfolk at least once a week. However, these findings are not incompatible: it is evident that these people do not regard dropping by a parent or brother's house as necessarily constituting part of their social life. This is especially the case among those respondents who regard *particular* relatives as leisure time companions, in addition to other relatives who they may 'drop by' or 'stop in on' once or twice a week for a coffee, a beer, or a chat. For example, a toolmaker whose father and in-laws lived in the area saw them nearly every day for 'talk – discussions – happenings of the day – ordinary day to day talk'. Yet of the five people with whom he spent most time socially four were non-relatives and one was his brother-in-law. When he and his wife got together with friends, which happened at least once a week, they would 'talk – visit in each other's homes – go out together sometimes – plays, a restaurant together – picnics'.

The finding that clerks, craftsmen and managers spend part of their leisure time with people from similar and dissimilar occupations to themselves cannot be explained, to any great extent, by reference to the sway of the extended family.

An alternative explanation of these friendship sets would be that they result from the class homogeneity of traditional working class and established middle class communities. In the North East especially, the cross-cutting influences of class and ethnicity have, in the past, contributed to the existence of tightly knit communities, ecologically distinct from other areas of the city, and internally devoid of large income, ethnic or occupational distinctions. The lower class Italian community of 'Cornerville' in Boston is perhaps the best known and documented in the literature of sociology.[5] To the extent, for example, that affluent craftsmen continue to live in such areas, and to the extent therefore that they remain ecologically separate from white collar workers, then we would expect the friendship sets of such people to reflect this ecological segregation. Such a hypothesis is especially attractive, as we have already seen in chapter 4 that affluent craftsmen are not living in the higher status neighbourhoods of the city that economically are within their reach.

Again, however, the data do not lend support to such an explanation. For in a city that has certainly in the past exhibited a high degree of spatial segregation in terms of ethnic and economic variables, there is little evidence that such segregation continues to exist. Table 57 gives important clues as to the dispersion of individuals in the various occupations throughout the city of Providence. Even within the managerial grouping, separate from clerks and craftsmen on so many dimensions of social class, a substantial proportion live next door to a blue collar worker. It would appear that the occupational composition of the areas of residence of clerical and craft workers are virtually identical: members of both categories would seem to live in areas where manual workers are in the majority, but where upper and lower level white collar workers represent a sizeable minority.

Not only are the occupational compositions of the communities in which respondents live far from homogeneous, it is also apparent that neighbours do not constitute a major source of friends or companions. 60 per cent of the total craft group and 73 per cent and 68 per cent of the the clerks and managers did not report a single neighbour as being one of the people with whom they spent time socially.[6] For the craft group as a whole, no more than 17 per cent included two or more neighbours as being amongst their close friends. Only two clerks and five managers did likewise. This minimal positition occupied by neighbours within friendship sets would seem to hold no matter how many leisure time companions a respondent might report. Craftsmen who might have five or six close friends showed no greater tendency to include one or two neighbours

Table 57.   *Occupations of neighbours*

	Brick-layers and Masons	Cabinet makers and Carpenters	Electricians	Tool-makers	Total Craft	Clerks	Managers
	Percentage						
Occupations of two next door neighbours							
Professionals & Managers	16	18	23	17	20	24	44
Clerical and Sales workers	10	15	11	12	12	11	6
Skilled craftsmen	29	24	26	29	26	26	16
Non-skilled and service workers	17	27	19	16	20	21	14
D.K., retired	28	16	21	26	22	18	20
Total per cent	100	100	100	100	100	100	100
Total number	70	98	112	108	388	88	76
*Exposure to white collar neighbours							
Neither neighbour white collar	48	37	43	47	43	43	21
One neighbour white collar	43	55	40	33	43	33	32
Both neighbours white collar	9	8	17	20	14	24	46
Total per cent	100	100	100	100	100	100	100
Total number	23	38	40	36	137	33	28

* Includes only those respondents reporting the occupations of *two* neighbours.

in that five or six than did people with only one or two leisure time companions. In total, out of the 695 friends reported by the craft sample only 133 (19 per cent) were neighbours. Similarly only 14 (9 per cent) of the clerks reported companions lived in the vicinity. As in our discussion of the influence of family, it is clear that community or neighbourhood cannot be seen as playing a significant role in shaping patterns of association.

A similar picture emerges when one looks at the number of workmates who are represented within individual friendship sets. Fully three quarters of the managerial and clerical sub-samples, and 68 per cent of the total craft group failed to name a single friend with whom they worked. In total 129 (19 per cent) of the 695 friends listed by the craft sample were also workmates. Similarly, of the 342 skilled craftsmen named by the total craft group as being among their leisure time companions, only 41 per cent were in the same trade as the respondent naming them. Indeed, for three of the craft groups the proportion was around one third, but in the case of the bricklayers and masons it was 60 per cent. This latter group is clearly the most occupationally isolated of the four craft groups. It will be remembered that bricklayers and masons had relatively fewer white collar and more unskilled blue collar friends than did any of the other manual groups in our sample. Nonetheless, the majority of craftsmen had almost twice as many friends who were in skilled crafts other than their own than they did friends possessing similar skills. This is a finding of considerable importance for the analysis. In order to claim that craftsmen and clerks are not members of the same social class, it is necessary to demonstrate that their relative isolation from each other is a result of forces emanating from their respective class situations rather than (or in addition to) mere occupational differences. For example, it would not be difficult to demonstrate that sociologists and architects are similarly isolated from each other's friendship sets, and yet in terms of the class structure both might be in an identical situation. In this instance the manner in which sociologists and architects practise their professions means that they are rarely exposed to each other and thus have little opportunity to develop friendships across occupational lines. Instead, the chances are high that sociologists will number a good many academics among their friends, while architects will recruit their companions largely from the building and related professions.

It is therefore important I show that the isolation of clerks and craftsmen from each other cannot be explained by reference to similar processes. The fact that electricians are mixing with masons, toolmakers, tinsmiths and mechanics away from the work situation more than they are mixing with other electricians, plus the fact that they are not spending time with clerks, goes a long way to demonstrate that indeed the line of demarcation separating clerks and craftsmen is a class, and not merely an occupational division.

Conclusion

It is evident that notwithstanding changes in real income and material possessions, in style of life and the structure of work tasks, in family size and aspirations for children, it is not possible to argue that individuals on alternate sides of the blue collar/white collar line now share a common class situation. This is despite the fact that clerks and craftsmen alike *view* each other as social equals. Likewise, it is difficult to regard managers as anything but a distinct and qualitatively different grouping.

Furthermore, the selectivity evidenced by clerks and managers alike in their choice of friends cannot be explained simply by reference to forces emanating from the family, the job or the community. To be sure these people do have leisure time companions who are drawn from one or the other of these groupings, but the majority of these companions are not relatives, workmates or neighbours.

Within the craft category the situation is somewhat different: while

Table 58. *Status of friends*

	Brick-layers and Masons	Cabinet makers and Car-penters	Elec-tricians	Tool-makers	Total Craft	Clerks	Managers
	Percentage						
Relatives	30	22	28	22	25	20	16
Neighbours	12	18	24	19	19	9	17
Workmates	24	21	18	13	19	15	11
*Other	34	39	30	46	37	56	56
Total per cent	100	100	100	100	100	100	100
Total number	124	178	203	190	695	157	138

* Regrettably, the data do not allow us to ascertain the degree of overlap, if any, existing betwen the first three categories of the table. This means, for example, that if a companion is both a relative and neighbour he will appear in both rows. The 'Other' category is therefore probably under-reported within every occupational grouping.

relatively small proportions of leisure time companions are relatives *or* workmates *or* neighbours, as Table 58 shows, *overall* such people account for around two thirds of the total number of friends mentioned by these respondents. Again, these blue collar workers would appear to be in a situation distinct from both the traditional working class and the established middle class. To be sure, their friendship circles are not based solely on familial, occupational or neighbourhood ties. But at the same time, they seem to be 'making' or 'finding' friends to a lesser extent than either upper or lower level white collar workers.

8   Conclusions

In general, the data I have presented indicate that statements about *the* middle class or *the* working class in American society are insufficiently precise, while hypotheses relating to the merging or blending or these two groupings into a single class or 'middle mass' are simply inaccurate. If anything, the situation is becoming more, not less, complex. In particular I have argued that there exists in the middle ranges of the American class structure an aristocracy of skilled labour, isolated both from the working class and from the lower reaches of the established middle class. It may be of value at this point to summarise some of the more important findings upon which I base this conclusion.

There can be little doubting the relative affluence enjoyed by skilled manual workers. In this particular study, their mean annual income was $7,590, while that of lower level clerical workers was $6,180. Indeed, more than 30 of the electricians and toolmakers received wages in excess of $10,000 per annum. In addition, these manual workers appeared to be in a more secure position economically than has, in the past, been the case. The work of Burns, discussed in chapter 2, shows that in the period 1898–1952, craftsmen's earnings were far more subject to changes in the volume of economic activity than were those of white collar workers. However, 85 per cent of the skilled workers in the present study considered their jobs to be 'quite secure', while only 17 per cent (nearly all bricklayers or carpenters) had been put out of work through no fault of their own at any time during the period 1962–7. Finally, the level of job satisfaction found amongst the craft sample was, if anything, *higher* than that experienced by the clerical employees.

To an extent the economic situation of these skilled craftsmen was reflected in an 'affluent' style of life, although the data indicate clearly that statements claiming that blue collar workers are adopting a middle class life style are as inaccurate as they are simplistic. In particular, it is important to make abundantly clear the distinction between behaving or acting in a certain way and the significance or meaning attached to that action by the subjects themselves. The importance of this distinction was perhaps most evident in the reasons given by craftsmen in explanation of their preference for buying rather than renting their homes. To be sure, in owning their own homes, these blue collar workers were behaving in a way that superficially could be regarded as indicative of the breakdown of class barriers. The reasons they gave for doing so, however, left little room for doubt that this was not the case.

Throughout much of the foregoing analysis I have been at pains to argue that craftsmen must be viewed as being in a class by themselves, largely as a result of their positit!on in the division of labour and the amount of formal education to which they had been exposed. And nowhere was the influence of these factors more apparent than in the analysis of the ways in which these people brought up their children, the hopes they had for them, and the extent to which those hopes were realised. For while blue collar parents may cherish high educational and subsequently, occupational aspirations for their offspring (though not nearly as high as those verbalised by the two sets of white collar parents), the fact that these people had themselves not been exposed to the world of higher education meant that they had little or no knowledge regarding how to prepare a son or daughter for success in that world. Indeed, I suggested, to the extent that blue collar parents rear their children to conform to externally imposed rules or standards, they are, in a sense, *preventing* them from achieving the educational and occupational success by which those same parents set so much store. As such the skilled blue collar family was seen as being directly associated with the perpetuation or maintenance of class differences from one generation to another. In contrast, the overwhelming majority of parents within the managerial sample had been undergraduates themselves and now move in an occupational sphere demanding initiative, independence and self-confidence; their children were accordingly brought up to internalise such values. Not surprisingly, therefore, the highest level of congruence between occupational and educational aspirations on the one hand, and achievement in these spheres on the other, was found amongst the families of these businessmen and executives.

Finally, the fact that America is not a middle class or even classless society is most readily apparent in the findings on patterns of association in which the blue and white collar workers, who are the subject of this study, were involved. And those patterns of association are clear and unambiguous: not only are craftsmen and clerks largely isolated from each other in the workplace, they also do not interact with each other to any extent outside of working hours. This is despite members of both groups possessing an image of class structure in which skilled manual and routine non-manual workers are viewed as members of the same class. In reality, however, skilled workers overwhelmingly chose other blue collar workers as friends, of whom the large majority were *also* skilled. In this instance congruity does exist between these people's view of the American class structure and the patterns of interaction in which they are involved: one half of the craftsmen regarded non-skilled workers as their social inferiors,

usually citing differences in income, education, or style of life in justification of this view. One respondent, for example, was quick to point
that he wouldn't have an unskilled worker in the house because such a man
would have 'failed' to learn a trade. Accordingly, only one fifth of the
leisure time companions reported by the total sample of craft workers were
non-skilled.

In this and earlier chapters, my central thesis has been to show that skilled
workers cannot be viewed as part of an amorphous 'middle mass', but
rather comprise a separate and distinct grouping within the American
class structure. As illustrative of this argument I give below 'portraits'
of two of the craftsmen in the study: a toolmaker and an electrician. I am
not, of course, claiming that *all* the people I interviewed exhibit every
one of these characteristics. Nor am I suggesting that these profiles can be
regarded as ideal types. They have been chosen simply because, in my
view, they indicate clearly some of the unique features of the position of the
skilled craftsman in contemporary American society.[1]

Peter Donovan, Toolmaker

The Donovans, a family of four, had only just moved into their house
in the north section of Providence when I interviewed them in 1967.
The house had cost over $17,500 and was the first they had owned in the
twelve years they had been married. Mrs Donovan has not worked since
their marriage although previously she operated a sewing machine in a
textile factory.

Mr Donovan works in a large factory just outside Providence making
precision tools which are themselves used in the making of cutlery.
He served a five year apprenticeship as well as attending a trade school
for a further period of twenty-four months. He is 'very satisfied' with his
job as 'it's creative – not repetitious at all', and although he considers
his chances of promotion to foreman to be 'good', he has no aspirations
in this direction. Mr Donovan works on average 52 hours per week, for
which he receives over $10,000 a year. He considers his job to be 'quite
secure' and has not lost any time, either because of industrial action or
because of slack business conditions, in the last five years. He will receive
a pension from his employer upon retirement. Although a member of
a trade union, Peter Donovan does not attend meetings very often, and
does not view the union movement in ideological terms. In his view, unions
exist so that workers can engage in collective bargaining. He would not
donate money to a union drive in another part of the country, is happy
with the size of his pay cheque and thinks that in general employees are
fairly treated by their employers. In keeping with these views, Mr Donovan
is an independent politically 'because I believe in voting for the right
man', although he sees the Democratic party as coming closest to his

interests and in fact supported the Democratic candidate in the 1960 and 1964 presidential elections.

The Donovan's social life is not extensive. Neither husband nor wife belong to any clubs or organisations and although they spend time with friends at least twice a week this consists simply of chatting and watching television. Indeed, Mr Donovan reported that they never went to the cinema, theatre, or attended a concert and tended to eat out no more than once a month. They do have people to dinner, but they are more likely to be relatives than friends. In addition he sees his parents, who live locally, on average once a week. For his two week holiday each year they 'just stay home and relax'.

In terms of perception of class structure Mr Donovan sees himself and his family as middle class because he has 'quite a bit of education' (he is a high school graduate) and is 'earning above $8,000 a year'. Further-more, he considers craftsmen to be in a higher social class than office workers as the 'demand is great' for skilled workers and income is correspondingly high. These same reasons were offered in explanation of the view that craftsmen were also in a higher social class than non-skilled workers. This image of the social order corresponds closely with the kinds of people that are included amongst Mr Donovan's friendship sets. He named four people with whom he spent leisure time, none of whom were relatives – a mason, a toolmaker, a printer and a man who owned and ran a nursery. (At work Mr Donovan has no contact at all with people who work in the offices, interacting only with other toolmakers and periodically, a foreman.)

At the time of the interview the Donovans had a boy who had not yet started school and a girl who was in a parochial grammar school (the family is Catholic). Mr Donovan hopes that both children will become college graduates, although he also said he wouldn't mind if a son of his chose a manual or non-manual occupation after leaving school. Both the son and daughter were being brought up to possess 'respect, honesty and fear of God'. Neither parent was a member of the P.T.A. and Mr Donovan had 'no idea' which type of college he'd like his children to attend, although he did feel 'fairly strongly' that a college education was desirable.

Joseph Bertoldi, Electrician

None of Joseph Bertoldi's six children attended college, although all of them are high school graduates (a level not attained by either of their parents). Two of the boys are electricians like their father, while a third is a building contractor. The three girls are now married and not working outside the home. Nevertheless, they remain a close family, getting to-gether at least once a week to 'enjoy the grandchildren – eat and drink together' in the elder Bertoldis' basement recreation room. Less time is spent with non-related friends, although once or twice a month they 'go for a ride, stop and have something to eat'. Three of Mr Bertoldi's friends are also electricians, while a fourth is a carpenter. But although at work he 'sometimes comes into contact with clerks and bookkeepers, *none* of the people with whom he spends leisure time are non-manual workers. Like Mr Donovan, neither Joseph Bertoldi nor his wife belong to any voluntary organisations. Similarly they are neither cinema nor concert goers, but do visit the theatre about twice a year. Several magazines – *Look, Popular Science, Popular Mechanix* – are taken in the house, although neither husband nor wife spends any time during the week reading a book. A good deal of time is spent watching television, comedy and sport programmes being the most popular.

Mr Bertoldi is employed as a chief electrician by a large department store. He enjoys a good measure of freedom in the work situation, finds the work 'very interesting' and his pay 'fair' and thus, not surprisingly, is 'very satisfied' with his present situation. Although, in 1967, he was 60 years of age, and earning over $10,000 a year he fully expected his wage to increase in the future. In fact the only negative aspect of his job mentioned by Mr Bertoldi was the lack of opportunities for promotion.

Class situation, for Mr Bertoldi, was based very much on income. He regarded himself as a member of the middle class because 'I earn enough' and was very much aware that financially he was in a more fortunate position than either routine office workers or non-skilled manual workers. However, being in accord with Wilensky, in viewing the centre of the American class structure as comprising a large 'middle mass', Mr Bertoldi did not regard craftsmen as being members of a different social class from either clerks or semi-skilled and unskilled workers. Although his father, a silversmith, had been a Republican, both he and his wife regarded themselves as independents, with the Democratic party coming closer to their interests. He voted with the nation in the 1960 and 1964 Presidential elections, although in local elections had often supported Republican candidates, especially if they were endorsed by the union.

Like Peter Donovan, although Joseph Bertoldi was a member and a regular attender at union meetings, he appeared to have little conception of the union movement, of its link with a particular class. Unions were seen as existing to gain better wages and conditions for their members as well as maintaining, in electrical work, high standards of public safety. But working in a job he regarded as quite secure and earning a fair wage, Mr Bertoldi did not regard unions and management as having competing interests – 'They can't get anywhere going in opposite directions.'

In addition to putting forward the view that there exists an identifiable aristocracy of skilled labour within the middle ranges of the American class structure. I have also been concerned to show that lower level clerical workers on the one hand, and managers or executives on the other, cannot be regarded as sharing a membership in a single 'middle' class. Indeed, many of the data suggest that this former group have experienced greater and more widespread changes in their class situation than has the affluent skilled worker. Consequently a clear and identifiable line of demarcation separating what we may call the lower middle class from the established middle class is now apparent.

I have referred earlier in this chapter to the fact that in terms of income the routine non-manual worker earns considerably less than the skilled craftsman. Equally important is the fact that the relationship of the clerk to his work appears to be changing. The rationalisation and mechanisation of clerical tasks is making the role of a lower level white collar worker less and less distinct from that of a worker in light industry. This diminution in the opportunities for creativity, freedom and control in routine non-manual work was associated with the finding that the level of job satisfaction found amongst the clerical sample was, if anything, lower than that experienced by the skilled craftsmen. This represented a radical departure from the findings of earlier research, which has consistently shown white collar personnel to be deriving a greater amount of satisfaction or meaning from their jobs than blue collar workers.

In contrast, the managers in the sample enjoyed a set of occupational and economic advantages that was approximated by none of the clerks, and only very few of the craftsmen. In the large majority of cases family income exceeded $12,000; while levels of job satisfaction were uniformly high. However, the most important evidence which suggested that clerks are becoming increasingly isolated from managerial and supervisory groups showed that the opportunities for career mobility from the former to the latter type of occupation are fast diminishing. In the past, the ability of routine non-manual workers to rise to positions of authority has been a major factor making for a common identity between individuals at differing levels of the white collar hierarchy. However, increasing technical and managerial specialisation has meant that the 'general office experience' of the aspiring clerk is no longer a sufficient qualification for promotion.

This divergence in the market *and* work situations of clerks and managers is perhaps nowhere more readily apparent than in their respective political beliefs. Only one quarter of the managers were prepared to identify themselves with the Democratic party; whereas three fifths of the clerks felt able to do so. In fact, sizeable numbers of both occupational categories professed independence from party loyalties. However, when asked which party came closest to their interests the clerks were overwhelmingly Democratic: no more than 14 per cent of them displayed any degree of affinity with the G.O.P. In contrast, 41 per cent of the managers verbalised Republican party sympathies.

As in the case of the skilled craft group, differences in the structure and functioning of clerical and managerial families can be directly linked with the perpetuation of class differences. As a group, the clerks had significantly fewer children and started their families later than did the managers. Similarly, they were anxious to instill in their children a particular and distinct set of values, while harbouring exceedingly high aspirations for their success in later life. Again these differences must be associated with the routine white collar worker's position in the division of labour. For these same clerical parents were only marginally more successful than the blue collar parents in realising their parental ambitions. And as in the case of this latter grouping, the relative lack of success of lower level white collar parents in this regard must be largely attributed to the fact that they themselves have not been exposed to the institutions of higher education.

Finally, in terms of social interaction outside of the work situation, clerks exist almost totally isolated from people occupying positions in the higher echelons of industry or commerce. Although managers provided the only significant number of people viewing the division between the middle and working class as coinciding with the non-manual/ manual line, the white collar workers with whom they themselves spent leisure time were from a very limited part of the non-manual sector. Not only were 86 per cent of the total number of friends mentioned by the managers engaged in non-manual occupations; *no more than five per cent* of these friends were in lower level clerical or kindred occupations. Rather, these highly paid, college educated, managers were involved in friendship sets comprising people like themselves – people predominantly engaged in business or the professions, while the clerks spent their leisure time largely with other white collar workers in routine or lower level non-manual occupations. Companions working in upper level management or in one of the professions were few and far between.

As in the case of my analysis of the position of the skilled craftsman in American society, I give below two additional profiles: one of a clerk and one of a manager. As before, these are presented solely for purposes of illustration.

Richard Silvestri, Clerk

Richard Silvestri is a second generation American. Both his father and his wife's father were born in Italy, while he and his wife were born in Rhode Island. The third of four brothers, Richard Silvestri is the only one to be employed in a white collar occupation. After graduating from high school he did several jobs until going in the army where he learned bookkeeping and secretarial work. He is now, in his early fifties, a supply clerk in a large government agency. And although the job is secure (the only threats being 'death and taxes') and he works with 'interesting people', Mr Silvestri confesses to being 'somewhat dissatisfied' with his situation. To begin with, he does not find it easy to live on his salary of between $6,000 and $7,000: 'With economic conditions as they are and two children I should net $150 a week clear. The government gives plenty to other countries – they should start here.' Furthermore, although he would very much like promotion, he is uncertain and a trifle cynical about his chances. When asked what he had done that might be helpful in gaining promotion, he replied 'worked hard for 18 years', adding 'It's like a personality contest. If they like you, you get promoted – if not you stay on in the same job.'

Richard Silvestri considers himself a member of the working class: 'To be in the middle class you have to be a business man – you have to make or earn more money than I do.' He also regards craftsmen as occupying a higher social class than either office or non-skilled workers: 'If you have a trade you can be self-reliant.' Not surprisingly, therefore, he and his wife are Democrats – 'They represent the working people' – although he is not a member of a trade union.

Although neither of the Silvestri's two boys are yet in high school their father feels 'fairly strongly' that they should have a college education, probably at the state university. He has not yet started to plan for the finance of that education. Relationships with Mrs Silvestri's parents are close – they come over nearly every day, and 'sit around, watch T.V. and talk', although rarely staying for dinner. Indeed meals do not appear to be taken with either relatives or friends, although the Silvestris get together with a number of friends at least once a week in each other's homes 'to drink beer and play penny poker'. The people Mr Silvestri mentioned specifically were *all* office workers working in the same agency as himself. Apart from these evenings spent with friends, and frequent contact with Mrs Silvestri's parents, social life appears somewhat re-stricted. Neither Richard Silvestri nor his wife belong to any clubs or associations, nor are they active members of the church. Similarly they do not eat in restaurants or ever visit the cinema, theatre or attend a concert. Although neither adult spends any time in the week reading a book, they do have subscriptions to five magazines – including *Look*, *Reader's Digest* and *Newsweek* – and are keen television viewers.

James Headmoor, Assistant to Company President
After completing two years at Harvard, James Headmoor worked for a textile machinery company in Massachusetts for twenty-three years. He then moved to a post in the Massachusetts state government for a brief period before taking up his present position in Providence. This involves managing the initiation and development of new products, a job providing 'variety and challenge' – aspects of the job hampered only by the frust-ration of having to work with limited assets which means that he is some-

times not able to put his ideas into practice. The salary James Headmoor draws now in his early fifties is in excess of $15,000.

There are five children; the youngest is in only the fifth grade, while the eldest is about to graduate from college. Mr Headmoor expects his three sons 'at least' to graduate from college, but sets lower sights for his two daughters 'as long as they are acceptable as college material'. In fact it is one of the daughters who is in her senior year at a private liberal arts college. All of the children had trusts set up in their own names 'a number of years ago' to finance their higher education. Similarly, they were all brought up to possess honesty, courage and self-discipline. Their parents are members of three Parent Teacher Associations, attending meetings 'frequently'.

Mr Headmoor is a Republican, and indeed voted for Barry Goldwater in the 1964 Presidential election. He lives fairly near the centre of Providence in a large house (which he valued at above $25,000) and regards himself and his family as belonging to the upper middle class, 'a matter of income, type of work, the way we live and the things we like to do'. Finally, while aware of the fact that craftsmen now earned substantially higher incomes than routine office workers he considered them to be members of the same social class but superior to non-skilled, 'less talented' manual workers.

Both husband and wife are engaged in an active social life. Mr Headmoor works for a charitable organisation and a boys club and is a member of a country and a town club. Mrs Headmoor also belongs to the country club, as well as working for Planned Parenthood and an additional civic organisation. As a couple they eat in restaurants at least once a week and visit the cinema and theatre every two or three months. In addition the Headmoors get together with friends about twice a week: 'We visit homes, often for dinner, often play bridge afterwards; play husband and wife golf with couples, then have dinner – or tennis with couples.' The husbands of the couples in question include the headmaster of a small private school, a lawyer, a bank executive and a doctor of medicine.

I have noted earlier that the thesis of *embourgeoisement* is not new. This is, of course, also the case with regard to the central argument of this book, namely that there exists in the United States an 'aristocracy of skilled labour', largely isolated both from the working class and the lower ranges of the established middle class. In fact, the debate in the latter part of the nineteenth century on the 'bourgeois tendencies' of large numbers of American workers, often focused specifically on the skilled craftsmen, the division between skilled and non-skilled workers being regarded by many as one of the principal obstacles to the development of a unified working class in Western societies generally.[2] In the United States this division was reinforced and intensified by the fact that it coincided with ethnic divisions – craftsmen being recruited from the ranks of 'native' Americans or immigrants from Northern Europe; the non-skilled composed largely of recent arrivals from Ireland or Southern Europe. As Engels expressed it in 1892:

> Your great obstacle in America, it seems to me, lies in the exceptional position of the native workers... Now a working class has developed and has also to a great extent organised itself on trade union lines. But it still takes up an aristocratic attitude and wherever possible leaves the ordinary badly paid occupations to the immigrants, of whom only a small section enter the aristocratic trade unions. But these immigrants are divided into different nationalities and understand neither one another nor, for the most part, the language of the country. And your bourgeoisie knows much better even than the Austrian Government how to play off one nationality against the other: Jews, Italians, Bohemians, etc., against Germans and Irish, and each one against the other, so that differences in the standard of life of different workers exist, I believe, in New York to an extent unheard of elsewhere.[3]

That 'native workers' were in an 'exceptional position' cannot be doubted. For example, in Poughkeepsie, New York in 1850, 18 per cent of carpenters were foreign-born, as compared to 68 per cent of non-skilled manual workers. In 1880, the proportions were 26 per cent and 73 per cent respectively.[4] And while, as we have seen, the working class in *general* enjoyed at this time 'a prosperity no trace of which has been seen here in Europe for years now' it was the skilled craftsmen who most benefited from this prosperity. The Philadelphia Census of 1860 showed the 'mean wealth' of cabinet makers in the county to be $7,272, while that of carpenters was $3,755 and that of machinists $3,627. At the same time labourers possessed a 'mean wealth' of $180. Clerks were more fortunate, the figure in their case being $1,410.[5]

As writers such as Engels and Lenin were clearly aware, a large part of this disparity in the fortunes of skilled and non-skilled workers at this time can be explained with reference to the nature of the American trade union movement. For it was not until 1935, with the formation of the Committee for Industrial Organisation (C.I.O.), that the ordinary blue collar worker in America was given the opportunity of strong union representation. In contrast, there had been local organisation of skilled workers since the 1790s, while craft unions had been unified on a national basis since 1886.[6] To be sure, the Knights of Labour, which emerged in the 1870s, had sought to unite all wage earners in one large centralised union irrespective of skill level or industry. But this organisation, like many before it, was short lived, having failed to contain the conflict between the leaders of the craft unions and the leaders of the Knights. Essentially this conflict revolved around the issue of whether or not there existed a 'community of interests' between skilled and non-skilled workers. The leaders of craft unions clung stubbornly to the view that improvements made in the situation of the ordinary workmen could only threaten the privileged position of the skilled artisan. Craftsmen and non-skilled workers therefore had disparate, if not opposing interests. The editor of *Carpentry and Building* was voicing the opinion of many when proclaiming in 1886 that the 'mechanic and unskilled labourer have no interests in common, and whatever is gained by unskilled labour is at the expense of skilled labour'.[7] On the other hand, those attempting to organise the unskilled argued that the safest way of protecting the aristocracy of labour lay in improving the position of the remainder of the manual labour force. The achievement of adequate pay and working conditions for unskilled workers would remove the desire on the part of these people to move into the ranks of the skilled, thus enabling craftsmen more easily to maintain their privileged and secure status.

Conflict over this issue reached a head in 1886 when representatives of the major craft unions broke all ties with the Knights of Labour, setting up the American Federation of Labour (A.F.L.) under the presidency of Samuel Gompers. The A.F.L. was concerned explicitly and simply with the organisation of the skilled. Indeed, within many of these craft unions the line separating employer from employee was considered less significant than that distinguishing skilled and unskilled workers. The International Typographical Union for example, admitted to membership 'such employers who may be practical printers', while the Carpenters and Joiners National Union welcomed 'Those members who have been initiated as journeymen and afterwards become employers'.[8]

With the withdrawal of the craft unions from the Knights of Labour, membership and subsequently influence, dwindled. The unskilled were destined to wait another fifty years before gaining adequate union representation. Furthermore, as Engels observed, the successive waves of immigrants arriving on American shores between 1880 and 1910 served only to widen and reinforce the gap between the organised aristocracy of labour and the non-unionised and unskilled remainder of the manual labour force. The average proportion of skilled workers in the total immigration from 1899 to 1910 was 20 per cent: the vast majority of new arrivals were from rural backgrounds, possessing neither urban skills nor a command of the English language. They were thus ignored almost completely by the leaders of the craft unions that went to make up the A.F.L. Indeed, there were many instances of immigrant *craftsmen* being refused the protection of union membership. Fear on the part of 'native' skilled workers and their leaders that the growing supply of immigrant tradesmen would undermine their privileged position meant that a variety of ploys were adopted to maintain the status quo. Often newly arrived craftsmen were forced to pay crippling initiation fees (sometimes as high as $500); or they might be set a special examination by the union – an examination which large numbers would fail. Some unions went so far as to insist that all members be fully fledged U.S. citizens. Such were the ways by which the American aristocracy of labour safeguarded its position in the class structure.

However, as the twentieth century approached the maintenance of this privileged position became an increasingly difficult task for the leadership of the craft unions. The greatest threat was posed by the increasing mechanisation of the production process, which often meant the disappearance of what had been a craft occupation and the emergence in its place of a large number of fragmented and mechanical tasks that could be performed by non-skilled labour. At the 1897 A.F.L. convention, Gompers proclaimed: 'The artisan of yesterday is the unskilled labourer of tomorrow, having being displaced by the invention of new machines and the division and sub-division of labour.'[9] Increasingly schisms developed within the leadership of the A.F.L. Many argued that adherence to the principle of craft unionism was, by now, harming the very people it was designed to protect. In the face of rapid change in techniques of production the privileged situation of the craftsmen would only be maintained by compensatory changes in union structure. Nevertheless, despite an awareness of the threat facing the skilled artisan, Gompers refused to be separated from the principal of craft unionism. The setting up of industry-wide unions could only, in his eyes, lead to the eventual disregarding of the interests of the minority – the minority, of course, being skilled craftsmen. Finally, the long standing feuds within the A.F.L. over this issue (during which time membership declined markedly) broke into open conflict, the result of which was the setting up of the C.I.O. in 1935. This aimed at establishing industrial unions, embracing *all* workers in a particular industry, irrespective of occupation or skill level. 'Dual unionism' was now a reality. The division between skilled and non-skilled could be expected to diminish accordingly.

However, as should be abundantly clear from the foregoing chapters, I have argued that, at least at the present time in American society, craftsmen and non-skilled manual workers share anything but a common class situation: the term 'aristocracy of labour' would appear to be as applicable now as in the latter part of the nineteenth century. Indeed, in terms of their *position in the class structure* there is little evidence to suggest that the situation has ever been different. To be sure, craftsmen have experienced periods of economic deprivation; certain trades have become obsolete while others have risen to take their place. But such events cannot be taken to indicate that skilled and non-skilled workers have ever been merged into a single class. This was, however, the argument advanced by the Lynds after their second visit to Middletown in 1935. The depression had virtually removed the wage differential between craftsmen and non-skilled workers–in the building trades for example it amounted to only two cents per hour. Indeed, 'machine "generating" and machine "tending" had so far displaced the earlier hand skills that the line between skilled and unskilled worker had "become so blurred as to be in some shops almost non-existent"'. Correspondingly, the apprenticeship system had virtually fallen into disuse. The term 'working class' could therefore be taken to include *all* those individuals who work with their hands.[10]

With the advantages of hindsight, it is hardly necessary to point out that as an occupational group, craftsmen have not, as the Lynds predicted, been reduced to insignificant numbers. Indeed, within the male labour force 'craftsmen, foremen and kindred workers' rose from 18 per cent of the total in 1950 to 20 per cent in 1969. Non-skilled male workers fell from 29 per cent to 27 per cent of the total during the same period. Further-more, research in a number of areas of sociological investigation, most notably within the fields of industrial and occupational sociology, has shown the existence of crucial differences in the situations of craftsmen and non-skilled workers. The level of 'alienation' experienced, the content of occupational ideologies, power in the labour market, involvement in politics, and family life as well as the use of leisure time, have all been shown to differ considerably between skilled and non-skilled manual occupations (and, of course, between manual and non-manual oc-cupations).[11] And yet the possible *implications* of these studies for the analysis of the structure and composition of the working class in the United States have been almost completely ignored by American students of stratification. Indeed, it is difficult to see how many of the arguments put forward in the 1950s and 1960s, regarding the disappearance of class differentials, could have been seriously entertained by sociologists fam-iliar with the picture steadily being built up of the organisation of work (and the implications of that organisation) in American society. How could the thesis of *embourgeoisement* re-emerge when in *sociological* terms its basic premises ran directly counter to the findings of a large number of studies conducted on one or other aspect of the division of labour?[12]

The answer must lie very largely in the manner in which American sociologists have conceptualised social class in the last few decades, a conceptualisation owing much to the work of Warner and his associates. Two features of this approach are striking: first, as is well known, Warner associated class position with an *aggregate score*, depending upon house type, dwelling area, occupation and source of income.[13] As such the study of social class becomes the study of *individual attributes*, rather than the analysis of *social structure*. Secondly, by its very nature this approach placed emphasis upon groups of individuals as *consumers*, while paying little heed to them as *producers*. Positions in the class structure thus became equated with status scores or indices of style of life. Furthermore, it is important to note that this fundamentally non-sociological approach to the analysis of class structure stood in stark contrast to the theoretical positions adopted by sociologists working in the fields of industrial and occupational sociology. American sociology, in other words, exhibited a strange dualism. And one of the consequences of this dualism was the emergence of academic debate on the blurring or disappearance of class barriers.

In conclusion, then, I am arguing that future discussion regarding changes in the structure and composition of the working class in American society must adopt a view of class structure which lays stress upon the economic bases of social class. And by economic bases I am not referring merely to income, but to *position in the division of labour*. To be sure, the fact that manual and non-manual workers can now afford televisions or houses is important. But such surface similarities cannot be allowed to obscure basic differences in freedom or autonomy in the work situation, in *chances* of career mobility or the *ability* to provide a higher education for one's children. As I have tried to show, these and many other life chances are determined not simply by level of income, or exposure to television or other suburban dwellers. Rather they are crucially influenced by the individual's situation in the system of production.

This particular study has focused primarily on the class situation of routine non-manual workers and skilled craftsmen. Equally important are changes that may be occurring in the position of semi-skilled and unskilled operatives. The question of whether, in fact, automation will lead to the proletarianisation of large numbers of blue collar workers (thus widening the gap still further between the aristocracy of labour and the remainder of the working class), or whether it will facilitate a *general* improvement in the life chances of the manual labour force cannot at this time be settled. But it will only be settled if subsequent research focuses on changes in the productive as well as in the consumption roles of those groupings that go to make up the class structure of the United States.

Appendix: The Interview Schedule

The schedule used in the study is set out below. In fact many of the questions were pre-coded, the interviewer simply circling the appropriate answer. For example question 1 was coded 'Rhode Island 1; Other State 2; Other Country 3.' In addition the schedule contained several grids. As a case in point, in question 150 the interviewer had to indicate whether the respondent attended say, the theatre, every week, fortnight, month, three months, six months, year or never. For reasons of space however, I have omitted the details of the coding system and the grids from the version of the schedule reproduced here.

It will be noticed that no reference is made in the text to several of the questions contained in the schedule. There are at least two reasons why this is so. First, certain questions that were seen as being important in 1967 are now somewhat dated. Several of the questions on political and religious attitudes are of this nature. Secondly, in the five years that have elapsed since the schedule was written my own theoretical perspectives have changed. I have not therefore had recourse to certain questions that were directly linked to issues with which I have become less concerned. For example, I had intended to develop a scale of authoritarianism, but now consider such scales to be of little value.

The Schedule

As mentioned in the letter you received, this study is concerned with comparing and contrasting in some detail the 'way of life' of over 300 families in the Providence area. By 'way of life' we are talking about the kinds of jobs people have, and what they think about them, how they spend their leisure time, how they feel about certain current issues, and so on.

Before we start let me assure you once again that all your answers will remain completely anonymous. Your name appears nowhere on this set of questions as the study is only concerned with statistical totals rather than with specific individuals.

ALL INFORMANTS

1 First of all, can you tell me where you were born?
2 And where was your wife born?

IF HUSBAND BORN ABROAD, ASK QUES. 19–23 THEN SKIP TO QUES. 142a to END. ›

3 How long have you lived at this particular address?

IF MOVED WITHIN LAST 10 YEARS

OTHERS GO TO QUES. 8 ›

4 Did you own or rent the house or apartment at your previous address?
5 And was that somewhere else in Rhode Island or in another state?

IF PREVIOUSLY LIVED IN R.I.
6 Could you tell me roughly where in Rhode Island – just the names of the streets at the nearest corner, and the town will be fine.
7 Do you prefer this neighborhood to the one where you lived previously or not?

ALL INFORMANTS

8 What specifically do you like or dislike about this neighborhood?
Get both likes AND dislikes

9 How many members of your household are there?
10 Is anybody else living in your home apart from your wife, yourself and your children? If so may I ask who else?
11 How many rooms do you have, not counting bathrooms?
12 How many separate bedrooms are there?
13 Are you living in an apartment here or do you have the whole house?
14 And is it your own house/apartment, or do you rent it?

ALL INFORMANTS

15a *Ask those RENTING:*
Would you like to own your own home or do you prefer to rent?

Ask HOME OWNERS:
Most people seem to think there are both advantages and disadvantages in renting and owning one's own home. From your experience would you say that the advantages of owning your own home outweigh the disadvantages, or vice versa?
15b What makes you say that?

IF INFORMANT PRESENTLY RENTS:

OTHERS GO TO QUES. 18 ›

16 Do you rent this house/apartment Furnished or Unfurnished?
17 Could you tell me roughly how much you pay each month for *rent plus heating*? Leave out gas and electricity. If *you* pay for heat just average it out over the year, and tack it on to your rent. Just tell me the letter that corresponds most nearly to this combined cost.

HAND CARD A

A Under $50	H $100–119
B $50–59	I $120–129
C $60–69	J $130–139
D $70–79	K $140–149
E $80–89	L $150+
F $90–99	No Response
G $100–109	

IF INFORMANT OWNS HOME:

18 Could you tell me roughly what the present value of this house is? I mean, what it would bring if you sold it to-day? Just tell me the letter on the card that corresponds most nearly to its present value.

HAND CARD B

A Under $5000	F $15000–17495
B $5000–7495	G $17500–19995
C $7500–9995	H $20000–24995
D $10000–12495	I $25000
E $12500–14995	No Response

ALL INFORMANTS

And now I'd like to ask you a few questions about your job.

19 Are you employed or self employed? *If both, determine principal source of income.*

20 Can you tell me what you actually do for a living?

21a Is that your only job, or do you some-times or always have a part-time job or spare time work as well?

If part or spare time work:
21b What is your part (or spare) time job(s) and when do you work at it?

22 Would you describe to me briefly what you actually *do* in your present job? I mean, your main job.

23a Have you ever been employed in a different *occupation* than the one you are in at present?

If yes:
23b Can you tell me what that occupation was, and when you were in it? (*Probe*: Was that the only other oc-cupation you've ever been in?)

IF HUSBAND BORN ABROAD, SKIP TO QUES. 142a to END. ❯

24 How did you learn to do your job – did you serve an apprenticeship, 'pick it up' as you went along, go to a trade or business school, or what?

25 Where there any minimum require-ments you had to have to start the job, or training for the job? I mean, did you have to be a high school graduate, take any tests, or anything?

26 How long does it take to become fully skilled in your job?

ALL INFORMANTS *NOT* SELF EMPLOYED

27 Roughly speaking, how many people work at the same firm or place as you?

ALL INFORMANTS SELF EMPLOYED

28 Do you have other people working for you? If so, how many people work for you?

ALL INFORMANTS

29 How interesting do you find your job – would you say *very interesting, quite interesting, not very interesting,* or *not at all interesting*?

30 What do you like best about your job?

31 And what do you like least?

32 Would you say you looked upon your job as being something you enjoy do-ing for its own sake – as something you are personally involved with, or do you look upon it more as a way of earning the money to be able to do the things you really enjoy doing?

33 So, how satisfied are you with your present job; would you say *Very satis-fied, Quite satisfied, Somewhat dis-satisfied,* or *Very dissatisfied*?

ALL INFORMANTS NOT SELF EMPLOYED

SELF EMPLOYED GO TO QUES. 40 ❯

34a Ask *craft* informants:
What about the idea of promotion – would you like to be promoted to a job 'higher up' such as foreman or manager, or would you rather stay in your present job?
Ask *clerical* informants:
What about the idea of promotion – would you like to be promoted to a job 'higher up' such as a manager, or would you rather stay in your present job?

If WOULD like promotion, ask:
34b Have you done anything that you think will be helpful to you in gaining promotion – I mean things like evening or correspondence courses, or discus-sions with the management where you work? If so, may I ask what you have done?

35a What would you say are your chances of promotion in your present job? Would you say they were *Good, Fair, Poor,* or *None*?

If promotion changes fair or good, ask:

35b What is the top position that you can expect to reach?

If promotion chances poor or none, ask:

35c Why do you think so?

36 Have you ever owned your own business?

37a Do you hope to go into business for yourself in the future?

If Yes, ask:

OTHERS GO TO QUES. 38a ❯

37b Why would you like to start your own business?

37c Have you done anything in the way of *planning* for your own business yet – I mean have you started saving or been to anyone for advice, or aren't your plans that far along yet?

If have started planning, ask:

37d What have you done?

ALL INFORMANTS NOT SELF EMPLOYED

38a Who is your *immediate* superior at work – I mean, who do you take your orders from?

38b Do you ever come into *actual contact* with anyone higher up than him – if so, whom?

If informant comes into contact with others:

38c Where and when do you come into contact with this/these person(s)? *Get specific answers*

39a For *craft* workers ask:
At *work* do you ever come into *actual contact* with any of the men who work in the offices? Would you say *Often, Sometimes, Rarely,* or *Never*?
For *clerical* workers ask:
At *work* do you ever come into *actual contact* with manual workers, such as skilled craftsmen or semi or unskilled workers? Would you say *Often, Sometimes, Rarely,* or *Never*?

If contact is EVER made, ask:

39a *Where* and *when* do you come into contact with them?
(*Probe*: Anywhere else?)

ALL INFORMANTS

40 Are any of the people you work with relatives of yours?
If yes, specify which relatives

41 Do any of the of the people you work with live in this area (as East Side, East Providence) – If so, how many would you say lived in this area?

42 Are you involved in any kind of shift work or do you always work roughly the same hours?

43 Basically, are you paid at an hourly rate, or do you get a fixed weekly or monthly wage or salary?

44 Do you get extra or overtime pay if you stay longer at work than usual, work more than a certain number of hours, or go in to work on a day when you usually don't have to work?

45 Do you usually work any overtime?

46 So how many hours do you usually work in an *average* week? (Including any overtime that you might do?)

47 On the average do you work a 5, a $5\frac{1}{2}$, or a 6 day week?

ALL INFORMANTS NOT SELF EMPLOYED

48a Do you consider the wage your firm pays you to be a fair one or not?

If wage not considered fair:

48b Why do you think it is unfair?

ALL INFORMANTS

49 *In general* do you think working people are usually fairly and squarely treated by their employers, or that employers sometimes take advantage of them?

50a Do you think it is more realistic to look at a large firm somewhat like a football team – with each person doing his bit toward the success of the enterprise – or is it more realistic to see it composed of two *opposed* parts – managers on the one side and workers on the other?

50b Why do you say that?

51 Is there any way in which a check is kept on what time you arrive at and leave work – for example, do you have to punch a time clock?

ALL INFORMANTS NOT SELF EMPLOYED

52 How secure would you say your present job is – Would you say it was *completely secure, quite secure, not very secure,* or *not at all secure*?

53 How much notice, or how many day's pay in lieu of notice, would your employer *have* to give you if he wanted to fire you?

ALL INFORMANTS

54a Have you been put out of work through no fault of your own – I mean 'laid off' at any time during the last five years?

If yes, ask:

54b Could you tell me when and for how long?

55a Have you been on strike at any time during the last five years?

If yes, ask:

55b Could you tell me when this was, how long you were on strike, and why you were on strike?

56 Provided you remain in the same job, do you expect your wages to *increase, decrease,* or *remain unchanged* as you get older?

57a If you are unable to work because of illness, do you still draw pay from your business or your employer?

If yes, ask:

57b How Long can you go on drawing sick pay?

58a Does your firm or employer contribute to any health schemes for you, such as Blue Cross, Blue Shield, or Major Medical Insurance?

If yes, ask:

58b What fraction of the total cost of that insurance does your firm or employer pay – *less than half, half, more than half,* or *all of it*?

59 Do you have any (other) health insurance that you've taken out yourself? If so, what do you have?

60a Will you draw any pension when you retire, *apart from* Social Security, either from your employer or from a union?

If yes, ask:

60b Do you contribute to that pension out of your regular earnings?

61 Some people say there is not much opportunity in America today – that the average man doesn't have much chance to really get ahead. Others say that there's plenty of opportunity and anyone who works hard can go as far as he wants. How do you feel about this?

Much Opportunity
Some Opportunity
Not Much Opportunity
No Real Opportunity
D.K.

62 With which of these four statements do you come closest to agreeing?

HAND CARD C

A Labour unions in this country are doing a fine job.

B While they do make some mistakes, on the whole unions are doing more good than harm.

C Although we need labor unionism in this country, the way they are run now they do more harm than good.

D This country would be better off without any labor unions at all.

E Don't Know, Undecided

63 What do you see as the prime *purpose* of Trade Unions?

64a Are you a member of a Trade Union?

If yes, ask:

64b How often do you attend union meetings – would you say *often, sometimes, rarely,* or *never*?

65 Suppose there is a section of the country where very few workers are unionized. A drive is started to unionize the companies there. People all over the country are asked to give money to support the drive. Some people think they should give money; others think they shouldn't. How do you think you would feel about this? (This would be in addition to any union dues you may already have paid.)

And now I'd like to ask you a few questions about any jobs your wife might have had before or after you got married.

66a First of all, did your wife work before you got married?

If yes, ask:

66b What did she do – if she held more than one job perhaps you could tell me the three she held for the longest time?

67a Is she working now?

If yes, ask:

OTHERS GO TO QUES. 71 ⌄

67b What is she doing now?

68 Is your wife's present job full or part time?

69 And is she paid by the hour, or does she get a weekly or monthly wage or salary?

70a Has she held any other kinds of job *since* your marriage?

If yes, ask:

70b What were they?

IF WIFE IS NOT CURRENTLY WORKING (QUES. 67a)

71a Has your wife worked at any time since you got married?

If yes, ask:

71b What did she do?

ALL INFORMANTS

72a About what was your *total* family income *before taxes* last year – 1966 – earned by you *and* your wife? *Leave out* any income your children may have earned. Just tell me the letter on the card that comes closest to the right amount.

If *wife* not *working, probe*: And you yourself earned that amount, right?

HAND CARD D

A	Under $2000	I	$9000–9999
B	$2000–2999	J	$10000–10999
C	$3000–3999	K	$11000–11999
D	$4000–4999	L	$12000–12999
E	$5000–5999	M	$13000–13999
F	$6000–6999	N	$14000–14999
G	$7000–7999	O	$15000 and up
H	$8000–8999		

IF WIFE WORKS, ASK:

72b How much of that total family income was earned by your wife?
Probe: And the rest was earned by you, right?

And now I'd like to ask you some questions about politics in general as well as how you feel about one or two specific political issues.

73a Did you vote in the Presidential election in 1964?

If yes, ask:

73b How did you vote? Did you vote for Goldwater or Johnson?

74a What about 1960? Did you vote in the Presidential election then?

If yes, ask:

74b Who did you vote for then, Nixon or Kennedy?

75 How interested would you say you were in politics – would you say that you were *Very interested, Quite interested, Not very interested,* or *Not at all interested?*

76a *In general,* do you consider yourself to be a *Democrat,* a *Republican,* or an *Independent?*

If Independent, ask:

76b If you *had* to choose between Republican and Democrat, which party would you say came closer to your interests?

77a Have you always (been an Independent) supported the Democratic/Republican Party?

If yes, ask:

77b What are the main reasons you have always (been an Independent) supported the Democratic/Republican Party?

If no, ask:

77c Why did you change?

ASK DEMOCRATS AND INDEPENDENTS QUES. 78a, THEN 78b

78a So, *in general* what kinds of *people* do you think support the *Democratic* Party?

ASK REPUBLICANS QUES. 78b, *THEN GO BACK AND ASK 78a*

78b What kinds of *people* do you think support the *Republican* Party?

ALL INFORMANTS

79 What party do you think most of the people who live in this neighborhood support?

80 Do you know what party your three closest friends support?
(*Probe: All 3 of them* are Democrats/Republicans?)

81 Do you know what party your parents supported in general?

82 What party does your wife support in general?

83 And finally, do you know what party her parents supported?

Now perhaps I could ask you about one or two more specific political issues.

84 Politicians often characterize themselves either as hawks or doves with regard to the war in Vietnam. Where do you stand on this issue – do you see yourself more as a hawk or a dove?

85 Do you think the United States is giving *enough economic aid* to underdeveloped countries, *too much aid,* or *not enough aid?*

86a Would you like to see the United States develop closer ties with Russia?

86b Do you think that Communist China should be admitted to the United Nations?

87 What do you think about the ever increasing amount of automation in this country – do you think it will lead to a better standard of living for everybody, or do you think it will cause hardship for a large number of people through unemployment?

88 In your opinion, should the right of free speech in America include the right for someone to make speeches criticizing what the President is doing in Vietnam?

89 In your opinion, should the right of free speech include the right for someone to make speeches against religion?

90 And finally, in your opinion should the right of free speech include the right for someone to make speeches against Negroes?

91 Which of these two statements do you most agree with?

HAND CARD E

1. The most important job for the government is to make it certain that there are good opportunities for each person to get ahead on his own.

2. The most important job for the government is to guarantee every person a decent and steady job and standard of living.
3. Don't Know or Undecided

---

92 In strikes and disputes between working people and employers do you usually side with the workers or with the employers?

93 In England and several other European countries public utilities like the gas, electric, and telephone companies as well as the railroads are owned by the government. Would you like or dislike to see this happen in this country?

94 In the last year or so do you think the Negro drive for Civil Rights has been going *too fast*, *too slow*, or at about the *right speed*?

95 The O'Connor Plan has been in the news recently. This is designed to do away with racial imbalance in Providence schools by bussing children, irrespective of their parents wishes, to schools in areas of Providence other than those in which they live. What do you think of this plan – do you agree with it or not?

96 There's also been a lot of talk recently about *fair housing*. How do you feel about this? Do you think landlords should be made to rent their apartments to Negroes even if they don't want to – or not?

97a What were your reactions when the government set up *Medicare* for the elderly last year? Did you *approve*, or *disapprove*?

If approval, ask: (*if disapproval, ask only 97c*) ⌄
97b Would you like to see Medicare extended to the whole population?
97c Why do you say that?

ALL INFORMANTS

98 What would you say was the *minimum* amount of education a young *man* must have to get on in the world these days?
(If "college", *probe*, Is "some college" enough, or must he be a college graduate?)

99a Do you think it is as important for young *women* to have as much education as young men?
99b Why do you say that?
100 So what would you say was the main *value* of education – I mean, what does the person who *is* educated have over the person who *isn't*?
101a Let's assume that a son of yours was

actually choosing a job at the moment. Would you rather he chose a *manual* or a *non-manual* job?
(*Probe:* Well, assuming he had no clear idea of what he wanted to do?)
101b Why do you say that?
(*Probe:* Any other reason?)
102a What about if he had the choice of a *Plumber's* job at $150 per week, or a *Bookkeeper's* job at $120 per week?
102b What would you prefer about the *plumber's/bookkeeper's* job?
(*Probe:* Anything else?)
103 What do you think is the ideal number of children for the AVERAGE American family?
If Other, Specify

104a Some people enjoy belonging to various clubs and organizations and others don't. Do you belong to any clubs, associations, or organizations like the kinds listed on the card, or to any others that aren't listed?

If yes, ask:
104b Could you tell me specifically which clubs, associations, or organizations you belong to?

HAND CARD F

Youth Groups (Scout Leaders etc.)
Church Connected Groups
Fraternal Organizations and Auxiliaries
Veterans Organizations
Nationality Groups
Sport or Hobby Clubs
Firm Recreational Clubs
Neighborhood Associations
Women's or Men's Social Clubs
Charitable Organizations
Political Associations

104c All together, how many of their meetings do you go to in an average month– *none, one, two, three,* or how many?

ALL INFORMANTS

105a Does your wife belong to any clubs, associations, or organizations like the ones on the list you've just seen?

If yes, ask:
105b Do you know which one she belongs to?
105c Again, all together, how many meetings would you say she goes to in an average month – *none, one, two, three* or how many?

ALL INFORMANTS
BELONGING TO ANY CLUB
OR ASSOCIATION
106a Are you or your wife an officer in any of the clubs or organizations that we've talked about?

If yes, ask:

106b Could you tell me what position you hold and in what organization?

ALL INFORMANTS

107 No one would deny that people living in America are different from one another in a great number of respects. People differ in age, occupation, the amount of money they earn, religion, color, and many, many more characteristics. Which of these differences do you think is the most important in America today?
Probe: What makes you say that?

108 There is quite a lot of talk these days about different *Social Classes* and many people seem to think that this is one of the most important dividing characteristics. If you were asked what social classes there are in America today, what would you say?

109 If you *had* to say, what social class would you say you and your family were in?
Do NOT read out list.

110 Some people seem to think there are *FOUR* social classes in the United States: the *Middle Class*, the *Lower Class*, the *Working Class*, and the *Upper Class*, If you had to choose one of these terms, which one would you say you and your family were in?
(Repeat terms if necessary)

111 *Ask informants identifying with MIDDLE class:*
You wouldn't then call yourself a *working* class person – why is that?

Ask informants identifying with the WORKING class:
You wouldn't then call yourself a *middle* class person – why is that?

ALL INFORMANTS

112 Again, if you had to use these four names, what class would you say your *parents* were in?

113 What about your *wife's* parents?

114 Would you say that you were about an average (*middle*) (*working*) class person or nearer the top or bottom of this class?
(Use term chosen by the informant)

115 In deciding which social class a person belongs to, which of the things on that card do you think it is *most important* to know?

HAND CARD G

Family Background

Income
Country of Origin
Education
Occupation
Way he spends his money
Religion
All
N.A./D.K.

---

116 So what *sort* of people are in the (working) (middle) class – how would you describe a (working) (middle) class person?
(Use term informant chose)

117 How about the (working) (middle) class – how would you describe a (working) (middle) class person?
(Use term NOT chosen by informant)

118 In your opinion what is the dividing line between the working class and the middle class? Where does the working class end and the middle class begin?

HAND CARD H

119 Will you mark on that card what you consider to be the relative size of the upper class, the middle class, the working class, and the lower class in Providence. In other words, what percentage of Providence do you think is Upper class, what percentage is Middle class, and so on. Just draw lines across at the various dividing lines.

120a It is often said that nowadays skilled craftsmen are doing better than men who work in offices. Do you think this is true?

120b Why do you say that?

120c So would you say skilled craftsmen and office workers are now in the same social class, or not?

(If no, probe for HIGHER or LOWER class)

If craftsmen in LOWER class, ask:
120d Why do you say that?

ALL INFORMANTS

121a It is *also* often said nowadays that some *unskilled* and *semi-skilled* workers are doing as well as *skilled craftsmen*. Do you think this is true?

121b So would you say that some unskilled and semi-skilled workers are now in the same social class as skilled craftsmen, or not?

If craftsmen in HIGHER class, ask:
121c Why do you say that?

ALL INFORMANTS

122 How long have you been married?
123 And do you have any children?
IF NO CHILDREN AT ALL SKIP TO QUES. 142 ⟩

INFORMANTS WITH CHILDREN

124a Have you or your wife ever read any books on how to bring up children?

If yes:
124b Do you remember what any of them were called?
124c Have you ever discussed any of these books with your friends or relatives?
125 Have you, or will, you or your wife give(n) your child(ren) any kind of religious training at home?
126 Have any of them gone to Sunday School or religious instruction classes or do you expect that any of them will?
127 Did you, do you, or will you, encourage your child(ren) to pray, or not?
128 Are any of your children *in* school or still *too young* for school?
IF NONE, SKIP TO QUES. 134 ⟩

IF ANY CHILDREN STILL IN SCHOOL

129a What grade(s) will he/she/they be in next school year?
129b If any in college, which College(s)?
130a Do you or your wife belong to a Parent-Teacher Association?

If yes, ask:
130b How often would you say either of you attend P.T.A. meetings – *never, rarely, occasionally,* or *frequently?*
If BOYS in school or still too young for school
131 How far in school would you like your son(s) to go?
(If 'to college', *probe.* 'How *far* in college would you like him/them to go?')

If GIRLS in school or still too young for school
132 What about your daughter(s) – how far would you like her/them to go in school?
(If 'to college', *probe.* 'How *far* in college would you like her/them to go?')

If informant wants ANY children to go to college
133a How strongly do you feel that your son(s)/daughter(s)/children should have a college education if they have the ability? Would you say you feel *very strongly, fairly strongly,* or *not too strongly?*
133b Have you already begun to set money aside especially to pay for his/her (their) college education?
If yes: Specify in what form
133c Have you any ideas about the TYPE of college you'd like him/her/them to go to, or haven't you thought about that yet?

ALL INFORMANTS WITH CHILDREN

134 Have any of your children *left* school?
IF NO, SKIP TO QUES. 136 ⌄

IF ANY CHILDREN HAVE LEFT SCHOOL

135a How far did he/she/they go in school?
135b If college – which College(s)?
135c What are they doing now – I mean, what are their occupations?
(Get occupation ONLY, NOT place of work)

ALL INFORMANTS WITH CHILDREN

136 Do, or did, any of your children attend or do you expect them to attend a *parochial* school?
137 Do, or did, any of your children attend, or do you expect them to attend a *private* school?
138 Do (did), any of your children attend, or do you expect any of them to attend any summer camps?
139 Do, or did, any of your children have, or do you expect them to have lessons on a musical instrument?
If Yes, which instrument(s)?
140 What do you think are the two or three most important qualities of character a parent should teach a child?
141a What do (or did) you usually do if one of your children disobeys(ed) you and does (did) something you have (had) clearly told him not to do?
141b And what happens (ed) if he/she does (did) it again?

ALL INFORMANTS

And now I'd like to ask you a few questions about your leisure time activities.

142a First of all, does your family have a car?
(Probe for how many)

If yes, ask:
142b What kind of car(s) is it (are they)?
143 In a normal week do you or your wife spend any time just reading a book?
144a Do you or your wife have a public library card?

If husband has card, ask:
144b How often do you go to the library?

If wife has card, ask:
144c How about your wife – how often does she go to the library?
145 Do you *regularly* get any magazines in your home? If so, would you tell me which magazines you get, and whether you buy them at the newstand or have a subscription to them?
146 Do you belong to any book clubs? If so, may I ask which ones?
Specify

If husband or wife a book reader ASK
147 Can you remember the names of the books you and/or your wife read most recently?

ALL INFORMANTS

148a Do you or your wife have any savings – in the form of a savings account at the bank, stocks and bonds in industry or government bonds?
Probe for TYPE *of savings*

If yes, ask:

HAND CARD I

148b Could you tell me the letter on this card that corresponds roughly to the *total* amount you have saved up to now? That is, in *all* forms of savings?

A $1–249	G $2000–2499
B $250–499	H $2500–4999
C $500–749	I $5000–7499
D $750–999	J $7500–9999
E $1000–1499	K $10000 or more
F $1500–1999	

149 What are your three favorite T.V. shows?
150 I'd like to read you a short list of things some people like to do in the evenings or on weekends. Could you tell me if you like to do any of these things and about how often you are able to do them ... every week, month, year?
Movies
Theatre
Sports Event
Restaurant
Concert
151 How do you usually spend holidays

such as Christmas and Thanksgiving – I mean, where do you spend them and who with?
152 How do you usually spend your vacations – do you like to visit relatives, go away, travel, relax at home or what? *(If 'go away', probe:* Where to? How long?)
153 Do you ever play golf?
154a Could you tell me if your house has any of the things on that card?

HAND CARD J

Color TV
Washing Machine
Clothes Dryer
Dishwasher
Air Conditioner
Stereo Equipment
F.M. Radio

For those items not already owned by informant, ask:
154b Do you expect to get any of these within the next two or three years?
155 If you were suddenly given a $2,000 *bonus* tomorrow, what would you do with the additional money?
156 Can you tell me the jobs or occupations of the people you spend most time with socially. Don't tell me their names. They can be relatives.
157 Do you actually work with any of these people? If so, how many?
158 Are any of them neighbors? Again, if so, how many of them are neighbors?
159a Can we talk about friends who are NOT relatives first – how often do you get together with friends you're *not* related to?

If informant EVER *sees non-related friends, ask:*
159b What do you usually do when you get together with friends, do you usually go out somewhere, visit each other's homes, just chat, play cards, watch TV, or what?
Probe for WHAT *is done and* WHERE.
160a What about *relatives* – how often do you get together with relatives?

If informant EVER *sees relatives, ask:*
160b Which relatives do you see most often?
160c And what do you usually do when you get together with relatives?
Probe for WHAT *is done and* WHERE

ALL INFORMANTS

161a Do you ever have people over for dinner in your home?

IF NO, GO TO QUES. 162 ⟩
If yes, ask:
161b How often would you say you had

people over for dinner – *once a week, once a month*, or what?

161c Are these people more often *friends*, or *relatives*, or *both about equally*?

If MORE OFTEN friends or relatives, ask alternative NOT chosen by informant:

161d Do you EVER have (friends) (relatives) over for dinner: would you say *occasionally, hardly ever*, or *never*?

ALL INFORMANTS

162 Do you and your wife ever have a cocktail before dinner – would you say *often, rarely, sometimes*, or *never*?

163 Do you know the jobs or occupations of your two next door neighbors?

164 How friendly are you with your next door neighbors? Would you say *very friendly, quite friendly*, or *not at all friendly*?

165 What about this neighborhood *in general*, would you say that you know *nearly everyone, quite a few* of your neighbors, *only two or three of them*, or *none at all*?

166 What religion are you?

167 How often, if at all, do *you* yourself, go to church (synagogue)?

168a How about your wife – does she attend church *more* or *less often* than you?

168b So how often does she go to church (synagogue)?

169a All things considered, would you say that your interest in religion has *increased, decreased*, or *remained about the same* over the last few years?

If change either way, ask:

169b Why do you think that has happened?

ALL INFORMANTS

170 What about your wife – has her interest in religion *increased, decreased*, or *remained about the same* over the last few years?

171 So, how important would you say religion was to your family? *Very important, quite important, not very important, or not important at all*?

172 Did either your wife or yourself attend either a parochial or a church related school for any time during your period of education?

173 In your family do you ever say grace (a prayer) before meals?

174 Have you ever discussed family, or other problems, with a priest or clergyman?

175 Would you prefer that any children you might have marry someone of the same religion as yourselves, or don't

you mind?

176 In your family do you ever pray together?

177a What were your reactions to the 1963 Supreme Court decisions banning Bible reading and prayers in public schools? Did you approve or disapprove?

177b Why do you think that?

178a Do you approve of religious leaders becoming involved in issues that are not *directly* concerned with religion – such as Medicare, Civil Rights, or the war in Vietnam?

178b Why do you say that?

179a Do you and your wife ever discuss religion or religious issues together?

If yes, ask:

179b What *kinds* of religious issues do you discuss?

ALL INFORMANTS

Finally, I'd like to ask one or two biographical questions, and then I won't take any more of your time.

180 May I ask your approximate age? Just tell me the letter on the card that most nearly approximates it?

HAND CARD K

A 20–24	F 45–49
B 25–29	G 50–54
C 30–34	H 55–59
D 35–39	I 60+
E 40–44	

181 Do you have any brothers? If so, can you tell me what they do for a living – what are their jobs?

182 And, if your wife has any brothers, could you tell me what they do for a living – what are their jobs?

183 How far did you go in school?

184 And your wife, how far did she go in school?

185 And what is (was) your father's job or occupation?
(If several jobs, get one worked at longest)

186 Can you tell me where your father was born?

187 And what about your mother?

188 And where was your *grandfather* on your *father's* side born?

IF INFORMANT'S FATHER OR GRANDFATHER WAS BORN ABROAD, ASK:

189a Do you think of *yourself* as being _____?
Use nationality of father or grandfather, as Irish, Italian, etc.

189b How important do you feel being
     _____ is to you – would you
     say you felt it was *Very important*,
     quite important, *not very important*, or
     not at all important?

189c Why do you say that? (*probe*: Any
     other reason?)

ALL INFORMANTS

190 And what is (was) your *father-in-law's*
     occupation?

*(If several jobs, get one worked at
longest)*

191 And, can you tell me where your wife's
     father was born?

192 What about your wife's mother, where
     was she born?

193 And finally, where was your wife's
     grandfather on her father's side born?

TERMINATE INTERVIEW

Notes to the Text

Preface

1. The most comprehensive study of contemporary changes in class structure conducted to date is English. See John H. Goldthorpe, David Lockwood, Frank Bechhofer and Jennifer Platt, *The Affluent Worker: Industrial Attitudes and Behaviour* (Cambridge, 1968); *The Affluent Worker: Political Attitudes and Behaviour* (Cambridge, 1968). *The Affluent Worker in the Class Structure* (Cambridge, 1969). See also an earlier study: Ferdynand Zweig, *The Worker in an Affluent Society: Family Life and Industry* (New York, 1962). For research conducted in Germany see H. Popitz, H. P. Bahrdt, E. A. Jures and H. Kesting, *Das Gesellschaftsbild des Arbeiters* (Tübingen, 1957); Richard F. Hamilton, 'Affluence and the Worker: The West German Case', *American Journal of Sociology*, 71 (1965). French studies include Pierre Belleville, *Une Nouvelle Classe Ouvrière* (Paris, 1963); Serge Mallet. *La Nouvelle Class Ouvrière* (Paris, 1963); A. Touraine, *La Conscience Ouvrière* (Paris, 1966); Richard F. Hamilton, *Affluence and the French Worker in the Fourth Republic* (Princeton, 1967).

Chapter 1, pp. 1–18

1. S. M. Lipset and Reinhard Bendix, 'Social Mobility and Occupational Career Patterns. I. Stability of Jobholding', *American Journal of Sociology*, 57 (1952), 371.
2. Karl Marx and Frederick Engels, *Selected Correspondence 1846–1895* (London, 1934), Engels to Florence Kelley Wischnewetsky, London, 3 June 1886, p. 449.
3. Furniture Workers' Union of America, Central Committee, *Normal Workday of Eight Hours* (New York, 1879), pp. 1–2, cited in Irwin Yellowitz, *The Position of the Worker in American Society, 1865–1896* (Englewood Cliffs, New Jersey, 1969), pp. 81–2.
4. Karl Marx and Frederick Engels, *Selected Works* (London, 1968), p. 226.
5. Lewis S. Feuer (ed.), *Marx and Engels Basic Writings on Politics and Philosophy* (Garden City, New York, 1959), p. 458.
6. Marx and Engels, *Selected Correspondence 1846–1895*, Engels to Sorge, London, 31 December 1892, p. 501.
7. *Ibid.* Engels to Florence Kelley Wischnewetsky, London, 3 June 1886, p. 449.
8. *Ibid.* p. 448.
9. *Ibid.* Engels to Schlüter, London, 30 March 1892, p. 497.
10. Kurt B. Mayer, 'The Changing Shape of the American Class Structure', *Social Research*, 30 (1963), 467. See also by the same author: 'Recent changes in the Class Structure of the United States', *Transactions of the Third World Congress of Sociology*, 3 (London, 1956); 'Diminishing Class Differentials in the United States', *Kyklos*, 12 (1959); *Class and Society* (New York, 1955), pp. 41–2. Writing at almost the same time as Mayer, Ogburn and Bernard made very similar, although less detailed claims, being more concerned with explaining why these changes in the distribution of income have come about. See William Fielding Ogburn, 'Technology and the Standard of Living in the United States', *American Journal of Sociology*, 60 (1955); 'Implications of the Rising Standard of Living in the United States', *American Journal of Sociology*, 60 (1955); Jessie Bernard, 'Class Organisation in an Era of Abundance: A New Principal of Class Organisation', *Transactions of the Third World Congress of Sociology*, 3 (London, 1956). See also John Brooks,

The Great Leap (London, 1967), chap. 5; Gilbert Burck and Sanford Parker, 'The Changing American Market', *Fortune* (August 1953); 'The Rich Middle Income Class', *Fortune* (May 1954).

11. Mayer, 'The Changing Shape of the American Class Structure', p. 464.
12. Edmund Brunner and Wilbur C. Hallenbeck, *American Society: Urban and Rural Patterns* (New York, 1955), p. 253.
13. Herbert J. Gans, *The Urban Villagers* (New York, 1962).
14. The view that suburbs geared towards middle income households would automatically bring together manual and non-manual workers was often, in the early 1950s, little more than an untested assumption. Subsequent research has however shown it to be largely true. See, for example, Bernard Lazerwitz, 'Metropolitan Community Residential Belts, 1950 and 1956', *American Sociological Review*, 25 (1960).
15. William H. Whyte, Jnr, *The Organisation Man* (New York, 1956), p. 331. Whyte's argument was initially published as a series of articles in *Fortune*. See also David Riesman, 'The Suburban Dislocation', *Annals of the American Academy of Political and Social Science*, 314 (1957); 'The Lush New Suburban Market', *Fortune* (November 1953).
16. Gerhard Lenski, *The Religious Factor* (New York, 1961), pp. 48–9.
17. Harold L. Wilensky, 'Class, Class Consciousness, and American Workers', in William Haber (ed.), *Labour in a Changing America* (New York, 1966), p. 12.
18. S. M. Miller and Frank Riessman, 'Are Workers Middle Class?', *Dissent*, 8 (1961).
19. William M. Dobriner, *Class in Suburbia* (Englewood Cliffs, New Jersey, 1963), p. 59. See also the excellent study: Bennett Berger, *Working Class Suburb* (Berkeley and Los Angeles, 1960).
20. Richard F. Hamilton, 'The Behaviour and Values of Skilled Workers', in Arthur B. Shostak and William Gomberg (eds.), *Blue Collar World* (Englewood Cliffs, New Jersey, 1964); 'Income, Class and Reference Group', *American Sociological Review*, 29 (1964).
21. C. Wright Mills, *White Collar* (New York, 1956), pp. 192–8, 204–9, 272–5, 297.
22. Richard F. Hamilton, 'The Marginal Middle Class: A Reconsideration', *American Sociological Review*, 31 (1966), 199. (Note that Hamilton is adopting here a position significantly different from that put toward three years earlier. See 'The Behaviour and Values of Skilled Workers',) A similar viewpoint is held by Wilensky, who argues that whether it is the traditional lower middle class or the upper levels of the working class that is changing, the net result is the emergence of a 'new middle mass' encompassing members of both groups. It should be pointed out that while Wilensky presents data in support of his argument, these data come from a study which *by definition* groups together respondents earning above $5,000 a year but not exercising authority in the work situation. It is, therefore, not surprising that he finds himself able to treat them as a homogeneous grouping. See Harold L. Wilensky, 'Work, Careers and Social Integration', *International Social Journal*, 12 (1960); 'Orderly Careers and Social Participation: the Impact of Work History on Social Integration in the Middle Mass', *American Sociological Review*, 26 (1961); 'Class, Class Consciousness, and American Workers'. See also Berger, *Working Class Suburb*, pp. 94–8.
23. Perhaps the worst offenders in this regard were those writers subscribing to the 'end of ideology' thesis. Thus the *perceived* 'withering away of the strike' was explained in 1960 at least partially by reference to the fact that class differences, and therefore class antagonisms were in the process of disappearing. See Arthur N. Ross and Paul T. Hartman, *Changing Patterns of Industrial Conflict* (New York, 1960), especially pp. 44–5.
24. As this discussion can have little relevance outside of the context of this study, it has not been felt necessary to document statements with the use of footnotes. In fact the description of Providence and Rhode Island is based on the following sources: Sidney Goldstein and Kurt B. Mayer, *The People of Rhode Island, 1960* (Providence, 1963); Goldstein and Mayer, *Metropolitanization and Population Change in Rhode Island* (Providence, 1961); *Journal – Bulletin Almanac* (Providence, 1968); Duane Lockard, *New England State Politics* (Princeton, 1959); W. Thomas Bicknell, *The History of the State of Rhode Island and Providence Plantations* (New York: The American Historical Society, 1920); Elmer E. Cornwell, Jnr, 'Party Absorption of Ethnic Groups: The Case of Providence, R.I.', *Social Forces*, 38 (1960), 205–10; Paul F. Gleeson, *Rhode Island: The Development of a Democracy* (Providence, State Board of Education, 1957); Lilian B. Miner, *Our State:*

Rhode Island (Providence, The Oxford Press, 1925). David Patten, *Rhode Island Story* (Providence, Providence Journal Company, 1954).

25. Rather, for the sociologist, age is relevant in the explanation of social behaviour via the concept of the generation. In these terms, an age group may go through certain 'decisive relevant experiences', which may affect the behaviour of members of that age group, or generation, throughout their life cycles. See Karl Mannheim 'On the Problem of Generations', in *Essays in the Sociology of Knowledge* (London, 1952); Rudolph Heberle, 'The Problem of Political Generations', in *Social Movements* (New York, 1951).

Chapter 2, pp. 19–44

1. Robert K. Burns, 'The Comparative Economic Position of Manual and White Collar Employees', *The Journal of Business*, 27 (1954).
2. Kurt B. Mayer, 'Recent Changes in the Class Structure'.
3. In the early 1960s Hamilton cast doubts upon the validity of the income data cited by Mayer, charging that the relative affluence of the contemporary blue collar worker was more apparent than real. However, using data drawn from the 1960 United States Census, and taking into account Hamilton's reservations, I was able to reaffirm that all economic differentials separating clerical workers and skilled craftsmen had disappeared. See Richard F. Hamilton, 'The Income Difference Between Skilled and White Collar Workers', *British Journal of Sociology*, 14 (1963); Gavin Mackenzie, 'The Economic Dimensions of Embourgeoisement', *British Journal of Sociology*, 18 (1967).
4. In 1971 a 'Special Section' of the *Monthly Labour Review* was devoted to 'Blue-collar/white collar pay trends'. This contained a number of articles, written primarily by economists and showed clearly that while, during the decade 1959-69, the earnings of blue collar workers in general advanced less rapidly than those of white collar workers as a whole, craftsmen again experienced a *higher* median rate of increase than did clerks. Thus, in the United States, in 1969 the median income for clerks was $8,252, while that of craftsmen was $8,938. (Both figures refer to male heads of households.) Again, in those instances where they work, clerical wives would seem to make a larger contribution to family finances than blue collar wives. The median family incomes for craft and clerical families were almost identical: $11,161 and $11,293 respectively. See especially Arthur Sackley and Thomas W. Gavett, 'Analysis of Occupational Wage Differences', *Monthly Labour Review*, (June, 1971); Robert L. Stein and Janice Hedges, 'Earnings and Family Income', *Monthly Labour Review* (June, 1971).
5. Nelson Foote, 'The Professionalisation of Labour in Detroit', *American Journal of Sociology*, 58 (1953).
6. Ely Chinoy, *Automobile Workers and the American Dream* (Boston, 1965), p. 44.
7. Mills, *White Collar*, pp. 272–5, 307. There exists evidence to suggest that the limitation of promotion opportunities for lower level clerical workers is not only occurring in the United States. Lockwood, writing seven years after Mills, pointed out that identical processes of administrative rationalisation were occurring in Britain and suggested that to varying degrees, such processes were 'conducive to the blockage of clerical promotion and to *the isolation of a separate clerical class*' (emphasis mine). See David Lockwood, *The Blackcoated Worker* (London, 1958), p. 142. Lockwood's hypothesis is lent added weight by some of the findings of study conducted in Scotland in the mid 1950s by Sykes. This author found 'the one major factor' in which the economic situations of manual and clerical workers differed was in terms of differential opportunities for promotion. But again the situation appeared to be in the process of changing: during the actual research most of the clerks joined a trade union, while in its early stages only four out of 96 said they approved of such organisations for clerks. This reversal Sykes explained by reference to reduced promotion expectations brought about by the introduction of a management trainee scheme. See A.J.M. Sykes, 'Some Differences in the Attitudes of Clerical and of Manual Workers', *Sociological Review*, 13 (1965). Similarly, Mumford and Banks found the introduction of computerisation made low level clerical workers far more pessimistic about their chances of promotion. See Enid Mumford and Olive Banks, *The Computer and the Clerk* (London, 1967). espec. pp. 90–2. However, Crozier, in a study of six Parisian insurance companies, did not find evidence of any widespread diminution of clerical promotion possibilities and clearly still regards this as a major difference in the situation

of blue and white collar workers. Similar findings are reported by the authors of the Luton study, previously referred to. See Michael Crozier, *The World of the Office Worker* (Chicago, 1971), pp. 32–4; Goldthorpe *et al.*, *Industrial Attitudes and Behaviour*, pp. 119–31.

8. Crozier, *The World of the Office Worker* , p. 34.
9. See Kurt B. Mayer and Sidney Goldstein, *The First Two Years: Problems of Small Firm Growth and Survival* (Washington, 1961).
10. Chinoy, *Automobile Workers and the American Dream*, p. 86.
11. *Ibid*.
12. Possibly the best critique of the methodology of research into job satisfaction is Arthur Kornhauser, 'Psychological Studies of Employee Attitudes', in S. D. Hoslett (ed.), *Human Factors in Management* (Parkville, Mo., 1946).
13. Crozier, *The World of the Office Worker*, p. 89.
14. The most useful review of some of these studies is: Robert Blauner, 'Work Satisfaction and Industrial Trends in Modern Society', in Reinhard Bendix and S. M. Lipset (eds.), *Class, Status and Power* (second edition) (London, 1967).
15. *Ibid*. p. 476.
16. This does not mean that these men are idealists; indeed, the evidence suggests that they were able to discuss the positive aspects of their jobs in instrumental rather than extrinsic terms *because*, to an extent, income at least is not problematical. When asked to describe their jobs in terms of a source of income *or* of instrinsic satisfaction only a small proportion were prepared to come down on the side of intrinsic benefits only. The majority of all craft groups said they saw their jobs as being something they enjoyed for its own sake *and* as a way of earning the money to be able to do the things they really enjoyed doing. The same is true for the large proportion of the clerks and managers.
17. In a study of 742 white collar employees undertaken soon after the second World War Morse found that clerical jobs 'which are more varied and require more skill and more decision-making' were correlated with higher levels of intrinsic satisfaction than those that were not. See Nancy Morse, *Satisfactions in the White Collar Job* (Michigan, 1953), p. 65. The implications of office mechanisation for the behaviour and values of clerical workers have been recognised at least since the First World War, although systematic analysis of these implications is relatively recent. I have already referred to Speier's assertions that office machinery was making the job of an office worker less and less distinct from that of a worker in light industry, and thereby contributing to a general 'downgrading' of the clerical worker. This process had already been portrayed graphically by Sinclair Lewis in his first major novel. See Hans Speier, 'The Salaried Employee in Modern Society', *in Social Order and the Risks of War* (New York, 1952) and Sinclair Lewis, *The Job* (New York, 1917). See also H. A. Rhee, *Office Automation in Social Perspective* (Oxford, 1968), W. H. Scott (ed.), *Office Automation: Administrative and Human Problems* (Paris, 1965); Mumford and Banks, *The Computer and the Clerk*.
18. Mills, *White Collar*, p. 194.
19. *Ibid*. pp. 196, 205.
20. *Ibid*. p. 207.

Chapter 3, pp. 45–73

1. Dennis H. Wrong, 'Trends in Class Fertility in Western Nations', in Bendix and Lipset (eds.), *Class, Status and Power* (second edn). For a general discussion of the relationship between fertility and social class, see: Dennis H. Wrong, *Population* (New York, 1956); Frank W. Notestein, 'Class Differences in Fertility', in Bendix and Lipset (eds.), *Class, Status and Power* (first edn) (Glencoe, Illinois, 1953); Conrad Taeuber and Irene Taeuber, *The Changing Population of the United States* (New York, 1958); Charles Westoff, 'Differential Fertility in the United States: 1900–1952', *American Sociological Review*, 19 (1954).
2. See especially Wrong, 'Trends in Class Fertility in Western Nations', and Kurt Mayer, 'Fertility Changes and Population Forecasts in the United States', *Social Research*, 26 (1959); N. B. Ryder, 'Variability and Convergence in the American Population', *Phi Delta Kappan*, 41 (1960).
3. Wrong, 'Trends in Class Fertility in Western Nations', p. 360.

4. This interpretation is given added weight by the almost identical findings of the Luton study. See Goldthorpe *et al.*, *The Affluent Worker in the Class Structure*, pp. 126–9.

5. Arsene Dumont, *Dépopulation et Civilisation* (Paris, 1890), cited in Charles F. Westoff, 'The Changing Focus of Differential Fertility Research: the Social Mobility Hypothesis', in Joseph J. Spengler and Otis Dudley Duncan (eds.), *Population Theory and Policy* (Glencoe, Illinois, 1956), p. 404.

6. Ronald Freedman, 'American Studies of Family Planning and Fertility: a Review of Major Trends and Issues', in Clyde Kiser (ed.), *Research in Family Planning* (Princeton, 1952). See also W. J. Gibbons, 'The Catholic Value System in Relation to Human Fertility', in G. F. Mair (ed.), *Studies in Population* (Princeton, 1949); Ronald Freedman, Pascal Whelpton and John Smith, 'Socio-Economic Factors in Religious Differentials in Fertility', *American Sociological Review*, 26 (1961).

7. Goldstein and Mayer, *The People of Rhode Island, 1960*, p. 11.

8. Respondents were also asked what they thought was the ideal number of children for the average American family. The pattern of their answers is in accord with their own family policies: the mean number of children cited by all three major occupational groupings was a little over three. Less than one quarter of the craftsmen and clerks (and only 16 per cent of the managers) considered families containing four or more children desirable.

9. In addition, 54 per cent of the craftsmen, 70 per cent of the clerks (but only 34 per cent of the managers) have a brother or brother-in-law on the other side of the manual/non-manual line to themselves. Similarly, 48 per cent of the blue collar sample have at least one brother in a job other than skilled manual work, i.e. white collar or non-skilled manual occupations, in about equal proportions.

10. A review and synthesis of nineteen studies carried out between 1928 and 1957 enabled Bronfenbrenner to conclude: 'The most consistent finding . . . is the more frequent use of physical punishment by working class parents. The middle class, in contrast, resort to reasoning, isolation, and what Sears and his colleagues have referred to as "love-oriented" discipline techniques.' See Urie Bronfenbrenner, 'Socialisation and Social Class Through Time and Space', in Eleanor E. Maccoby *et al*, *Readings in Social Psychology* (New York, 1958).

11. Melvin L. Kohn, *Class and Conformity: A Study in Values* (Homewood, Illinois, 1969), chap. 6.

12. Perhaps not entirely unrelated is the fact that managers were also the group using books on child rearing to the greatest extent (either Spock or Bessell). 84 per cent of managerial parents used at least one such book. The comparable proportions of craftsmen and clerks were 60 per cent and 45 per cent. In addition the large majority of managers reported discussing such books or manuals with friends or relatives. The numbers of blue and lower level white collar parents doing likewise were far fewer.

13. Robert S. Lynd and Helen Merrell Lynd, *Middletown* (New York, 1929), pp. 143–4. On the other hand, there was evidence to suggest that traditional working class male segregation within these nuclear units was weakening. In discussing discipline, for example, only four craftsmen gave answers suggesting that they did not view this as the mutual responsibility of *both* parents. Three of these manual workers clearly regarded discipline as the province of the mother – one carpenter having as his ultimate deterrent the threat to 'surrender' a wayward child to his mother.

14. See, for example, Evelyn Duvall, 'Conceptions of Parenthood', *American Journal of Sociology*, 52 (1946); David F. Aberle and Kaspar D. Naegele, 'Middle Class Fathers' Occupational Role and Attitudes Towards Children', *American Journal of Orthopsychiatry*, 22 (1952); Daniel Miller and Guy Swanson, *The Changing American Parent* (New York, 1958); Kohn, *Class and Conformity*. This latter writer has focused upon three components of work situation which are associated with a middle class orientation toward self-direction and a working class emphasis upon conformity to external authority. These are: the extent to which individuals are closely supervised at work; the degree to which work tasks require initiative, thought and independent judgement; the extent to which work tasks allow for a variety of approaches. Unfortunately, my own data do not allow us to distinguish between the various aspects of occupational circumstances.

15. Controlling for income, age, ethnicity and exposure to the middle class via wife's occupation appeared to have little effect. Admittedly, however, in several instances

numbers were very small and I cannot therefore express absolute confidence in these negative findings.

16. Kohn, *Class and Conformity*, p. 190.
17. See, for example, the secondary analysis of a number of studies and public opinion surveys: Herbert H. Hyman, 'The Value Systems of Different Classes: A Social Psychological Contribution to the Analysis of Stratification', in Bendix and Lipset (eds.), *Class, Status and Power* (first edn), as well as an excellent review of the literature: Olive Banks, *Sociology and Education* (London, 1968), chaps. 4, 5.
18. Before being asked to discuss aspirations for their own children, if any, *all* respondents were asked whether they thought it was important for young women to have as much education as young men. 56 per cent of the total craft group thought that there should be parity in educational opportunities and achievements. 64 per cent and 71 per cent of the clerical and managerial groups respectively answered in similar vein.

    Distinguishing characteristics of those craftsmen 'subscribing' to the notion of educational parity between the sexes *and* of those viewing a college education as desirable for their own daughters were the level of schooling attained by both parents and the holding of a white collar occupation on the part of the mother. 34 per cent of craftsmen with daughters in school and who themselves had not graduated from high school wanted those daughters to complete college. The comparable proportion among craft high school graduates was 62 per cent. Almost identical differences are obtained in a comparison of those craft families where the mother has or has not herself completed high school, and in those where the mother is currently employed in a manual or non-manual occupation. These findings are in direct accord with those of earlier studies. See, for example, Elizabeth G. Cohen, 'Parental Factors in Educational Mobility', *Sociology of Education*, 38 (1965); R. L. Simpson, 'Parental Influence, Anticipatory Socialisation and Social Mobility', *American Sociology Review*, 27 (1962); I. Kraus, 'Aspirations Among Working Class Youth', *American Sociological Review*, 29 (1964).
19. The first question simply asked respondents to explain why they thought it was, or was not, 'as important for young *women* to have as much education as young men'. (See note 18 above.) The wording of the second question, again asked of *all* respondents, was: 'So what would you say was the main *value* of education – I mean, what does the person who *is* educated have over the person who *isn't*?'
20. The tendency for working class parents to view education as a means to an end and middle class families to regard it as an end in itself has been noted previously. See for example: Joseph A. Kahl 'Educational and Occupational Aspiration of "Common Man" Boys', *Harvard Educational Review*, 23 (1953); Gerald Handel and Lee Rainwater, 'Persistence and Change in Working-Class Life Style', in Shostak and Gomberg, *Blue Collar World*.
21. Given this perceived relation between education and occupational success, it is not surprising that almost to a man, those blue and lower level white collar workers who did *not* think education was as important for women as for men, explained their attitude in terms of the relative lack of need of a job or career for females. These men were realists: insofar as women marry at an early age, bear and rear children and keep house, preparing them for a job to which they will devote only a small fraction of their lives is a waste.
22. The main reasons offered by these managers (71 per cent of the total) in explanation of their view were: vocationally oriented reasons – 22 per cent; advantages for marriage or motherhood – 52 per cent; more cultured, refined, able individual – 36 per cent.
23. See Kahl, 'Educational and Occupational Aspirations'; Cohen, 'Parental Factors in Educational Mobility'.
24. Small numbers prevent adequate comparisons on these questions between white and blue collar employees. Only seven clerks had a son receiving full-time schooling; for managers the figure was 12. The majorities of both groups were P.T.A. members, although we can say little with any certainty regarding their frequencies of attendance. The same is true for members of these occupational groups with daughters attending grammar or high schools; four out of eight clerks and six out of ten managers in this situation belonged to a P.T.A.
25. The pattern of responses elicited from the managerial group was not substantially different, although rather more than half reported that they would save or invest such a sum. Only one respondent mentioned buying or improving a house. The financial position of the large majority of these people was such that a windfall of $2,000 was not needed to be 'put toward' any one particular item.

26. An added factor is, of course, the *quality* of schooling. In this regard 42 per cent of the managerial parents were having, or planned to have their children privately educated. The comparable proportion of craft and clerical parents were 9 per cent and 19 per cent. Conversely 45 per cent of craftsmen with children (and 54 per cent of their clerical counterparts) had sent, or intended to send them to a Catholic Parochial school. Only 13 per cent of the managers had made a similar choice.

Chapter 4, pp. 74–94

1. 'Worker Loses his Class Identity', *Business Week* (11 July 1959); Burck and Parker, 'The Changing American Market'. See also 'The Rich Middle Income Class', *Fortune* (May 1954).
2. Mayer, *Class and Society*, p. 41; Lenski, *The Religious Factor*, p. 49; Wilensky, 'Class, Class Consciousness and American Workers', p. 13. See also Whyte, Jnr, *The Organisation Man*, pp. 330–44; W. H. Miernyk, *Trade Unions in the Age of Affluence* (New York, 1962); Riesman, 'The Suburban Dislocation'.
3. U. S. Department of Labor, *How American Buying Habits Change* (Washington D. C., 1959), p. 6.
4. See for example, W. Lloyd Warner *et al.*, *The Social Life of a Modern Community* (New Haven, Conn., 1941), chap. 11; *Social Class in America* (Chicago, 1944), chap. 2.
5. J. A. Kahl, *The American Class Structure* (New York, 1957), pp. 203–4.
6. Mayer, *Class and Society*, p. 47.
7. It is also worthy of note, that 45 per cent of craftsmen live in single dwellings, while only one third of the clerks are in as fortunate a position. Instead, exactly one half of this latter group live in apartments while only 36 per cent of the craftsmen do likewise. The remainder live in duplex or semi-detached houses. Not surprisingly, over 80 per cent of the managers live in a single family unit.
8. The small number of people who said that they preferred to rent in nearly all cases gave one or both of two reasons for this: renting was cheaper, at least in the short run; home-ownership carried with it too many responsibilities involving upkeep. A larger number of blue than of white collar respondents mentioned economic reasons, although differences were not large.
9. Goldstein and Mayer, *The People of Rhode Island, 1960*, pp. 39, 41, 80–1.
10. For two reasons these rankings cannot be regarded as absolute. First, the 37 census tracts within Providence have been ranked on the basis of data gathered in 1960. We could thus expect changes, albeit minor ones, to have occured in the period 1960–7. Secondly, the use of the city of Providence as a basis for comparison is partially misleading insofar as not all of the respondents live in that city. Nonetheless, my primary concern is with the *relative* positioning of clerks and craftsmen. As part of the general discussion therefore, the exercise would appear useful and valid.
11. Almost exactly half of the clerks in the sample lived next door to at least one blue collar worker while a similar proportion of craftsmen had a clerical employee as a neighbour. See chap. 7, Table 57: *Occupations of Neighbours.*
12. The relatively high level of residential stability of the sample is perhaps worthy of note. Only around one third of all three major occupational groupings had moved house in the four years prior to 1967, while around one half of each group had lived in their present dwelling for over ten years. In addition, of those respondents who had moved house within the previous ten years the majority of craftsmen and of managers had not moved to a neighbourhood scoring higher on the Index of Social Rank. Of the 94 craftsmen who had moved house during this period 39 per cent had moved to a higher status area, 36 per cent had moved to a neighbourhood of equal prestige while one quarter had come to live in a neighbourhood scoring lower on the scale than their previous area of residence. This was not so in the case of the clerical workers who had been mobile, 59 per cent of whom had moved to an area of higher status and only 6 per cent moving downward. Despite this relative lack of 'upward mobility' in terms of neighbourhood ranking the large majority of craftsmen and managers said they preferred their present neighbourhood to their previous one (50 per cent of clerks reported similarly).
13. Louis Wirth, 'Urbanism as a Way of Life', *American Journal of Sociology*, 44 (1938), 22; Charles and Mary Beard, *The Rise of American Civilisation*, vol. 2 (New York, 1927), p. 730,

quoted in Mirra Komarovsky, 'The Voluntary Associations of Urban Dwellers', *American Sociological Review*, 11 (1946.)

14. See especially, Murray Hauskneckt, *The Joiners* (New York, 1962). Earlier studies, in addition to Komarovsky, 'The Voluntary Associations', include: William G. Mather, 'Income and Social Participation', *American Sociological Review*, 6 (1941); Floyd Dotson, 'Patterns of Voluntary Association Among Urban Working Class Families', *American Sociological Review*, 16 (1951); Leonard Reissman, 'Class, Leisure and Social Participation', *American Sociological Review*, 19 (1954); Wendell Bell and Maryanne Force, 'Social Structure and Participation in Different Types of Formal Associations', *Social Forces*, 34 (1956).

15. While, as is abundantly clear, the home must be seen as the centre of leisure time spent with friends, it would be misleading to imply that this is exclusively the case. In fact around one quarter of each of the three major occupational groups reported leisure time activities that took them outside of the home. Within both the craft and clerical groups eating out with friends appeared to be the most popular, 10 per cent of both categories going to restaurants with friends. 13 per cent of the managerial category said that they often went to a play or movie with friends while only twelve craftsman and three clerks did likewise. Larger numbers of craftsmen went out bowling, drinking or engaged in particular interests, such as square dancing, together with their friends. But in all occupational groupings numbers doing such things were small and certainly do nothing to modify the picture that has emerged so far: the large part of leisure time takes the form of mutual visiting.

16. Mirra Komarovsky, *Blue-Collar Marriage* (New York, 1964), p. 316.

17. See Bernard Rosenberg and David Manning White (eds.), *Mass Culture, the Popular Arts in America* (New York, 1957), espec. sect. 3, 'Mass Literature'; Reissman, 'Class, Leisure and Social Participation'.

18. Respondents were asked the titles of the books they had read most recently. This enabled not only a comparison of literary tastes, but also provided a way of checking whether or not people who claimed to be book readers actually were. The results suggest that the numbers not telling the truth were small. The groups with the largest proportions of people who could not name the book they read most recently were the toolmakers and managers. The former were the craft group claiming the largest number of bookreaders (48 per cent) while the latter represented the single largest proportion of readers within any of the six occupational groups (71 per cent). It is probable that both these figures are a little optimistic.

19. Arthur B. Shostak, *Blue-Collar Life* (New York, 1969), p. 196.

20. '*Popular Mechanix*' is Part of Today!', *The New York Times*, 18 August 1966, p. 60, quoted in Shostak, *Blue-Collar Life*, p. 196.

21. Rosenberg and White, *Mass Culture*, p. 342.

22. Saxon Graham, 'Class and Conservatism in the Adoption of Innovations', *Human Relations*, 9 (1956). In my own sample, in all three major occupational groups there is no relationship between television ownership and income.

23. Berger, *Working Class Suburb*, p. 75; Komarovsky, *Blue-Collar Marriage*, p. 342.

24. Shostak, *Blue-Collar Life*, p. 188.

Chapter 5, pp. 95–115

1. Studies which have documented this relationship include: Paul Lazarsfeld *et al.*, *The Peoples's Choice* (New York, 1948); Bernard Berelson *et al.*, *Voting* (Chicago, 1954); Angus Campbell *et al.*, *The Voter Decides* (Evanston, Illinois, 1954); Angus Campbell *et al.*, *The American Voter* (New York, 1960); S. M. Lipset, *Political Man* (London, 1960); Heinz Eulau, *Class and Party in the Eisenhower Years* (New York, 1962); Robert R. Alford, *Party and Society* (Chicago, 1963).

2. Alford, *Party and Society*, chap. 8.

3. Lipset, *Political Man*, p. 304.

4. It might be emphasised that up to the time at which respondents were asked to discuss their political loyalties and ideologies, the concept of class had not been included in the wording of any question in the interview schedule.

5. Due to the small numbers of individuals involved, it is not possible to examine in any systematic manner the reasons proffered for Republican support. Indeed only 22 people of the total sample of 276 considered themselves to be 'pure' Republicans.

6. See for example, on the relevance of income: Lipset, *Political Man*, chap. 7; on education V. O. Key, Jnr, *Politics Parties and Pressure Groups* (fifth edn) (New York, 1964) pp. 586–9; Campbell *et al.*, *The American Voter*, pp. 475–81.

7. Comparisons were made between high school graduates and non-high school graduates and those earning family incomes of less than, and in excess of, $9,000 per annum.

8. Vance Packard, *The Status Seekers* (New York, 1959), p. 213; S. M. Lipset and R. Bendix, *Social Mobility in Industrial Society* (London, 1959), pp. 67–8.

9. Whyte, *The Organisation Man*, p. 332. In fact the data suggest that wife's occupation is important in influencing political ideology: having a wife *currently* in white collar employment is associated with a move away from the Democratic party, but towards independence rather than the Republicans. 66 per cent of craftsmen with a wife in manual employment considered themselves to be Democrats. Among those whose wives were office workers only 41 per cent supported this party. However, as only 19 per cent of the manual sample had wives presently in white collar jobs, their influence was only slight.

10. David Easton and Robert D. Hess, 'The Child's Political World', *Midwest Journal of Political Science*, 6 (1962), 237–8; Herbert Hyman, *Political Socialization* (Glencoe, Illinois, 1959), p. 19. It should be emphasised that by using the concept of political socialisation, one is not bound to accept some of the more naive or extreme statements made by people working in this area. I am for example, making no claims that political socialisation is a functional requirement for political stability, or that political ideas learned in the home are fixed or immutable. For a discussion of these and other related issues, see Richard E. Dawson and Kenneth Prewitt, *Political Socialisation* (Boston, 1969); David Marsh, 'Political Socialisation: The Implicit Assumptions Questioned', *British Journal of Political Science*, 1 (1971).

11. For additional evidence on this point see: Harold L. Wilensky and Hugh Edwards, 'The Skidder. Ideological Adjustments of Downwardly Mobile Workers', *American Sociological Review*, 24 (1959); Lenski, *The Religious Factor*, p. 142.

12. Surprisingly, this is not a disproportionately high figure. Perhaps the most sophisticated study of mobility to date, that of Blau and Duncan, found 67.5 per cent of clerical workers to have originated from blue collar or farm families. See Peter M. Blau and Otis Dudley Duncan, *The American Occupational Structure* (New York, 1967), p. 39. Data were gathered from a national sample in 1962.

13. Murray S. Stedman and Susan W. Stedman, 'The Rise of the Democratic Party in Rhode Island', *New England Quarterly*, 24 (1951), 337.

14. Alford, *Party and Society*, pp. 55–6.

15. J. Q. Wilson and E. C. Banfield, 'Public-Regardedness as a Value Premise in Voting Behaviour', *American Political Science Review*, 58 (1964).

16. Stedman and Stedman, 'The Rise of the Democratic Party in Rhode Island', pp. 333–4.

17. Lockard, *New England State Politics*, p. 313.

18. Little can really be determined from the 1964 vote, where the extremism of Goldwater meant that the large majority of both religions were forced to vote for Johnson. While 50 per cent of the Protestant skilled craftsmen voted for Nixon only 9 per cent did so for Goldwater.

19. Raymond E. Wolfinger, 'The Development and Persistence of Ethnic Voting', *American Political Science Review*, 59 (1965); Michael Parenti, 'Ethnic Politics and the Persistence of Ethnic Identification', *American Political Science Review*, 61 (1967).

20. Wolfinger, 'The Development and Persistence of Ethnic Voting', p. 905. This point had been suggested earlier by Lubell: see Samuel Lubell, *The Future of American Politics* (New York, 1952), p. 75. It is, however, important to note the distinction between an ethnic group as a whole identifying with a particular party, and successful members of that group gaining access to positions of power in the alternative party. Although the evidence is clear that Italians as a group support the Democratic party, Rhode Island Italians with aspirations for leadership have gone into the Republican party more than the Democrats. Cornwell has compared the ethnic make-up of Providence Ward Committees between 1904 and 1957, and shown that while the Irish gradually gained seats almost entirely as Democrats, the Italians moved into both parties. In 1957 the Italians had 35 per cent of all

Republican Ward Committee seats and only 22 per cent of the Democratic. This he explains by the reluctance of the Irish to share this newly won status with even more recent arrivals. However, the mass of Italians do not appear to have defected to vote for their countrymen. It would seem that the nationality of a candidate is largely irrelevant in explaining his support. It may be an added fillip, but nothing more. See Cornwell, 'Party Absorption of Ethnic Groups: The Case of Providence, R.I.'; Lockard, *New England State Politics*, p. 319.

21. Parenti, 'Ethnic Politics and the Persistence of Ethnic Identification', p. 721.

Chapter 6, pp. 116–148

1. Richard Centers, *The Psychology of Social Classes* (New York, 1961).
2. Discussion of the problems and advantages inherent in investigating respondents' images of class in an unstructured manner can be found in Goldthorpe *et al.*, *The Affluent Worker in the Class Structure*, Appendix C; Jennifer Platt, 'Variations in Answers to Different Questions on Perceptions of Class', *Sociological Review* (New series), 19, (1971).
3. Mills, *White Collar*, p. 240.
4. Centers, *The Psychology of Social Classes*, pp. 85–7.
5. Surprisingly, contact with individuals on the other side of the blue collar/white collar line seems to have no relevance. The same is true for the promotion possibilities inherent in occupational role, as well as wife's occupation. I had hypothesised that all three of these variables, providing as they do, access to individuals in different class situations, would be positively correlated with class identification.
6. It will be noticed that on this question respondents were asked specifically about their perceptions of the class structure of Providence, whereas earlier reference was to the four classes in the United States. For the large majority of the sample, experience of class differences takes place at the community level. It was for this reason that in this particular question I referred to Providence rather than to the nation as a whole. There is no reason to suspect that this has led to distortion. It would seem that in terms of stratification, Providence is regarded simply as a microcosm of the United States generally, the one difference being that the people I interviewed were more at ease in discussing the relative sizes of classes in the former instance than they would have been in the latter.
7. This hypothesis gains a measure of support from Berger who claims that 'In working class lexicon, the term "lower class" is reserved for people who are not quite respectable', Berger, *Working Class Suburb*, p. 81.
8. Elizabeth Bott, *Family and Social Network* (London, 1957), p. 165. This readiness to claim membership in the largest class in the society has been found by a number of other writers. Indeed, Oeser and Hammond refer to it as the 'expansion effect'. More recently Goldthorpe has gone further, suggesting: 'the "expansion effect" is most probable where stratification is being interpreted primarily in "money" terms by members of a group experiencing upward economic mobility'. See O. A. Oeser and S. B. Hammond, *Social Structure and Personality in a City* (London, 1954), pp. 281–3; F. M. Martin, 'Some Subjective Aspects of Social Stratification', in David Glass (ed.), *Social Mobility in Britain*, (London, 1954), pp. 61–4; John H. Goldthorpe, 'L'image des classes chez les travailleurs manuels aisés', *Revue Français de Sociologie*, 11 (1970), 322, fn. 14.
9. In fact four questions were devoted to this problem: (1.) After respondents had identified with either the working or middle class according to Center's classification, they were asked to explain their choice: 'You wouldn't then call yourself a working (or middle) class person – why is that?' (2.) 'So what *sort* of people are in the working (or middle) class – how would you describe a working (or middle) class person?' (3.) 'How about the middle (or working) class–how would you describe a middle (or working) class person?'' (Respondents were asked to discuss their 'own' class first.) (4.) 'In your opinion what is the dividing line between the working class and the middle class? Where does the working class end and the middle class begin?' All four questions were open-ended. Table 42 is based on responses only to questions 2 and 3 above. In the event that an interviewee used more than one criterion in defining a middle or working class person, preference was given first to descriptions couched in terms of occupation, then to descriptions based on criteria of income and/or education, and finally to those referring to style of life.

10. It is interesting to note that Centers obtained largely similar results. Only 4 per cent of his national sample regarded white collar work as an essential criterion of middle class status although 23 per cent did equate manual labour with the working class. 'The suggestion is strong that if (salaried or white collar work) has ever in itself been a factor in identifying people with the middle class it has become much less important and is much less important now', Centers, *The Psychology of Social Classes*, p. 100. Similarly, the affluent production workers studied by Goldthorpe *et al.* placed much greater emphasis on 'money' than occupation as the determinant of class position, although other English studies have not produced findings in accord. See Goldthorpe *et al.*, *The Affluent Worker in the Class Structure*, pp. 145–7; Martin, 'Some Subjective Aspects of Social Stratification', pp. 58–64; W. G. Runciman, *Relative Deprivation and Social Justice* (London, 1966) pp. 161–2.

11. Berger, *Working Class Suburb*, p. 85.

12. Despite the overwhelming affirmative response to this question, there were a few informants – 20 craftsmen, three managers and four clerks – who did not think craftsmen were doing better than men who work in offices. The majority of the reasons given for this response were so varied as to be unclassifiable into general categories. The one general reason given by eight of the 27 was the fact that in some aspect of market situation – year round work, fringe benefits – the clerk maintained an advantage over the craftsman.

13. Nevertheless, it is significant that fewer managers insisted on the relevance of the manual/non-manual when asked to compare the class situations of craftsmen and clerks than was the case in their more general portrayal of the working and middle classes. No definitive explanation can be offered for this 'weakening' of position. It is possible however that these people were thinking of hourly paid semi-skilled workers when linking manual employees and the working class. When asked to incorporate highly skilled tradesmen into their image of class structure a proportion were forced to move away from their previous standpoint. The images of class structure held by craftsmen and clerks have, of course, been far more consistent.

14. Of the 20 craftsmen who did *not* think they were in the same social class as clerical workers, six gave reasons having to do with the fact that skilled manual jobs still did not have the status, standing or prestige of white collar jobs. However, the responses give the distinct impression that the craftsman is reporting how he thinks clerks view the situation, a view that he does not necessarily regard as being legitimate. An electrician explained: 'It's just that the white collar worker feels superior – they just have that attitude,' while a toolmaker remarked: 'People who work in offices – even though they are below a craftsman in wages – tend to feel they are in a higher, upper class.' Two of the seven managers continuing to see a manual/non-manual break gave similar reasons. The majority of the managers in this group of seven gave the superior education of the clerk in explanation of their view. The fact that craftsmen have to work harder and longer for their money, that promotion possibilities are greater in the white collar groups, and that clerks and craftsmen don't associate with one another, were also mentioned. But as one manager pointed out: 'this will change in the future'.

15. Quoted in Mills, *White Collar*, p. 301.

16. Hostile descriptions of unions were relatively uncommon. What few there were referred to their present 'behaviour' or structure rather than to unionism *per se*. Remarks such as 'actually I think they are getting out of hand'; 'they're becoming too commercialised and have a tendency to run the shops and dictate to management' are representative. As would be expected, with one exception, the craftsmen who are hostile to unions are themselves non-members.

17. In this regard, Bott has suggested that in instances where individuals conceptualise class in terms of life style (as in fact my respondents do) rather than in terms of power, then, *by definition*, there will be pressures towards the setting up of at least a three class hierarchy – one's equals, one's superiors and one's inferiors. Lockwood has made the same point in his discussion of the 'differential traditionalist' worker, in which he sees an inferior class as 'almost a necessary condition for the protection of his own (the differential worker's) sense of self-esteem'. While this latter explanation rests upon a somewhat dubious psychology it does underlie the pressure towards images of three or more classes amongst individuals who see the bases of class as being continuous variables such as income, education or style of life. See Bott, *Family and Social Network*, p. 176; Lockwood, 'Working Class Images of Society', pp. 252–3.

18. Lockwood, 'Working Class Images of Society', p. 260.

Chapter 7, pp. 149–161

1. Berger, *Working Class Suburb*, pp. 66, 68.
2. See for example, Blau and Duncan, *The American Occupational Structure*, pp. 67–75; Edward O. Laumann and Louis Guttman, 'The Relative Associational Contiguity of Occupations in an Urban Setting', *American Sociological Review*, 31 (1966); Alexander Stewart, Robert Blackburn and Kenneth Prandy, 'Measuring the Class Structure', *forthcoming*.
3. See Clyde H. Coombs, *A Theory of Data* (New York, 1964). I am grateful to Alexander Stewart and Kenneth Prandy, sociologists in the Department of Applied Economics in the University of Cambridge, for their guidance and help in the use of this technique.
4. That distance 1 – 4 is less than distance 5 – 6 is incompatible with the fact that distance 1 – 5 is greater than distance 4 – 6. On a one dimensional solution distance 1 – 5 would be distance 1 – 4 plus distance 4 – 5; distance 4 – 6 would be distance 5 – 6 plus distance 4 – 5, and since 1 – 4 is less than 5 – 6, 1 – 4 plus 4 – 5 cannot be greater than 5 – 6 plus 4 – 5.
5. W. F. Whyte, *Street Corner Society* (Chicago, 1955).
6. Respondents were not restricted only to neighbours living next door. Rather, in this question, they were encouraged to use their own definition of the term 'neighbour'.

Chapter 8, pp. 162–175

1. Needless to say, names, and several other irrelevant details, are ficticious.
2. The point was perhaps argued with most vehemence by Lenin: 'The Mensheviks of the West have acquired a much firmer footing in the trade unions; there the *craft-union, narrow-minded, selfish, case-hardened, covetous, and petty-bourgeois "labour-aristocracy", imperialist-minded, and imperialist-corrupted*, has developed into a much stronger section than in our country' (italics his). See V. I. Lenin, *Selected Works* (London, 1969), p. 540.
3. Marx and Engels, *Selected Correspondence 1846–1895*, Engels to Schlüter, London, 30 March 1892, pp. 496–7.
4. Clyde Griffen, 'Workers Divided: The Effect of Craft and Ethnic Differences in Poughkeepsie, New York, 1850–1880', in Stephen Thernstrom and Richard Sennett (eds.), *Nineteenth Century Cities* (New Haven, 1969).
5. Stuart Blumin, 'Mobility and Change in Ante-Bellum Philadelphia', in Thernstrom and Sennett, *Nineteenth Century Cities*.
6. For a more detailed account of the exclusivity of American craft unions see for example: Philip S. Foner, *History of the Labour Movement in the United States*, vol. 3 (New York, 1964); Miernyk, *Trade Unions in the Age of Affluence*; Selig Perlman, *A History of Trade Unionism in the United States* (New York, 1937); Lloyd Ulman, *The Rise of the National Trade Union* (Cambridge, Mass., 1966).
7. Quoted in Yellowitz, *The Position of the Worker in American Society*, p. 92.
8. *Ibid.* p. 32.
9. Quoted in Foner, *History of the Labour Movement*, vol. 3, p. 198.
10. Lynd and Lynd, *Middletown in Transition*, pp. 64–6, 245.
11. On the relationship between work situation and level of 'alienation' see, for example, Robert Blauner, *Alienation and Freedom* (Chicago, 1964); on occupational ideologies and degree of power in the labour market: Theodore Caplow, *The Sociology of Work* (New York, 1954), Lee Taylor, *Occupational Sociology* (New York, 1968); on orientations towards politics: S. M. Lipset *et al.*, *Union Democracy* (Glencoe, Ill. 1956); and on the influence of the job on family life: W. Fred Cottrell, *The Railroader* (Stanford, Calif., 1940).
12. This is not entirely the case with regard to recent discussion of the 'proletarianisation' of the routine white collar worker. In this instance some cognisance has been made of changes occuring in the market and work situation of the clerical employee, and the implications of those changes for class structure discussed. See Mills, *White Collar*, chaps. 9–10. Nonetheless, Mills's contribution cannot really be compared with the more systematic and scholarly analyses of the position of the low level white collar worker undertaken by writers in other countries. See, for example, Speier, 'The Salaried Employee in Modern Society'; F. D. Klingender, *The Condition of Clerical Labour in Britain* (London, 1935); Lockwood, *The Blackcoated Worker*.
13. See, for example, Warner, *et al.*, *Social Class in America*, chap. 1. For a sociological critique of this type of approach see G. K. Ingham, 'Social Stratification: Individual Attributes and Social Relationships', *Sociology*, 4 (1970).

Bibliography

Aberle, David F. and Naegele, Kaspar D., 'Middle Class Fathers' Occupational Role and Attitudes Towards Children', *Americal Journal of Orthopsychiatry*, 22 (1952).

Alford, Robert R., *Party and Society*, Chicago, 1963.

Axelrod, Morris, 'Urban Structure and Social Participation', *American Sociological Review*, 21 (1956).

Bain, George, *The Growth of White Collar Unionism*, London, 1970.

Banks, Olive, *Sociology and Education*, London, 1968.

Beard, Charles and Mary, *The Rise of American Civilisation*, vol. 2, New York, 1927.

Bell, Wendell and Force, Maryanne, 'Social Structure and Participation in Different Types of Formal Associations', *Social Forces*, 34 (1956).

Belleville, Pierre, *Une Nouvelle Classe Ouvrière*, Paris, 1963.

Bensman, Joseph and Vidich, Arthur, *The New American Society*, Chicago, 1971.

Berelson, Bernard *et al.*, *Voting*, Chicago, 1954.

Berger, Bennett, *Working Class Suburb*, Berkeley and Los Angeles, 1960.

Bernard, Jessie, 'Class Organisation in an Era of Abundance: A New Principle of Class Organisation', *Transactions of the Third World Congress of Sociology*, 3, London, 1956.

Bernstein, Irving, *The Lean Years, A History of the American Worker 1920–1933*, Boston, 1966.

Bicknell, Thomas W., *The History of the State of Rhode Island and Providence Plantations*, New York, 1920.

Blau, Peter M. and Duncan, Otis Dudley, *The American Occupational Structure*, New York, 1967.

Blauner, Robert, *Alienation and Freedom*, Chicago, 1964.

'Work Satisfaction and Industrial Trends in Modern Society', in Reinhard Bendix and S. M. Lipset (eds.) *Class, Status and Power* (second edn.), London, 1967.

Blumin, Stuart, 'Mobility and Change in Ante-Bellum Philadelphia', in Stephen Thernstrom and Richard Sennett (eds.), *Nineteenth Century Cities*, New Haven, Con., 1969.

Bott, Elizabeth, *Family and Social Network*, London, 1957.

Bronfenbrenner, Urie, 'Socialisation and Social Class Through Time and Space', in Eleanor E. Maccoby *et al.*, *Readings in Social Psychology*, New York, 1958.

Brooks, John, *The Great Leap*, London, 1967.

Browder, Earl, *Marx and America*, London, 1959.

Brown, Richard and Brannen, Peter, 'Social Relations and Social Perspectives Amongst Shipbuilding Workers – A Preliminary Statement', *Sociology*, 4 (1970).

Brunner, Edmund and Hallenbeck, Wilbur C., *American Society: Urban and Rural Patterns*, New York, 1955.

Burck, Gilbert and Parker, Sanford, 'The Changing American Market', *Fortune*, August 1953.

Burns, Robert K., 'The Comparative Economic Position of Manual and White Collar Employees', *The Journal of Business*, 27 (1954).

Campbell, Angus *et al.*, *The Voter Decides*, Evanston, Ill., 1954.

The American Voter, New York, 1960.

Caplow, Theodore, *The Sociology of Work*, New York, 1954.

Centers, Richard, *The Psychology of Social Classes*, New York, 1961.

Chinoy, Ely, *Automobile Workers and the American Dream*, Boston, 1965.

Christman, Henry M., *The American Journalism of Marx and Engels*, New York, 1966.

Cochran, Thomas C., *Social Change in Industrial Society, Twentieth Century America*, London, 1972.

Cohen, Elizabeth G., 'Parental Factors in Educational Mobility', *Sociology of Education*. 38 (1965).

Coombs, Clyde H., *A Theory of Data*, New York, 1964.

Cornwell, Elmer E., Jnr, 'Party Absorption of Ethnic Groups: The Case of Providence, R.I.', *Social Forces*, 38 (1960).

Cottrell, W. Fred, *The Railroader*, Stanford, Calif., 1940.

Crozier, Michel, *The World of the Office Worker*, Chicago, 1971.

Dahl, Robert A., *Who Governs?: Democracy and Power in an American City*, New Haven, Conn., 1961.

Dahrendorf, Ralf, 'Recent Changes in the Class Structure of European Societies', *Daedalus*, 93 (1964).

Dawson, Richard E. and Prewitt, Kenneth, *Political Socialisation*, Boston, 1969.

Dobriner, William M., *Class in Suburbia*, Englewood Cliffs, N. J., 1963.

Dotson, Floyd, 'Patterns of Voluntary Association Among Urban Working Class Families', *American Sociological Review*, 16 (1951).

Dufty, N. F. (ed.), *The Sociology of the Blue-Collar Worker*, Leiden, 1969.

Dumont, Arsene, *Dépopulation et Civilisation*, Paris, 1890.

Duvall, Evelyn, 'Conceptions of Parenthood', *American Journal of Sociology*, 52 (1946).

Easton, David and Hess, Robert D., 'The Child's Political World', *Midwest Journal of Political Science*, 6 (1962).

Eulau, Heinz, *Class and Party in the Eisenhower Years*, New York, 1962.

Fava, Sylvia Fleis, 'Subarbanism as a Way of Life', *American Sociological Review*, 21 (1956).

Feuer, Lewis S. (ed.), *Marx and Engels Basic Writings on Politics and Philosophy*, New York, 1959.

Fischer, George (ed.), *The Revival of American Socialism*, New York, 1971.

Foner, Philip, S., *History of the Labour Movement in the United States*, vol. 3, New York, 1964.

Foote, Nelson, 'The Professionalisation of Labour in Detroit', *American Journal of Sociology*, 58 (1953).

Freedman, Ronald, 'American Studies of Family Planning and Fertility: a Review of Major Trends and Issues', in Clyde Kiser (ed.), *Research in Family Planning*, Princeton, 1952.

Freedman, Ronald, Whelpton, Pascal and Smith, John, 'Socio-Economic Factors in Religious Differentials in Fertility', *American Sociological Review*, 26 (1961).

Fürstenberg, Friedrich, 'Structural Changes in the Working Class; A Situational Study of Workers in the Western German Chemical Industry', in J. A. Jackson, (ed.), *Social Stratification*, Cambridge, 1968.

Gans, Herbert J., *The Urban Villagers*, New York, 1962.

The Levittowners, New York, 1967.

Gibbons, W. J., 'The Catholic Value System in Relation to Human Fertility', in G. F. Mair (ed.), *Studies in Population*, Princeton, 1949.

Ginzberg, Eli and Berman, Hyman, *The American Worker in the Twentieth Century*, Glencoe, Ill., 1963.

Gleeson, Paul F., *Rhode Island: The Development of a Democracy*, Providence, 1957.

Goldstein, Sidney and Mayer, Kurt B., *Metropolitanization and Population Change in Rhode Island*, Providence, 1961.

The People of Rhode Island, 1960, Providence, 1963.

Goldthorpe, John H., 'Attitudes and Behaviour of Car Assembly Workers: A Deviant Case and a Theoretical Critique', *British Journal of Sociology*, 17 (1966).

'The Affluent Worker and the Thesis of Embourgeoisement: Some Preliminary Research Findings', *Sociology*, 1 (1967).

'L'image des classes chez les travailleurs manuels aisés', *Revue Française de Sociologie*, 11 (1970).

Goldthorpe, John. H. and Lockwood, David, 'Not So Bourgeois After All', *New Society*, 1 (1962).
  'Affluence and the British Class Structure', *The Sociological Review* (new series), 4 (1963).
Goldthorpe, John H., Lockwood, David, Bechhofer, Frank, and Platt, Jennifer., *The Affluent Worker: Industrial Attitudes and Behaviour*, Cambridge, 1968.
  The Affluent Worker: Political Attitudes and Behaviour, Cambridge, 1968.
  The Affluent Worker in the Class Structure, Cambridge, 1969.
Goodman, Jay S., *The Democrats and Labour in Rhode Island 1952–1962*, Providence, 1967.
Gorz, André, *Stratégie Ouvrière et Néocapitalisme*, Paris, 1963.
  'Work and Consumption', in Perry Anderson and Robin Blackburn (eds.), *Towards Socialism*, London, 1965.
Graham, Saxon, 'Class and Conservatism in the Adoption of Innovations', *Human Relations*, 9 (1956).
Greer, Scott, 'Catholic Voters and the Democratic Party', *Public Opinion Quarterly*, 25 (1961).
Griffen, Clyde, 'Workers Divided: The Effect of Craft and Ethnic Differences in Poughkeepsie, New York, 1850–1880', in Stephen Thernstrom and Richard Sennett (eds.), *Nineteenth Century Cities*, New Haven, Conn., 1969.
Hamilton, Richard F., 'The Income Difference Between Skilled and White Collar Workers', *British Journal of Sociology*, 14 (1963).
  'Income, Class and Reference Group', *American Sociological Review*, 29 (1964).
  'The Behaviour and Values of Skilled Workers', in Arthur B. Shostak and William Gomberg (eds.), *Blue Collar World*, Englewood Cliffs, N, J., 1964.
  'Affluence and the Worker: The West German Case', *American Journal of Sociology*, 71 (1965).
  'The Marginal Middle Class: A Reconsideration', *American Sociological Review*, 31 (1966).
  Affluence and the French Worker in the Fourth Republic, Princeton, 1967.
Handel, Gerald and Rainwater, Lee, 'Persistence and Change in Working-Class Life Style', in Arthur B. Shostak and William Gomberg (eds.), *Blue Collar World*, Engelwood Cliffs, N, J., 1964.
Hausknecht, Murray, *The Joiners*, New York, 1962.
Heberle, Rudolph, *Social Movements*, New York, 1951.
Hoos, Ida, 'The Impact of Automation on Office Workers', *International Labour Review*, 82 (1960).
Hörning, Karl H. (ed.), *Der 'neue' Arbeiter*, Frankfurt am Main, 1971.
Hyman, Herbert H., 'The Value Systems of Different Classes; A Social Psychological Contribution to the Analysis of Stratification', in Reinhard Bendix and S. M. Lipset (eds.), *Class, Status and Power* (first edn), Glencoe, Ill., 1953.
  Political Socialization, Glencoe, Ill., 1959.
Ingham, G. K., 'Social Stratification: Individual Attributes and Social Relationships', *Sociology*, 4 (1970).
Journal – Bulletin Almanac, Providence, 1968.
Kahl, Joseph A., 'Educational and Occupational Aspirations of "Common Man" Boys', *Harvard Educational Review*, 23 (1953).
  The American Class Structure, New York, 1957.
Key, V. O., Jnr, 'A Theory of Critical Elections', *Journal of Politics*, 17 (1955).
  Politics Parties and Pressure Groups (fifth edn), New York, 1964.
Klingender, F. D., *The Condition of Clerical Labour in Britain*, London, 1935.
Kohn, Melvin L., 'Social Class and Parent–Child Relationships: An Interpretation', *American Journal of Sociology*, 68 (1963).
  Class and Conformity: A Study in Values, Homewood, Ill., 1969.
Komarovsky, Mirra, 'The Voluntary Associations of Urban Dwellers', *American Sociological Review*, 11 (1946).
  Blue-Collar Marriage, New York, 1964.
Kornhauser, Arthur, 'Psychological Studies of Employee Attitudes', in S. D. Hoslett (ed.), *Human Factors in Management*, Parkville, Mo., 1946.
Kornhauser, Arthur, Mayer, Albert J. and Sheppard, Harold, *When Labor Votes*, New York, 1956.

Kraus, I., 'Aspirations Among Working Class Youth', *American Sociological Review*, 29 (1964).

Lane, David, *The End of Inequality?*, Harmondsworth, England, 1971.

Lane, Robert E., *Political Life*, New York, 1959.

Laumann, Edward O., *Prestige and Associations in an Urban Community*, Indianapolis, 1966.

Laumann, Edward O. and Guttman, Louis, 'The Relative Associational Contiguity of Occupations in an Urban Setting', *American Sociological Review*, 31 (1966).

Lazarsfeld, Paul *et al.*, *The People's Choice*, New York, 1948.

Lazerwitz, Bernard, 'Metropolitan Community Residential Belts, 1950 and 1956', *American Sociological Review*, 25 (1960).

Leggett, John C., *Race, Class and Labour*, New York, 1968.

Lenin, V. I., *Selected Works*, London, 1969.

Lenski, Gerhard, *The Religious Factor*, New York, 1961.

Levine, Gene N., *Workers Vote*, Totowa, N.J., 1963.

Levitan, Sar A. (ed.), *Blue Collar Workers, A Symposium on Middle America*, New York, 1971.

Lewis, Sinclair, *The Job*, New York, 1917.

Lipset, S. M., *Political Man*, London, 1960.

Lipset, S. M. and Bendix, Reinhard, 'Social Mobility and Occupational Career Patterns. I. Stability of Jobholding', *American Journal of Sociology*, 57 (1952).

Social Mobility in Industrial Society, London, 1959.

Lipset, S. M., Trow, Martin and Coleman, James, *Union Democracy*, Glencoe, Ill., 1956.

Lipsitz, Lewis, 'Work Life and Political Attitudes: A Study of Manual Workers', *American Political Science Review*, 58 (1964).

Litwak, E., 'Geographical Mobility and Extended Family Cohesion', *American Sociological Review*, 25 (1960).

Lockard, Duane, *New England State Politics*, Princeton, 1959.

'Ethnic Elements in New England Politics', in Charles Press and Oliver Williams (eds.), *Democracy in Fifty States*, Chicago, 1966.

Lockwood, David, *The Blackcoated Worker*, London, 1958.

'The "New Working Class"', *European Journal of Sociology*, 1 (1960).

'Sources of Variation in Working Class Images of Society', *Sociological Review*, 14 (1966).

Lubell, Samuel, *The Future of American Politics*, New York, 1952.

Lynd, Robert S. and Lynd, Helen Merrell, *Middletown*, New York, 1929.

Middletown in Transition, New York, 1937.

Mackenzie, Gavin, 'The Economic Dimensions of Embourgeoisement', *British Journal of Sociology*, 18 (1967).

'The Class Situation of Manual Workers: The United States and Britain', *British Journal of Sociology*, 21 (1970).

Mallet, Serge, *La Nouvelle Classe Ouvrière*, Paris, 1963.

Mann, Michael, *Consciousness and Action Among the Western Working Class*, London, 1973.

Mannheim, Karl, *Essays on the Sociology of Knowledge*, London, 1952.

Marsh, David, 'Political Socialisation: The Implicit Assumptions Questioned', *British Journal of Political Science*, 1 (1971).

Martin, F. M., 'Some Subjective Aspects of Social Stratification', in David Glass (ed.), *Social Mobility in Britain*, London, 1954.

Marx, Karl and Engels, Frederick, *Selected Correspondence 1846–1895*, London, 1934.

Letters to Americans 1848–1895, New York, 1953.

Selected Works, London, 1968.

Mather, William G., 'Income and Social Participation', *American Sociological Review*, 6 (1941).

Mayer, Kurt B., *Class and Society*, New York, 1955.

'Recent Changes in the Class Structure of the United States', *Transactions of the Third World Congress of Sociology*, 3, London, 1956.

'Fertility Changes and Population Forecasts in the United States', *Social Research*, 26 (1959).

'Diminishing Class Differentials in the United States', *Kyklos*, 12 (1959).

'The Changing Shape of the American Class Structure', *Social Research*, 30 (1963).

Mayer, Kurt B. and Goldstein, Sidney, *The First Two Years: Problems of Small Firm Growth and Survival*, Washington, 1961.

Michels, Robert, *Political Parties*, New York, 1962.

Miernyk, William H., *Trade Unions in the Age of Affluence*, New York, 1962.

Miller, Daniel and Swanson, Guy, *The Changing American Parent*, New York, 1958.

Miller, S. M. and Reissman, Frank, 'Are Workers Middle Class?', *Dissent*, 8 (1961).

'The Working Class Subculture: A New View', in Arthur B. Shostak and William Gomberg, *Blue Collar World*, Englewood Cliffs, N.J., 1964.

Mills, C. Wright, *White Collar*, New York, 1956.

Miner, Lilian B., *Our State: Rhode Island*, Providence, 1925.

Morais, H. M., 'Marx and Engels on America', *Science and Society*, 12(1948).

Morse, Nancy, *Satisfactions in the White Collar Job*, Michigan, 1953.

Mumford, Enid and Banks, Olive, *The Computer and the Clerk*, London, 1967.

New York Times, *Social Profile: U.S.A. Today*, New York, 1970.

Notestein, Frank W., 'Class Differences in Fertility' in Reinhard Bendix and S. M. Lipset (eds.), *Class, Status and Power* (first edn.), Glencoe, Ill., 1953.

Oeser, O. A. and Hammond, S. B., *Social Structure and Personality in a City*, London, 1954.

Ogburn, William Fielding, 'Technology and the Standard of Living in the United States', *American Journal of Sociology*, 60 (1955).

'Implications of the Rising Standard of Living in the United States', *American Journal of Sociology*, 60 (1955).

Packard, Vance, *The Status Seekers*, New York, 1959.

Parenti, Michael, 'Ethnic Politics and the Persistence of Ethnic Identification', *American Political Science Review*, 61 (1967).

Parkin, Frank, *Class Inequality and Political Order*, London, 1971.

Parsler, R., 'Some Social Aspects of Embourgeoisement in Australia', *Sociology* 5 (1971).

Patten, David, *Rhode Island Story*, Providence, 1954.

Perlman, Selig, *A History of Trade Unionism in the United States*, New York, 1937.

Platt, Jennifer, 'Variations in Answers to Different Questions on Perceptions of Class', *Sociological Review* (new series), 19 (1971).

Popitz, H., Bahrdt, H. P., Jures, E. A. and Kesting, H., *Das Gesellschaftsbild des Arbeiters*, Tübingen, 1957.

Rainwater, Lee, 'Persistence and Change in Working Class Life-Style', in Arthur B. Shostak and William Gomberg (eds.), *Blue Collar World*, Englewood Cliffs, N.J., 1964.

Reissman, Leonard, 'Class, Leisure and Social Participation', *American Sociological Review*, 19 (1954).

Rhee, H. A., *Office Automation in Social Perspective*, Oxford, 1968.

Riesman, David, 'The Suburban Dislocation', *Annals of the American Academy of Political and Social Science*, 314 (1957).

Rosenberg, Bernard and White, David Manning (eds.), *Mass Culture, the Popular Arts in America*, New York, 1957.

Ross, Arthur N. and Hartman, Paul T., *Changing Patterns of Industrial Conflict*, New York, 1960.

Rubinow, I. M., *Was Marx Wrong?*, New York, 1914.

Runciman, W. G., *Relative Deprivation and Social Justice*, London, 1966.

Ryder, N. B., 'Variability and Convergence in the American Population', *Phi Delta Kappan*, 41 (1960).

Sackley, Arthur and Gavett, Thomas W., 'Analysis of Occupational Wage Differences', *Monthly Labour Review*, 1971.

Scott, W. H. (ed.), *Office Automation: Administrative and Human Problems*, Paris, 1965.

Sexton, Patricia and Sexton, Brendan, *Blue Collars and Hard Hats*, New York, 1971.

Shostak, Arthur B., *Blue-Collar Life*, New York, 1969.

Simpson, R. L., 'Parental Influence, Anticipatory Socialisation and Social Mobility', *American Sociological Review*, 27 (1962).

Speier, Hans, 'The Salaried Employee in Modern Society', in *Social Order and the Risks of War*, New York, 1952.

Stedman, Murray S. and Stedman, Susan S., 'The Rise of the Democratic Party in Rhode Island', *New England Quarterly*, 24 (1951).

Stein, Robert L. and Hedges, Janice, 'Earnings and Family Income', *Monthly Labour Review*, 1971.

Stewart, Alexander, Blackburn, Robert and Prandy, Kenneth, 'Measuring the Class Structure', *forthcoming*.

Sykes, A. J. M., 'Some Differences in the Attitudes of Clerical and of Manual Workers', *Sociological Review*, 13 (1965).

Taeuber, Conrad and Taeuber, Irene, *The Changing Population of the United States*, New York, 1958.

Taylor, Lee, *Occupational Sociology*, New York, 1968.

Touraine, A., *La Conscience Ouvrière*, Paris, 1966.

Ulman, Lloyd, *The Rise of the National Trade Union*, Cambridge, Mass., 1966.

U.S. Department of Labour, *How American Buying Habits Change*, Washington, D.C., 1959.

Warner, W. Lloyd *et al.*, *The Social Life of a Modern Community*, New Haven, Conn., 1941.
Social Class in America, Chicago, 1944.
Democracy in Jonesville, New York, 1949.

Weinstein, James. *The Decline of Socialism in America, 1912–25*, New York, 1967.

Westergaard, John H., 'The Withering Away of Class, a Contemporary Myth', in Perry Anderson and Robin Blackburn (eds.), *Towards Socialism*, London, 1965.

Westoff, Charles, 'Differential Fertility in the United States: 1900–1952', *American Sociological Review*, 19 (1954).
'The Changing Focus of Differential Fertility Research: the Social Mobility Hypothesis' in Joseph J. Spengler and Otis Dudley Duncan (eds.), *Population Theory and Policy*, Glencoe, Ill., 1956.

Whyte, W. F., *Street Corner Society*, Chicago, 1955.

Whyte, William H., Jnr, *The Organisation Man*, New York, 1956.

Wilensky, Harold L., 'Work, Careers and Social Integration', *International Social Science Journal*, 12 (1960).
'Orderly Careers and Social Participation: the Impact of Work History on Social Integration in the Middle Mass', *American Sociological Review*, 26 (1961).
'Mass Society and Mass Culture', *American Sociological Review*, 29 (1964).
'Class, Class Consciousness and American Workers', in William Haber (ed.), *Labour in a Changing America*, New York, 1966.

Wilensky, Harold L. and Edwards, Hugh, 'The Skidder: Ideological Adjustments of Downwardly Mobile Workers', *American Sociological Review*, 24 (1959).

Willener, Alfred, *Images de la société et classes sociales*, Berne, 1957.

Wilson, J. Q. and Banfield, E. C., 'Public-Regardedness as a Value Premise in Voting Behaviour', *American Political Science Review*, 58 (1964).

Winch, Robert and Greer, Scott, 'Urbanism, Ethnicity and Extended Familism', *Journal of Marriage and the Family*, 30 (1968).

Wirth, Louis, 'Urbanism as a Way of Life', *American Journal of Sociology*, 44 (1938).

Wolfe, Bertram, *Marx and America*, New York, 1934.

Wolfinger, Raymond E., 'The Development and Persistence of Ethnic Voting', *American Political Science Review*, 59 (1965).
'Worker Loses his Class Identity', *Business Week*, 11 July, 1959.
'The World of the Blue Collar Worker', *Dissent*, 19 (1972).

Wright, Charles R. and Hyman, Herbert H., 'Voluntary Association Membership of American Adults: Evidence from National Sample Surveys', *American Sociological Review*, 23 (1958).

Wrong, Dennis H., *Population*, New York, 1956.
'Trends in Class Fertility in Western Nations', in Reinhard Bendix and S. M. Lipset (eds.), *Class, Status and Power* (second edn.), London, 1967.

Yellowitz, Irwin, *The Position of the Worker in American Society, 1865–1896*, Englewood Cliffs, N.J., 1969.

Zweig, Ferdynand, *The Worker in an Affluent Society: Family Life and Industry*, New York, 1962.

Index

Aberle, David F., 192 n. 14
Achievements, of children (*see also* Aspirations for children), 68–72
Alford, Robert R., 95, 108
Alienation (*see also* job satisfaction), 32
'American dream', *see* self-employment
American Federation of Labour, 172–3
Areas of residence (*see also* Community structure), 58–61
Aristocracy of labour, 163–6, 170–5
Aspirations
  'bourgeois', 2–3, 170–1
  for children's educational success, 47–8, 57–63
  for children's occupational success, 47–8, 63–8

Bahrdt, H. P., 188 n. 1
Banfield, E. C., 108
Banks, Olive, 43, 190 n. 7, 191 n. 17, 193 n. 17
Beard, Charles, 81
Beard, Mary, 81
Bechhofer, Frank, 188 n. 1, 190 n. 7, 192 n. 2, 197 n. 2, 198 n. 10
Bell, Wendell, 195 n. 14
Belleville, Pierre, 188 n. 1
Bendix, Reinhard, 105, 188 n.1, 191 nn.1, 14, 193 n.17
Berelson, Bernard, 195 n.1
Berger, Bennett, 92, 133, 149, 189 n.19, 197 n.7
Bernard, Jessie, 188 n.10
Bicknell, W. Thomas, 189 n. 24
Blackburn, Robert, 199 n. 2
Blau, Peter, 196 n. 12
Blauner, Robert, 191 n.14, 199 n.11
Blumin, Stewart, 199 n. 5
Bott, Elizabeth, 197 n. 8, 198 n. 17
Bronfenbrenner, Urie, 192 n. 10
Brooks John, 188 n. 10
Brunner, Edmund, 189 n. 12
Burck, Gilbert, 189 n. 10, 194 n. 1
Burns, Robert K., 19–20
Business Week, 74

Campbell, Angus, 195 n. 1, 196 n. 6
Caplow, Theodore, 199 n. 11
Catholicism, *see* religious differences
Centers, Richard, 119–20, 198 n. 10
Children
  aspirations for, 47–8, 57–63

numbers of, *see* Family size
socialisation of, 51–7, 192 n. 12
Chinoy, Ely, 27, 32
Class, concept of, 174–5
Class consciousness/class conflict (*see also* Images of class structure), 138–46
Cohen, Elizabeth G., 23, 193 n. 18
Committee for Industrial Organisation, 171–3
Community structure
  influence of (*see also* Areas of residence), 158–61
Coombs, Clyde H., 150
Cornwell, Elmer, 189 n. 24, 196 n. 20
Cottrell, W. Fred, 199 n. 12
Crozier, Michael, 34, 190 n. 7, 191 n. 8

Dahl, Robert A., 109, 112–13
Democratic party
  and ethnic/religious minorities, 107–14
  perceived bases of support, 103–4
  personal reasons for support, 101–2
  support for, 96–9
de Tocqueville, Alexis, 81
Dinner parties, 87–8
Dobriner, William M., 189 n. 19
Dotson, Floyd, 195 n. 14
Dumont, Arsene, 48
Duncan, Otis Dudley, 192 n. 5, 196 n. 12
Duvall, Evelyn, 192 n. 14

Easton, David, 196 n. 10
Education
  of children, 57–63
  conception of, 59–63, 193 n. 21
  influence of, 56–7, 72, 193 n. 18
Edwards, Hugh, 196 n. 11
Embourgeoisement, 3–6, 75, 174
Engels, Frederick, 2–3, 171, 188 n.n. 2, 4, 6–9
Ethnic groups
  influence of, 18, 107–14
  in sample, 7–9, 16–17
Eulau, Heinz, 195 n. 1
'Exceptionalism', 1–3, 171

Family size, 46–8, 192 n. 8
Feuer, Lewis S., 188 n. 5
Foner, Philip S., 199 n.n. 6, 9
Foote, Nelson, 190 n. 5
Force, Maryanne, 195 n. 14
Fortune, 74, 189 nn. 10, 16

Freedman, Ronald, 192 n. 6
Friends, *see* Leisure time, Interaction, Workmates

Gans, Herbert J., 4
Gavett, Thomas W., 190 n. 4
Gibbons, W. J., 192 n. 6
Glass, David, 197 n. 8
Gleeson, Paul F., 189 n. 24
Goldstein, Sidney, 78, 189 n. 24, 191 n. 9, 192 n. 7
Goldthorpe, John H., 188 n. 1, 190 n. 7, 192 n. 2, 197 nn. 2, 8, 198 n. 10
Gomberg, William, 189 n. 20, 193 n. 20, 195 nn. 19–20, 24
Gompers, Samuel, 172–3
Graham, Saxon, 195 n. 22
Griffen, Clyde, 199 n. 4
Guttman, Louis, 199 n. 2

Hallenbeck, Wilbur C., 189 n. 12
Hamilton, Richard F., 188 n. 1, 189 n. 22, 190 n. 3
Hammond, S. B., 197 n. 8
Handel, Gerald, 193 n. 20
Harrington, Michael, 4
Hartman Paul T., 189 n. 23
Hausknecht, Murray, 195 n. 14
Heberle, Rudolph, 190 n. 25
Hedges, Janice, 190 n. 4
Hess, Robert D., 196 n. 10
Home ownership
 extent of, 74–6
 perceived benefits of, 76–7
Hoslett, S. D., 191 n. 12
Hyman, Herbert H., 106, 193 n. 17

Images of class structure (*see also* class consciousness/class conflict) classes as groups, 147–8
 criteria/bases of middle class, 130–3
 criteria/bases of working class, 125–30
 non-manual/manual line, 133–6
 number of classes, 117–25
 relative sizes of classes, 120–5
 self-placement, 118–20
 skilled/non-skilled line, 136–8
Income
 contribution of wife, 20–2
 fluctuations in, 22
 manual/non-manual differentials, 3–4, 19–22, 162, 167, 190 nn. 3–4,
Index of dissimilarity, 149–50
Index of social rank, 78
Ingham, G. K., 199 n. 13
Interaction
 content of, 152–60
 patterns of, 149–52, 163–4, 168

Job satisfaction, 32, 34–43, 191 n. 16–17
Job security (*see also* unemployment), 22–4
Jures, E. A., 188 n. 1

Kahl, Joseph A., 23, 75, 193 n. 20
Kesting, H., 188 n. 1
Key, V. O. Jnr, 196 n. 6

Kin, relations with, 48–51
Kiser, Clyde, 192 n. 6
Klingender, F. D., 199 n. 12
Knights of Labour, 171–3
Kohn, Melvin L., 54, 192 n. 14, 193 n. 16
Komarovsky, Mirra, 87, 92, 195 n.n. 13–14
Kornhauser, Arthur, 191 n. 12
Kraus, I., 193 n. 18

Lane, David, 45 n.
Laumann, Edward O., 199 n. 2
Lazarsfeld, Paul, 195 n. 1
Lazerwitz, Bernard, 189 n. 15
Lenin, V. I., 171, 199 n. 2
Leisure time (*see also* 'life style')
 activities, 81–94, 195 n. 15
 spent with friends, 84–8, 149–61
 spent with kin, 48–51, 87–8, 155–61
Lewis, Sinclair, 191 n. 17
Life style, 5, 74–94, 162–3
Lipset, S. M., 95, 105, 188 n. 1, 191 n.n. 1, 14, 193 n. 17, 195 n. 1, 199 n. 11
Lenski, Gerhard, 5, 74, 196 n. 11
Lockard, Duane, 109, 189 n. 24
Lockwood, David, 147–8, 188 n. 1, 190 n. 7, 192 n. 2, 197 n. 2, 198 n.n. 10, 17, 199 n. 12
Lubell, Samuel, 196 n. 20
Lynd, Helen Merrell, 192 n. 13, 199 n. 10
Lynd, Robert S., 192 n. 13, 199 n. 10

Maccoby, Eleanor E., 192 n. 10
Mackenzie, Gavin, 190 n. 3
Magazine subscriptions (*see also* mass media) 90–2
Mair, G. F., 192 n. 6
Mallet, Serge, 188 n. 1
Mannheim, Karl, 190 n. 25
Martin, F. M., 197 n. 8, 198 n. 10
Marx, Karl, 2, 188 n.n. 2, 4–9
Mass media, impact of, 5
Mather, William G., 195 n. 14
Matriarchal families, 49, 192 n. 13
Mayer, Kurt B., 3–4, 20–1, 74–5, 78, 189 n. 24, 191 n. 9, 192 n. 7
Methodology, 12–18
Miernyk, W. H., 194 n. 2, 199 n. 6
Miller, Daniel, 192 n. 14
Miller S. M., 189 n. 18
Mills, C. Wright, 30, 42–3, 119, 129, 189 n. 21, 199 n. 12
Miner, Lilian B., 189 n. 24
Mobility
 geographical, 51
 social, 50–1, 106, 192 n. 9
Morse, Nancy, 191 n. 17
Mumford, Enid, 43, 190 n. 7, 191 n. 17

Naegele, Kaspar D., 192 n. 14
Notestein, Frank W., 191 n. 1

Oeser, O. A. 197 n. 8
Office mechanisation (*see also* job satisfaction) 42–3, 191 n. 17
Ogburn, William Fielding, 188 n. 10
Organisations, membership in, 81–4

Overtime, 26–7

Packard, Vance, 105
P.T.A., membership in, 70
Parenti, Michael, 112–13, 197 n. 21
Parker, Sanford, 189 n. 10, 194 n. 1
Patten, David, 190 n. 24
Pension schemes, 25–6
Perlman, Selig, 199 n. 6
Platt, Jennifer, 188 n. 1, 190 n. 7, 192 n. 2, 197. n. 2. 198 n. 10
Political affiliation
  changes in, 96–8
  general, 96–100, 167
Political assimilation, 109, 112–14
Political 'independence', 96–9, 102–3
Political socialisation, 102, 106–7
Popitz, M., 188 n. 1
Prandy, Kenneth, 199 n. 2
Profiles of respondents, 164–6. 168–70
'Proletarianisation', of white collar workers, 6, 199 n. 12
Promotion
  attitudes towards, 29
  blockage of, 30, 190 n. 7
  chances of, 27–31
Protestantism. *see* Religious differences
Providence, 7–12, 78, 107–8

'Qualities of character', *see* Socialisation, patterns of

Rainwater, Lee, 193 n. 20
Reading habits, 88–90
Religious differences
  in family size, 48
  in political affiliation, 107–14
Republican party
  perceived bases of support, 104–5
  personal reasons for support, 196 n. 5
  support for, 96–9
Rhee, H. A., 191 n. 17
Riesman, David, 189 n. 16, 194 n. 2
Riessman, Frank, 189 n. 18
Reissman, Leonard, 195 n. 14
Rosenberg, Bernard, 195 nn. 17, 21
Ross, Arthur N., 189 n. 23
Runciman, W. G., 198 n. 10
Ryder, N. B., 191 n. 2

Sackley, Arthur, 190 n. 4
Sample frame, *see* Methodology
Saving, 71
Schlüter, K., 188 n. 9, 199 n. 3
Scott, W. H., 191 n. 17
Self-employment
  experience of, 31
  plans for, 32–4
Sennett, Richard, 199 nn. 4–5

Shostak, Arthur B., 189 n. 20, 193 n. 20, 195 nn. 19–20, 24
Sickness benefits, 24–5
Simpson, R. L., 193 n. 18
Smith, John, 192 n. 6
Socialisation, patterns of, 51–7, 163, 168, 192 n. 12
Sorge, F. A., 188 n. 6
Speier, Hans, 191 n. 17, 199 n. 12
Spengler, Jospeh J., 192 n. 5
Stedman, Murray S., 109, 196 n. 13
Stedman, Susan W., 109, 196 n. 13
Stein, Robert L., 190 n. 4
Stewart, Alexander, 199 n. 2
Suburbanisation, effects of, 4–6
Supervisory style, 32, 39–40
Swanson, Guy, 192 n. 14
Sykes, A. J. M., 190 n. 7

Taeuber. Conrad, 191 n. 1
Taeuber, Irene, 191 n. 1
Taylor, Lee, 199 n. 11
Television viewing (*see also* mass media), 92–4
Thernstrom, Stephen, 199 nn. 4–5
Touraine, A., 188 n. 1
Trade unions
  conflict within, 171–3
  involvement in, 142–4
  perceptions of, 144–6

Ulman, Lloyd, 199 n. 6
Unemployment, experience of, 24
Unfolding technique, 150–2
U.S. Department of Labour, 74

Voting, 99–100

Warner, W. Lloyd, 18, 74–5, 174–5
Westoff, Charles, 191 n. 1, 192 n. 5
Whelpton, Pascal, 192 n. 6
White, David Manning, 195 nn. 17, 21
Whyte, W. F., 199 n. 5
Whyte, William H. Jnr, 5, 194 n. 2, 196 n. 9
Wilensky, Harold L., 74, 189 n. 22, 196 n. 11
Wilson, J. Q., 108
Wirth, Louis, 81
Wischnewetsky, Florence Kelley, 188 n. 7
Wolfinger, Raymond E., 112–13
Work situation
  differences in 64–5
  influence of, 6, 41–3, 55–6, 64–5, 128–9, 152–5, 175
Workmates, relations with, 38, 159–61
Wrong, Dennis, 199 nn. 1–3

Yellowitz, Irwin, 188 n. 3, 199 n. 7